The Islamic Finance Industry

Islamic finance has emerged to meet the financial needs of people who seek a different approach to conventional banking and finance. Due to its late inception, Islamic finance has often been regarded as an "infant industry" compared to its traditional counterparts. Even though the Islamic finance industry is still classified as nascent, it has shown rapid growth in the last decade or so.

The primary objective of this book is to highlight the main issues and challenges the Islamic finance industry faces and to offer practical solutions. First, the book classifies the main components of Islamic finance such as money and banking, capital markets, fintech, microfinance, and insurance, as well as morality and governance. Second, all of the chapters are combined according to their relationship and link with each other so as to provide readers with a unique and holistic overview of the subject. The chapters are written by well-renowned experts in the field.

As well as offering readers theoretical information about each subject under discussion, it advances practical solutions that can contribute to the development of each field. This book answers questions such as how money is created by banks; what the business model of Islamic banking should look like; whether Islamic microfinance institutions are sustainable; what the likely framework of takaful should be; what the potential role of fintech could be in reshaping the Islamic financial system; and where and whether morality fits in the financial system.

This book will attract the attention of students, researchers, practitioners, regulators, and policymakers.

Burak Çıkıryel is a Dr. research assistant in the Department of Islamic Economics and Finance, Social Science University of Ankara, Turkey.

Tawfik Azrak is an assistant professor in the Department of Islamic Economics and Finance, Social Science University of Ankara, Turkey.

Islamic Business and Finance Series

Series Editor: Ishaq Bhatti

There is an increasing need for western politicians, financiers, bankers, and indeed the western business community in general to have access to high quality and authoritative texts on Islamic financial and business practices. Drawing on expertise from across the Islamic world, this new series will provide carefully chosen and focused monographs and collections, each authored/edited by an expert in their respective field all over the world.

The series will be pitched at a level to appeal to middle and senior management in both the western and the Islamic business communities. For the manager with a western background the series will provide detailed and up-to-date briefings on important topics; for the academics, postgraduates, business communities, manager with western and an Islamic background the series will provide a guide to best practice in business in Islamic communities around the world, including Muslim minorities in the west and majorities in the rest of the world.

Islamic Finance in the Financial Markets of Europe, Asia and America
Faiza Ismail

The Informal Economy and Islamic Finance
The Case of Organization of Islamic Cooperation Countries
Shabeer Khan

Digital Transformation in Islamic Finance
A Critical and Analytical View
Edited by Yasushi Suzuki and Mohammad Dulal Miah

The Islamic Finance Industry
Issues and Challenges
Edited by Burak Çıkıryel and Tawfik Azrak

For more information about this series, please visit: www.routledge.com/Islamic-Business-and-Finance-Series/book-series/ISLAMICFINANCE

The Islamic Finance Industry
Issues and Challenges

Edited by
Burak Çıkıryel and Tawfik Azrak

LONDON AND NEW YORK

First published 2023
by Routledge
4 Park Square, Milton Park, Abingdon, Oxon OX14 4RN

and by Routledge
605 Third Avenue, New York, NY 10158

Routledge is an imprint of the Taylor & Francis Group, an informa business

© 2023 selection and editorial matter, Burak Çıkıryel and
Tawfik Azrak; individual chapters, the contributors

The right of Burak Çıkıryel and Tawfik Azrak to be identified as
the authors of the editorial material, and of the authors for their
individual chapters, has been asserted in accordance with sections 77
and 78 of the Copyright, Designs and Patents Act 1988.

All rights reserved. No part of this book may be reprinted or
reproduced or utilised in any form or by any electronic, mechanical,
or other means, now known or hereafter invented, including
photocopying and recording, or in any information storage or
retrieval system, without permission in writing from the publishers.

Trademark notice: Product or corporate names may be trademarks
or registered trademarks, and are used only for identification and
explanation without intent to infringe.

British Library Cataloguing-in-Publication Data
A catalogue record for this book is available from the British Library

Library of Congress Cataloging-in-Publication Data
Names: Çıkıryel, Burak, editor. | Azrak, Tawfik, editor.
Title: The Islamic finance industry : issues and challenges / edited by
Burak Çıkıryel and Tawfik Azrak.
Description: New York, NY : Routledge, 2023. |
Series: Islamic business and finance | Includes bibliographical
references and index.
Identifiers: LCCN 2022057167 (print) | LCCN 2022057168 (ebook) |
ISBN 9781032455013 (hardback) | ISBN 9781032455020 (paperback) |
ISBN 9781003377283 (ebook)
Subjects: LCSH: Financial services industry—Islamic countries. | Banks
and banking—Islamic countries. | Banks and banking—Religious aspects—
Islam. | Capital market—Islamic countries. | Islam—Economic aspects.
Classification: LCC HG3368.A6 I8594 2023 (print) | LCC HG3368.A6
(ebook) | DDC 332.10917/67—dc23/eng/20221128
LC record available at https://lccn.loc.gov/2022057167
LC ebook record available at https://lccn.loc.gov/2022057168

ISBN: 978-1-032-45501-3 (hbk)
ISBN: 978-1-032-45502-0 (pbk)
ISBN: 978-1-003-37728-3 (ebk)

DOI: 10.4324/9781003377283

Typeset in Bembo
by codeMantra

Contents

List of Figures	vii
List of Tables	ix
List of Graphs	xi
The Editors	xiii
List of Contributors	xv
Foreword	xix

1 Introduction   1
TAWFIK AZRAK

2 Islamic Banks as Creators of Money   7
ÖMER FARUK TEKDOĞAN

3 The Advantages of Islamic Banking and Financial Markets   28
MABID ALI AL-JARHI

**4 Suggestions for Banking Business Models of Islamic
Banking: Current Issues and Practical Solutions for Future**   44
ZEYNEB HAFSA ORHAN

**5 Financial Sustainability of Islamic Microfinance
Institutions (MFIs)**   65
MURAT YAŞ AND YI CHEN

**6 Contemporary Issues in Takaful Sector and Possible
Solutions**   81
HAKAN ASLAN

**7 Issues in Technology: An Analysis of the Potential
Role of Fintech in Reshaping the Islamic Financial System**   100
MOHAMMAD GHAITH MAHAINI

vi *Contents*

8 Morality of Finance: An Islamic Economics Approach 117
HARUN ŞENCAL AND İSA YILMAZ

**9 Issues and Practical Solutions of Shariah Governance
in Islamic Financial Institutions** 134
BURAK ÇIKIRYEL

Index 153

Figures

1.1	Islamic Finance Asset Growth	2
1.2	Islamic Finance Assets Distribution	3
2.1	Creation of Loans and Deposits by Banks	11
2.2	Creation of Loans by Traders	13
2.3	Demonstration of Interbank Clearing	15
2.4	M2 Money Supply and Loans Given in Türkiye, 03/2020–10/2020	16
2.5	Islamic Banks' Consolidated Cash and Reserves Holdings against Deposits, Türkiye versus Indonesia, 10/2020	18
2.6	Credit Terms for Mortgage Financing, Islamic Bank versus Conventional Bank, Türkiye	18
2.7	Consumer Loans Granted by Participation Banks in Türkiye, 2019/1–2020/9	20
4.1	The Scheme of IAP	56
4.2	A Suggestion for an Islamic Investment Bank	59
6.1	Modus Operandi of Takaful	87
6.2	Proposed Takaful Model: *Wakalah*-Cooperative	93
7.1	Islamic Fintech within the Framework of the Islamic Financial System	104
9.1	General Framework of Shariah Governance	144

Tables

2.1	The Share of Financial Institutions in Turkish Financial System in Terms of Asset Sizes – 09/2017	9
4.1	The Business Model of Mit Ghamr Savings Bank	53
5.1	Financial Institutions in Indonesia	66
6.1	Categorization of Issues in Takaful	92
8.1	Value-Based Intermediation Objectives	128

Graphs

4.1 Growth in Islamic Banking Asset Size, 2012–2019 (trillion dollars) 50

The Editors

Dr. Burak Çıkıryel is a research assistant at the Social Sciences University of Ankara in the Department of Islamic Economics and Finance. He graduated from Bursa Uludağ University, Department of Economics, in 2013. He completed his Master in Islamic finance from International Centre for Education in Islamic Finance (INCEIF) in 2017 in Kuala Lumpur, Malaysia. He holds a PhD from Sakarya University, Department of Islamic Economics and Finance. He is the co-editor of the Journal of Islamic Economics. He has conducted numerous academic projects, publications, and conferences in the areas of his research interests, including macroeconomic policy, banking, and finance aspects under the domain of Islamic economics. He has been working at the Social Sciences University of Ankara in the Department of Islamic Economics and Finance since 2019.

Asst. Prof. Dr. Tawfik Azrak is a Certified Shariah Advisor and Auditor (CSAA) and Islamic finance and banking expert with over nine years of experience. Dr. Azrak has been working as an assistant professor at the Social Science University of Ankara – Turkey, since May 2018. Early in his career, he worked at the International Shariah Research Academy for Islamic Finance (ISRA) for two years and did practical training in the Shariah department at Asian Finance Bank. He had published several projects and research papers dealing with various issues related to accounting and Islamic finance, both in Arabic and English languages.

He achieved his PhD in Islamic Banking and Finance from the International Islamic University of Malaysia (IIUM) and a master's degree in Islamic Finance from The Global University of Islamic Finance (INCEIF), where he got a scholarship from the Islamic Research and Training Institute (IRTI). His bachelor's degree was from Damascus University in Economics in the year 2010.

Contributors

Prof. Dr. Mabid Ali Al-Jarhi is currently a professor of economics and finance at Ankara Social Sciences University (ASBU) and Marmara University, Istanbul. He received the following honors and awards: IsDB Prize in Islamic Economics (2019), International Prize Award Mehmet Akif İnan Vakfı (2019), İslam İktisadı Araştırma Ödülü, IKAM (2021). His past experiences are more than 60 years, including the following:

- Head of Training and Financial Expert, Emirates Islamic Bank Dubai
- Director, IsDB Economics and Policy Planning Department
- Former President, International Association for Islamic Economics, London
- Senior Economist and Head of Research, Arab Monetary Fund, AMF
- Senior Economist, the Economic Studies Institute, AMF
- Secretary-General of the Council of Arab Governors of Central Banks
- Editor of the Joint Arab Economic Report, Published by the Arab Monetary Fund
- Director-General of the IsDB Islamic Research and Training Institute, IRTI, ISDB
- Financial Advisor and Head of Training, Emirates Islamic bank
- Economic Expert, Institute of National Planning, Cairo
- Former President, International Association for Islamic Economics (www.iaie.net)

In addition, he has teaching experiences from different universities in the world.

Asst. Prof. Dr. Hakan Aslan is the director of the Research Centre of Islamic Economics and Finance, Head of Islamic Economics and Finance Department Faculty of Political Sciences Sakarya University, Turkey. Hakan Aslan is a scholar focusing mostly on Islamic Insurance, Islamic Finance, and Islamic Capital Markets. Having completed his undergraduate education at the Department of Actuarial Sciences at Marmara University in 2009, he then proceeded to his postgraduate studies in the Department of Business Administration, Financial Markets, and Investment Management at the same university and was awarded his MSc degree in 2012 with a thesis on Sukuk. During this period, he has served as a research assistant at that department from 2011 to 2015. Later, he continued his education as a PhD student at the Department of Business Administration, Accounting and Finance at Marmara University. He has been to the International Islamic University Malaysia (IIUM) for a year as a visiting academic staff to develop his PhD thesis. He completed his PhD thesis titled "Factors affecting the development of takaful (Islamic insurance) system in Turkey: A mixed-method study." He attended the Islamic Finance Summer School at Durham University in the UK in 2018.

Dr. Yi Chen currently is an academic coach in an educational institution in China. She teaches Doctor of Business Administration (DBA) and Executive Master of Business Administration (EMBA) students to write academic theses. Yi Chen holds a PhD in Islamic Finance from INCEIF Malaysia. She also has obtained a master's degree in International Accounting and Financial Management from the University of Glasgow, UK and a bachelor's degree in English with a focus on international accounting from Jiangxi Normal University, China.

Asst. Prof. Dr. Mohammad Ghaith Mahaini is an assistant professor at Istanbul Sabahattin Zaim University in Turkey. He was also a research assistant at INCEIF, The Global University of Islamic Finance in Malaysia. Dr. Ghaith is involved in many product development-related researches and has authored books, research papers, and chapters in books on Islamic finance. Having served at various Islamic financial institutions for over 14 years, Dr. Ghaith has been exposed to the Islamic finance industry in the Middle East and Malaysia professionally and academically. He was awarded his PhD from the prestigious University of Malaya (UM). He is also a qualified Chartered Islamic Finance Professional CIFP-INCEIF (International Centre for Education in Islamic Finance) and holds a Post Graduate Diploma in Financial Management. Dr. Ghaith is also a graduate of Business Administration.

Assoc. Prof. Dr. Zeyneb Hafsa Orhan holds an undergraduate degree from Bahçeşehir University, İstanbul, Turkey, at the Economics Department. She did her master at Linköping University, Linköping, Sweden, on the subject of International and European Relations. Then she took her PhD degree from the International University of Sarajevo, Sarajevo, Bosnia and Herzegovina, at the Economics Department. Her PhD thesis is on the subject of risk analysis in Islamic banks. She is currently associate professor in banking at Istanbul Sabahattin Zaim University, İstanbul, Turkey.

Assoc. Prof. Dr. Harun Şencal holds a PhD in Islamic Finance from Durham University, UK. He graduated from the Computer Engineering Department of Yeditepe University in 2007 and obtained an MBA degree from the same university. He teaches both conventional and Islamic economic courses. He works as an assoc professor in the Economics Department at the Istanbul 29 Mayis University, Turkey. His main research area includes both qualitative and quantitative aspects of Islamic economics and finance. In particular, his research focuses on risk aspects of Islamic financial instruments and moral foundations of Islamic financial institutions, which are presented in several international conferences and published in journals.

Asst. Prof. Ömer Faruk Tekdoğan is an Assistant Professor at the Institute for Islamic Studies, Social Sciences University of Ankara. He received his BA degree in business administration from İstanbul University and his master's degree in economics from North Carolina State University. He completed his Ph.D. in Islamic Economics and Finance, at İstanbul University. Previously, he worked as Head of Department at Directorate General of Economic Programs and Research in the Ministry of Treasury and Finance, and as Policy Analyst in the Organization for Economic Co-operation and Development where his main research areas were Official Development Finance for infrastructure, investment, private sector development and regional connectivity. His research interests include Islamic economics and finance, monetary economics, banking, financial economics, and agent-based modeling.

Asst. Prof. Dr. Murat Yaş is an assistant professor in the Institute of Islamic Economics and Finance at Marmara University. He graduated from Boğaziçi University, Department of Economics, in 2012. In 2014, he was a visiting graduate student at the ICMA Center at the University of Reading and completed his master in Islamic Finance from INCEIF. He completed his PhD in Islamic Finance from INCEIF in 2020.

Assoc. Prof. Dr. İsa Yılmaz has a bachelor's degree in Economics and Management from Istanbul Bilgi University and the University of London double degree program with the academic direction provided by The London School of Economics and Political Science (LSE). He got a master's degree in Islamic Finance from the University of Durham (UK) and completed his PhD in Islamic Finance program at the University of Durham. Currently, he has been working at Istanbul Medeniyet University as assoc prof. dr in Economics Department.

He has several academic publications in the areas of his research interests, including economic development, financialization, and political economy aspects within the area of Islamic economics. In a wider sense, his research interests are on alternative economic and financial systems that envisage authentic models for developmental and welfare consequences for emerging economies. To address this, his interest area expands through the literature on the moral economy, political economy, philosophy of economics, and alternative banking and financial models.

Foreword

Especially after the 2008–2009 Global Financial Crisis (GFC), Islamic finance has been of great interest to policymakers and researchers not only from Muslim countries but from western countries as well. While some have noted a few differences between Islamic finance and conventional finance, others have advocated Islamic finance as a viable system that can replace the present ailing conventional financial system. Over the past years, there has been an expanding list of studies and research articles focusing on Islamic finance, starting with the theoretical and Shariah principles of Islamic finance to comparative analyses of Islamic finance and conventional finance and, more recently, to the socio-economic outcomes of Islamic finance. The focuses in the literature have predominantly been on Islamic banking, Islamic capital markets, and Takaful.

This book is a further contribution to the literature on Islamic finance. It comprises chapters contributed by well-known scholars in their specific fields of Islamic finance. The coverage of the book is comprehensive in that it covers key economic issues as well as puts forth current emphases on contemporary issues and the development of fintech and wraps up the book with the very foundations of Islamic finance related to morality and Shariah governance.

Working side-by-side and competing with conventional banks under the same regulatory and policy environments, Islamic banks have inevitably become involved in the money creation process. This point has been clearly emphasized. Still, the prohibition and absence of interest rates render Islamic finance to have economic advantages, which is theoretically demonstrated in this book. Drawing from the literature, the book also provides suggestions for the business model of Islamic banks. These three issues in Islamic banks are deliberated lucidly in three chapters following the introductory chapter.

Apart from the chapters on Islamic banks, this book also deliberates on issues in Islamic micro-financial institutions and Takaful, the two segments in Islamic finance that have received relatively less attention. The chapter that looks at fintech in reshaping Islamic finance is refreshing and forward-looking. Indeed, the discussion of Islamic finance, or even conventional finance, will not be complete without considering the implications of fintech and digitalization or Industrial Revolution 4.0.

Likewise, the discussion of Islamic finance, in particular, will not be complete without dealing with the issues of morality and Shariah governance. Islamic finance is value-based, driven by the teachings of Islam. As societal welfare takes precedence over individual benefits, moral values and Shariah governance are key for the attainment of Maqasid Shariah. In all, this book has made a substantial contribution in putting various aspects of Islamic finance and should prove to be a valuable reading not only for scholars in Islamic finance but for the general public and practitioners who are interested in Islamic finance.

Mansor H. Ibrahim
Deputy President Academic & Dean
INCEIF University, Malaysia

1 Introduction

Tawfik Azrak

1 Islamic Finance and Its Objectives

Based on Shariah teachings, the Islamic financial system promotes ethical values; hence it is not value-neutral, as is the case of the conventional financial system. The Islamic financial system endeavors to advocate Maqasid-based approach whereby public interest (Maslahah) is promoted, and harm (Mafsadah) is to be prevented. Islamic finance promotes productive activities and genuine trade and business transactions related to the real economic system (Dusuki 2011). This industry showed rapid growth in the last decade with all of its main components, such as Islamic banking, Islamic insurance, Islamic capital market, and Islamic money market.

Islamic finance provides financial services compliant with Shariah (Islamic law). It fosters financial markets to channel funds to the real economy by promoting the risk-sharing concept instead of risk transfer. For this, it employs contracts that impose risk-taking on all contractual parties and avoids gharar (high uncertainty), maysir (gambling), and riba (interest) or investments that cause harm to the society, such as tobacco, alcohol, and liquor. In addition, it promotes the fair distribution of wealth among society by encouraging Islamic social finance tools like Zakat (mandatory almsgiving), Sadakah (charitable giving), and Waqf (endowments).

The primary objective of Islamic finance is to provide and develop a financial environment that is in accordance with the principles of Shariah. Apart from this, the following are the summary of Islamic finance's main objectives.

- To design financial products and services in conformity with Shariah objectives, and these financial products and services are not only in line with contractual formalities of Shariah but also reflect the Shariah mindset (both form and substance),
- To foster risk-taking activities among participants and avoid risk-shifting mindset,
- To offer contemporary alternative financial products and services in conformity with Shariah,

DOI: 10.4324/9781003377283-1

- To contribute toward economic development and prosperity within the principles of Islamic justice,
- To facilitate efficient allocation of resources,
- To help achieve stability in the economy,
- To alleviate poverty and income inequalities,
- To remove social inequalities and to improve the standards of living.

2 Islamic Finance Outlook

As we mentioned in the previous paragraph, the Islamic finance industry showed rapid growth in the last decade. Based on the 2021 Islamic finance development report (Adil 2021), in the year 2020, the global assets for the industry maintained double-digit growth, rising 14% to $3.374 trillion. This is down from 15% growth in 2019, but it is a remarkable achievement considering the painful year the COVID-19 pandemic inflicted on our communities, societies, and economies (Figure 1.1).

As the first graph showed, the growth of Islamic finance assets was increasing from one year to another, and it reached around $3.400 trillion in the year 2020. It is expected that size of the sector in the year 2025 is to attain $3.374 trillion. These figures confirm that Islamic finance, in the near future, is a considerable candidate to take a bigger share of the pie of the financial sector (Figure 1.2).

Graph number 2 depicts the distribution of the assets among the main sectors in the Islamic finance industry in 2020. Islamic banking dominates the Islamic financial industry, obtaining the biggest share of the industry assets. The main reason why Islamic banking outperforms other sectors is that

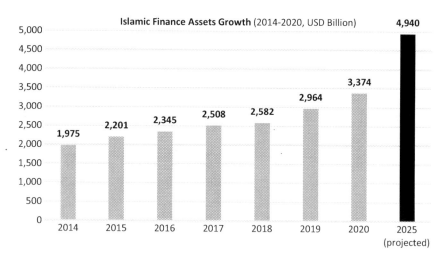

Figure 1.1 Islamic Finance Asset Growth.
Source: Islamic finance development report 2021.

Figure 1.2 Islamic Finance Assets Distribution.
Source: Islamic finance development report 2021.

Muslim communities around the world look for alternative institutions that provide their basic financial needs in a Shariah-compliant way. This situation results in an influx of customers to Islamic banks day after day from their conventional peers and consequently acquiring more assets. Sukuk come second and comprise 19% of Islamic finance assets. The demand for Sukuk arises due to the dire need for investment instruments in the Islamic financial industry and the limited investment opportunities that the Islamic financial markets have to channel surplus funds. Sukuk have become the most common Islamic financial instruments transacted in almost all financial markets worldwide, and their popularity has been increasing, especially in the recent decade. The remaining 11% was divided between Islamic funds, other Islamic Financial Institutions (IFIs), and Takaful (Islamic Insurance). The small ratios of other sectors indicate the dire need for their improvement and less public awareness about these sectors. Thus, the industry players should stimulate more investment in these sectors. This stimulation will lead them to take their rightful shares among Islamic finance assets distribution.

3 Objectives of This Book

The primary objective of this book is to highlight the main issues the Islamic finance industry faces nowadays and offer practical solutions to those issues. First of all, we have classified the main areas of Islamic finance, such as banking and takaful. Secondly, we have requested the relevant expert of each field to write a chapter that includes the issues and practical solutions related to that area. Afterwards, all the chapters were combined according to their relations and continuity with each other.

This book not only provides its readers with theoretical information about each subject but also offers practical solutions that can contribute to the development of each field. In this respect, we can claim that this book provides knowledge in theory and practice. Therefore, there is no doubt that this book will attract the attention of students, employees and employers working in the industry, and policymakers. This book can also be used (potential candidate) as a main and supplementary textbook in Islamic finance courses. Finally, this book endeavors to answer the following questions (these questions will provide readers with a brief overview of the book):

- How is money created by banks?
- How should money be created? What could be the possible structure of banking and financial markets (money and capital market)?
- What should the business model of Islamic banking be like?
- Are Islamic microfinance institutions sustainable enough?
- What should be the likely framework of takaful considering its issues and challenges?
- What could be the potential role of fintech in reshaping the Islamic financial system?
- Where does morality fit in the financial system?
- What could be the feasible structure of Shariah governance in IFIs?

4 Summary of the Chapters

In Chapter 2, Dr. Omer Faruk Tekdogan had clarified the money creation process of private banks and how and why Islamic banks are a part of this process. Then, he has briefly explained the full reserve banking system as the alternative to the fractional reserve system, which is the backbone of the money creation process and the centerline of both conventional and Islamic banks. The paper showed that many Islamic economists are aware of private money creation, and they advocate full reserve requirement for the banking system. However, he argued that many Islamic economists still have a misconception about Islamic banks since they deny the fact that Islamic banks are also creators of money.

In Chapter 3, Professor Dr. Mabid Ali Al-Jarhi has shown that Islamic finance starts from rejecting interest-based lending, and such rejection appears to be religiously justified equally in Islam, Christianity, and Judaism. The abhorrence of interest is also found in Buddhism and Hinduism. However, the school of analytical Islamic economics has developed its economic rationale. The classical loan contract, upon which the financial system of market capitalism is founded, has been built on a flawed theory. The use of the rate of interest is marred with serious inefficiencies. This chapter reviews the theoretical flaws underlying the classical loan contract and the inefficiencies surrounding interest rate use. Islamic finance alternatively provides finance in the form of money in return for equity or rights to share proportionately in future business profits and productions. Finance is also offered as goods and services delivered in return for a commitment to repay their value at a future date or spot money in return for future commodities delivery. The paper goes further to explain the economic advantages of such a system.

In Chapter 4, Assoc. Prof. Dr. Zeyneb Hafsa Orhan has come up with the new suggestion of business model for Islamic banks. First of all, this chapter aims to discuss the criticisms directed toward the banking business model in general and the current business model of Islamic banks in particular. Afterward, it proposes a peculiar business model of Islamic banks by considering related literature. In addition to considering the advancement in financial technology and its adoption, this chapter primarily discusses the significance of dynamic, efficient, and authentic Islamic banks.

In Chapter 5, Asst. Prof. Dr. Murat Yaş and Dr. Yi Chen offer a critical survey of semi-formal Islamic Microfinance Institutions in Indonesia, namely Baitul Maal Wat Tamwil (BMT) literature over the past 15 years. It reviews studies on the financial sustainability of BMTs in Indonesia through investigating their challenges and how they managed to overcome these barriers. By investigating one specific microfinance institution as a case study, this chapter has shed light on what could be the possible issues that Islamic microfinance institutions face and what could be the possible solutions offered to those issues.

In Chapter 6, Asst. Prof. Dr. Hakan Aslan attempted to emphasize the main issues that the contemporary takaful sector has encountered. The importance of this chapter came from reviewing contemporary discussions on takaful studies and takaful operations, highlighting issues in the takaful sector and attempts to offer proposals for these issues using qualitative techniques. In this chapter, the most problematic issues in the takaful sector have been discussed and categorized. Then, possible solutions are offered to those issues.

In Chapter 7, Asst. Prof. Dr. Mohammad Ghaith Mahaini employs qualitative and descriptive approaches in reviewing the potential role fintech can have in reshaping the Islamic financial framework. It analyzes the position of fintech in the Islamic financial framework and discusses the different categories of fintech solutions that could disrupt the Islamic finance industry. It also highlighted the main issues hindering the proliferation of Islamic fintech with feasible solutions.

In Chapter 8, Assoc. Prof. Dr. Harun Şencal and Assoc. Prof. Dr. İsa Yılmaz critically evaluate the three core concepts of the morality of Islam in relation to finance, namely indebtedness, accumulation, and interest, and explore their role in the global financial crisis of 2008. Second, the study traces the emergence and development of Islamic finance within the global financial system and discusses the role of instrumental morality in the convergence of the products and services (provided by the IFIs) toward conventional institutions. Furthermore, the study discusses whether the IFIs have been successful in terms of offering solutions to the moral problems arising due to the operations of the conventional financial sector, with particular attention to the core principles explored in the first part. Lastly, the study examines the current trends in Malaysia, Turkey, and the Islamic Development Bank to envisage the future direction of Islamic finance.

Finally, in Chapter 9, Dr. Res. Asst. Burak Çıkıryel attempts to address the issues of Shariah governance in IFIs. It begins with the definition of Islamic and conventional corporate governance and is followed by making a comparison between the two frameworks. The fundamentals of Islamic corporate governance are explained in detail, emphasizing the components of its institutional framework. Then, the stance of Islamic corporate governance on the shareholder versus stakeholder model was identified. After highlighting that Shariah governance can be considered as part of the Islamic corporate governance framework, the issues related to Shariah governance are discussed, paying more attention to the Shariah supervisory board. Finally, the article ends by proposing a new Shariah governance framework to overcome the current issues and bring a unique perspective on the Shariah supervisory process in IFIs.

References

Adil, Mustafa. 2021. "Islamic Finance Development Report 2021: Advancing Economies." *Refinitiv*. Retrieved March 14, 2022 (https://www.refinitiv.com/en/resources/special-report/islamic-finance-development-report).

Dusuki, Asyraf Wajdi. 2011. *Islamic Financial System: Principles & Operations*. 2nd ed. Kuala Lumpur: International Shariah Research Academy for Islamic Finance (ISRA).

2 Islamic Banks as Creators of Money

Ömer Faruk Tekdoğan

1 Introduction

Banks are financial intermediaries with some exclusive features, which differentiates them from other financial intermediaries. The foremost one is demand deposits that serve as a widely accepted means of payment and consist of a significant part of the money supply. Only banks have the privilege of private money creation, and this is restrained primarily by reserve requirements (Tobin, 1967) and by other legal and natural causes. Contrary to this phenomenon, there are common misconceptions about how money is produced today. The counterargument of "banks are financial intermediaries who collect deposits and then lend them to borrowers" is supported on academic grounds and by practitioners of the banking sector as well. This counterargument, in fact, does not rule out private money creation. The fractional reserve system and multiple deposit creation are the *sine qua non*-subjects of mainstream economics curriculum and textbooks, especially in monetary economics (Mishkin, 2004).

Islamic banks are also financial intermediaries playing in the same field as conventional banks, with the obligation of operating in accordance with Islamic law. Islamic banks are not permitted to deal with interest-bearing transactions. Therefore, they cannot undertake lending operations on the basis of predetermined rates of return. In theory, Islamic banks apply profit and loss sharing principles in their lending operations, such as mudarabah and musharakah (Khan & Mirakhor, 1989). In practice, however, Islamic banks heavily resort to murabaha financing because it is possible for banks to charge profits in the sense of time value of money, and the risks are relatively much lower in murabaha than mudarabah and musharakah (Anwar, 2003). Islamic banks, operating within the fractional reserve banking system, also create money following the same process of conventional banks. Islamic economists and jurists who have considered these issues either did not take this aspect of Islamic banking into account or denied it (Zaman, 2015a).

In this study, we try to identify in what ways money is created by private banks and Islamic banks as well. To this end, we start by briefly describing the tripartite relationship of money, bank, and credit. Then we elaborate

DOI: 10.4324/9781003377283-2

8 *Ömer Faruk Tekdoğan*

on the money creation process of banks and try to clear up whether Islamic banks do or do not create money. The last section covers the main points and studies about full reserve banking (FRB) as the debatable alternative solution to banks' money creation.

2 Money, Credit, and Development of the Banking System

Although it is still a controversial topic in economics, the private money creation of banks was put into words by many prominent economists in the past century. Irving Fisher is a well-known economist with his quantity theory of money and was the first to distinguish clearly between real and nominal interest rates. He argues that credit money was the principal for the severity of the Great Depression (Fisher, 1936). Milton Friedman, the father of monetarism, who received the 1976 Nobel Memorial Prize in Economic Sciences, proposed the elimination of banks' private money creation by separating the depository function from the lending function of them (Friedman, 1948). Frederick Soddy was a 1921 Nobel Prize winner in chemistry. He wrote four books from 1921 to 1934, in which he sketched a radical restructuring of global monetary relationships. Soddy believed that many people were suspicious about that money vastly exceeding in amount the total national money is created and destroyed by the moneylender with a stroke of the pen. He mocked people who still believed the banks could only loan their customers spare money (Soddy, 1961). In his remarks on the US economy after the global financial crisis, the US ex-President Obama was trying to calm down people who were asking that government money would be better spent going directly to families and businesses instead of banks by arguing that a dollar of capital in a bank can actually result in eight or ten dollars of loans to families and businesses, the multiplier effect as we know from banks' multiple deposit creation ("Obama's Remarks on the Economy," 2009).

An American economic historian, Abbott Payson Usher, argued that the essential function of a banking system is the creation of credit, and credit creation is clearly attested in Mediterranean Europe by decisive documentary evidence at the beginning of the 13th century (Usher, 1943). Three economists from the Bank of England described money creation in the modern economy where bank lending creates deposits, which means deposits are mostly created by commercial banks themselves (McLeay et al., 2014).

The banking system is the largest and most important part of the financial system in many countries. Like Türkiye, Greece, Finland, Estonia, and Spain which have the largest share of the banking sector in the financial sector in terms of asset size, with more than 70% shares. In contrast, the share of the banking sector in the financial sector in Luxembourg, the United States, and the Netherlands are below 30% (Hagino & Cavieres, 2013). For instance, according to asset sizes, the banking sector constitutes 88% of the financial

Islamic Banks as Creators of Money 9

Table 2.1 The Share of Financial Institutions in Turkish Financial System in Terms of Asset Sizes – 09/2017

Banks	88.0%
Insurance – pension funds	4.2%
Leasing	1.6%
Factoring	1.1%
Financing	1.0%
Others	4.2%

Source: Ministry of Development (2018).

system in Türkiye (Ministry of Development, 2018) and the share of financial institutions in Turkish financial system in terms of asset sizes is provided in Table 2.1 as an example. The financial system is simply composed of those who supply funds and those who demand funds. Financial intermediaries act as facilitators between these two groups. Financial intermediaries receive a fee from them, usually in the form of interest, in return for their service to reduce transaction costs and informational asymmetries while matching these two groups more easily.

From past to present, money and credit have functioned as a tool in the conduct of economic transactions. Contrary to what the classical economists suggest, Graeber (2011) asserts that we begin with what we now call virtual money, then we invented money, which has never completely replaced credit systems. Money and debt emerged at the same time. Therefore, a history of debt requires a history of money (Graeber, 2011).

While money and credit are both tools for the realization of exchange transactions, it is the unit of account that gives them functionality. From this point of view, we see that credit and barter come to the fore when money is scarce in terms of turning the wheels of the economy or when the unit of account loses its feature. The few examples of barter in modern communities are most commonly associated with monetary crises. For instance, in the German inflation of 1923, the 'butter' standard became a more reliable common measure of value (Davies, 2002). During the Middle Ages and in the early modern period, accounts were kept in terms of specific units, which were not means of payment but were units of value. In contrast, credit held in these accounting units might serve as means of payment[1] (Usher, 1943).

The banking system is located in the middle of money and credit because it is the primary mechanism that produces both of them. Credit transactions of non-bank financial institutions increase the loan supply but do not affect the money supply. On the other hand, as banks lend, they produce credit money and increase both the loan supply and the money supply. Therefore, we need to know the banking system's development in terms of deposit and credit creation. The stages of the continuous development of the banking system are outlined below.

At stage one, there are numerous small banks that are geographically semi-isolated. At this stage, banks are repositories for savings, i.e., deposits. Thus, deposits are not widely used as a means of payment. This means an expansion of lending would entail a substantial loss of reserves; therefore, banks are dependent on deposits for reserves and on reserves for lending. We can say deposits are exogenous to the banks, as they come from an increased supply of high-powered money due to depositors' cash/deposit preferences. At this stage, banks were intermediaries between saving and investment, as bankers claim of **financial intermediation theory**, and functioned like direct-lending institutions, where one has to have saved money before one lends it (Chick, 1992).

At stage two, there are fewer, but this time larger banks, which gained public confidence. At this stage, the consolidation of clearing arrangements enabled the shift to deposits as a means of payment. Now, deposits are not only savings but also transaction balances, moving from one bank to another but not leaving the system as a whole to any significant extent. This enabled the banking system to lend to a multiple of reserves, subject to a conventional or imposed reserve requirement, which is called **bank deposit multiplication** or **fractional reserve theory of banking** (Chick, 1992).

At stage three, the development of interbank lending mechanisms contributes to the efficient use of reserves. At stage four, the lender-of-last-resort principle is firmly established where the central bank has fully accepted responsibility for the stability of the financial system. Now, banks are more encouraged to expand lending beyond the reserve capacity of the system. Bank lending is constrained because the central bank provides reserves at a penalty rate higher than market interest rates (Chick, 1992). Endogenous money is, therefore, the result of institutional changes, which enabled the banking system to expand the supply of credit with no prior expansion of bank reserves. The introduction of liability management at stage five is considered a less fundamental version of money's endogeneity. This stage arose only because the central bank may not fully accommodate the demand for bank reserves. As a result of the last two stages, banks are no longer dependent on deposits or reserves in order to lend (Rochon & Rossi, 2013). The developments in the last two stages enhance bank lending in one hand, while introducing their own constraint on the other hand.

Here we see two theories coming forward: **financial intermediation theory** and **fractional reserve theory** (money multiplier) of banking. However, McLeay et al. (2014) underline two misconceptions about money creation: one is that banks act simply as intermediaries, lending out the deposits of depositors. The other one is that the central bank determines the quantity of loans and deposits in the economy by controlling the quantity of central bank money, which is the money multiplier theory. There is another theory, **credit creation theory,** according to which individual banks create credit in the form of deposits without solely lending out customers' deposited money (Werner, 2014).

3 Money Creation Process

Banks' deposit multiplication according to fractional reserve theory is shown in Figure 2.1. According to this theory, when money is deposited to a bank, the bank keeps a fraction of this deposit as a reserve requirement, which is imposed by the central bank and generally called required reserve ratio. We assume the required reserve ratio is 10%, all banks make loans for the full amount of their excess reserves, and the public prefers to keep all their money in deposits rather than carrying cash. At $t=0$, \$100 is deposited to Bank A by a depositor, which increases Bank A's reserves and deposit accounts to \$100. At $t=1$, Bank A lends out \$91 and keeps the remaining \$9 in its reserves. The borrower then spends the money for buying something, and the seller

t	Bank A		Bank B		Bank C		Bank D	
0	Reserves 100	Deposit 100						
1	Reserves 10 Loans 90	Deposit 100	Reserves 90	Deposit 90				
2	Reserves 10 Loans 90	Deposit 100	Reserves 9 Loans 81	Deposit 90	Reserves 81	Deposit 81		
3	Reserves 10 Loans 90	Deposit 100	Reserves 9 Loans 81	Deposit 90	Reserves 8,1 Loans 72,9	Deposit 81	Reserves 72,9	Deposit 72,9

Total Reserves:	$10 + 9 + 8,1 + 72,9$ ==>>>	**100**	
Total Deposit:	$100 + 90 + 81 + 72,9$ ==>>>	**343,9**	
Total Loans:	$90 + 81 + 72,9$ ==>>>	**243,9**	

Figure 2.1 Creation of Loans and Deposits by Banks.
Source: Authors.

12   *Ömer Faruk Tekdoğan*

(because of zero cash preference) deposits it in his deposit account at Bank B. This procedure repeats itself at each step and eventually at $t=3$, after three transactions, total reserves are equal to $100 (the initial cash amount deposited to Bank A), total loans created by the banking system is equal to $266.61, and total deposits is equal to $346.61. This classical textbook example continues to the final step, where total reserves remain the same while total loans reach $1.000 and total deposits reach $1.000. As a result, with a reserve base of $100, the banking system created many loans and deposits. In the event of a bank run where all depositors want to withdraw their deposits, the banking system will not be able to meet this demand.

If we only had traders as financial intermediaries instead of banks, the situation would be like in Figure 2.2. Let's assume, at time $t=0$, Trader A has $100 in cash. He lends out all this amount as he is not subjected to a required reserve ratio. After three steps, there is still $100 cash in the system, total loans created is $300, and the total amount borrowed is $300. If we compare this situation with the one in the banking system, the total loan amount is slightly higher (because of the absence of the required reserve ratio), and there was no deposit creation. As Menger (2009) pointed out, if a bank begins to decrease deposit creation, the gap would be immediately filled by a competing bank, or, if this is not possible, the commerce will create for itself other media of circulation to settle transactions, which will take the place of deposits (Menger, 2009). However, the most crucial difference between these two examples is that when banks grant loans and create deposits, this increases the money supply and disturbs the stability of the economy's unit of account. In terms of money supply, at the end of the second example, the total cash amount still equals $100. However, at the end of first example, through money creation, total deposits amount is $346.61 that is readily to be spent.

For the deposit multiplication example of the banking system, we assume a cash amount of $100 is deposited in the first place. However, credit creation theory asserts that there is no need for that. A researcher conducted an empirical study with a local bank in Germany to see how banks channel funds for lending. The bank's manager confirmed that neither he nor the bank's staff checked either before or during the granting of the loan whether they keep sufficient funds with the central bank. Furthermore, the bank also did not undertake any transfers or account bookings in order to finance the credit balance (Werner, 2014). This phenomenon is peculiar to banks. Because in bookkeeping terms, the creation of money is how banks provide the economy with a number of money units to facilitate the exchange of objects between the payer and the payee. Depending on the technological and institutional framework, money creation, which is always an endogenous phenomenon, may take different physical forms such as gold coins, paper money, or book-entry money (Rochon & Rossi, 2013).

It is the Electronic Fund Transfer (EFT) system that facilitates the money production of banks with today's technology. When a customer receives a loan from a bank, the loan amount is either deposited into the customer's

t	Trader A		Trader B		Trader C		Trader D	
0	Cash 100	Capital 100						
1	Cash 0 Loans 100	Capital 100	Cash 100	Borrowed 100				
2	Cash 0 Loans 100	Capital 100	Cash 0 Loans 100	Borrowed 100	Cash 100	Borrowed 100		
3	Cash 0 Loans 100	Capital 100	Cash 0 Loans 100	Borrowed 100	Cash 0 Loans 100	Borrowed 100	Cash 100	Borrowe d 100

Total Cash:		**100**
Total Loans:		**300**
Total Borrowing:		**300**

Figure 2.2 Creation of Loans by Traders.
Source: Authors.

deposit account at that bank or transferred to the customer's deposit account at another bank. In this case, the lending bank becomes liable to the counterpart bank as much as the deposit it generates. Each bank has a settlement account in the EFT system, and the funds in the banks' required reserve accounts are transferred to their EFT accounts every day when the system is opened. For example, in Türkiye, transfers can also be made between EFT reconciliation accounts and other bank accounts at the central bank. Banks' balances in the EFT system are transferred to the reserve deposit accounts at the end of the day, and their EFT accounts are reset. In order to reduce the liquidity needed in the EFT system, payments between banks can be instantly cleared. Therefore, in a system with two banks, if banks are indebted an equal amount of deposit money to each other through the system, the amount to be transferred back to the reserve deposit account will be the same as the beginning of the day through clearing, so there is no limit to the amount of deposit money in the short term because the deadline for maintaining the additional required reserve can take more than one month. In the EFT system, it is unlikely that banks will be indebted to each other in equal amounts; some of them will have a fund deficit at the end of the day, while some of them have surplus funds. One of the constraints in banks' deposit money creation is the cost to be incurred to close the fund deficit (Tekdogan, 2020a).

An earlier form of the EFT clearing system was great periodical fairs that were being held all over Europe during the Middle Ages, to which traders and bankers were coming from everywhere. In these fairs, debts and credits were being cleared without using a single coin and, by this way, merchants and traders could rely on a unit of account whose definition is stable, which was wholly independent of coin debasement (Rochon & Rossi, 2013). Another example is the clearinghouses of the USA, which were began to be established during the 1850s. Each bank opened an account only in the clearinghouse, instead of opening an account in each other bank individually. However, clearing operations continued to be made with gold. Clearinghouses started to issue bonds in exchange for gold in order to speed up the clearing process. Until the 1850s, banks were sending their porters to other banks to clear checks with a daily exchange and settlement. Each bank had bank accounts with other banks. Banks' porters were carrying ledger books, checks drawn on other banks, and bags of gold (Gorton, 1984).

A simple demonstration of interbank clearing can be seen in Figure 2.3. In a banking system of two banks, first, a customer of Bank A borrows $100 from his banks, and the loan amount is deposited in his account. In the second transaction, another customer borrows $200 from Bank A, and the total loan amount is being transferred to his account in Bank B. Thus, after the second transaction, total loans and total deposits of Bank A are equal to $300 and $100, respectively. Bank A is indebted to Bank B an amount of $200. However, deposit accounts in Bank B increase by $200. In the third transaction, a customer of Bank B borrows $300 and asks the bank to transfer it to his account in Bank A. After all, transactions are settled, Bank A's total loans and total deposits are $300 and $400 respectively, and Bank B's total loans and total deposits are $300 and $200, respectively. In total, an amount of $600 was lent out by creating $600 as credit money. The total cost for these transactions is $100, which Bank B should borrow from Bank A.

The close relationship between the money supply and loans given is shown in Figure 2.4. It is not interesting for those who argue that banks can lend more money as more money is deposited in bank accounts. However, Figure 2.4 starts when Türkiye was hit by the Covid-19 pandemic, and the

Bank A		Bank B	
Loans 100	Deposits 100		
Loans 300	Deposits 100	Clearing (Bank A) 200	Deposits 200
	EFT (Bank B) 200		
Loans 300	Deposits 400	Loans 300	Deposits 200
Clearing (Bank B) 300	EFT (Bank B) 200	Clearing (Bank A) 200	EFT (Bank A) 300
Loans 300	Deposits 400	Loans 300	Deposits 200
Interbank Lending 100			**Interbank Borrowing 100**

Figure 2.3 Demonstration of Interbank Clearing.
Source: Authors.

economy slowed down. Many people lost their jobs, relied on their savings, and the confidence in the Turkish Lira was low. The government pushed banks to increase lending by inventing the active ratio,[2] which was unique to banking practice. Public banks accelerated loan growth, loans increased from 2.769 billion TL to 3.657 billion TL, and deposits increased from 2.258 billion TL to 3.010 billion TL.

4 Islamic Banks also Create Money

It is argued that credit money is created as banks lend out loans and the most important difference between Islamic banks and conventional banks is that they do not give loans. However, Islamic banks are subject to the same regulatory framework as conventional banks. As such, they are part of the fractional reserve system. They create money like conventional banks through the same clearing mechanism via the EFT system, which was already explained in the previous section.

Islamic banks operate in competition with conventional banks in the capitalist system. They need to comply with Islamic rules, but they also need to fulfill the systemic requirements. For this reason, it is difficult for Islamic banks to survive without credit creation in the fractional reserve system (Hasan, 2014). Since central banks' mandate to control the money supply and

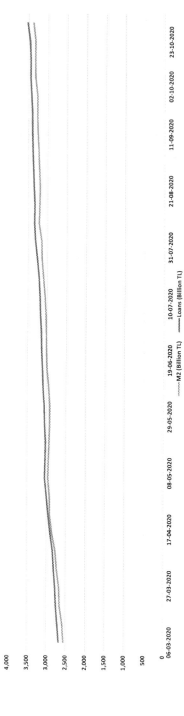

Figure 2.4 M2 Money Supply and Loans Given in Türkiye, 03/2020–10/2020.
Source: Central Bank of Republic of Türkiye.

prevent inflation dominates their relationship with the commercial banks, central banks treat Islamic banks at par with the conventional banks by obliging them to the same regulations relating to reserve requirements (Siddiqi, 1992). Although there are separate legal regulations for Islamic banks in some Islamic countries, the same mechanism enables them to operate on a fractional reserve basis.

The regulatory framework applied to all banks consists of a generic Basel Committee on Banking Supervision (BCBS) component, and this conceptual framework could be complemented by Islamic Financial Services Board (IFSB) prudential standards and guiding principles on Islamic banking to give effect to Shariah law compliance. IFSB standards are normally based on corresponding conventional standards of BCBS. In some countries such as Indonesia and Malaysia, a similar regulatory framework is adopted for Islamic and conventional banks, but separate guidelines and regulations are issued for areas that are specific to Islamic banking. The central bank (and an independent authority for microprudential regulation in some countries) is usually the institution responsible for the supervision of Islamic banks, just like conventional banks in the Islamic countries (Song & Oosthuizen, 2014).

In Türkiye, participation banks and conventional banks are defined as credit institutions in the Banking Act 5411, and they are both in the same regulatory framework based on the fractional reserve. Although Indonesia adopted the Islamic (Shariah) Banking Act, the case for the fractional reserve is not different from any other Islamic country. In both countries, Islamic banks operate on a fractional reserve basis, which can be seen in Figure 2.5. In a bank-run situation where all depositors rush to Islamic banks to withdraw their deposits, only 42% of demand deposits can be served in Türkiye, and 33% can be served in Indonesia. If time deposits are also taken into consideration, these ratios decrease to 19% and 16%, respectively. Note that Islamic banks' reserves kept at the central bank are not only against demand deposits, which are a component of M1 money supply, but also against other liabilities of Islamic banks, which are components of M2 and M3 money supply.

The statement that Islamic banks do not give loans is vague. What is meant here may be the use of the name financing or murabaha instead of the loan. Murabaha is an Islamic contract, and its permissibility is not questioned here. However, looking at the consequences, the redemption plan is clear from the beginning when an Islamic bank provides financing with murabaha, just as the principal and interest redemption plan is determined when a conventional bank lends. Either way, when a mortgage or vehicle financing is used, there is not much difference as well. For instance, Figure 2.6 compares the credit terms for mortgage financing offered by a participation bank and a conventional bank in Türkiye. Here is a difference in the form but not substance, and essentially the two operations have the same effects in the last instance. As Siddiqi (1992) argues, when Islamic banks finance trade through murabaha, much of the money paid out to sellers is bound to flow back to bank

TURKEY

				(Million TL)	Multiplier
Cash	15.730,80	Demand Deposits	144.440,85		2,4
Reserves	44.466,80	Time Deposits	180.745,18		
Total	**60.197,60**	**Total**	**325.186,03**		**5,4**

INDONESIA

				(Billion IDR)	Multiplier
Cash	5.947,04	Demand Deposits	227.394,78		3,0
Reserves	69.211,24	Time Deposits	236.797,83		
Total	**75.158,28**	**Total**	**464.192,61**		**6,2**

Figure 2.5 Islamic Banks' Consolidated Cash and Reserves Holdings against Deposits, Türkiye versus Indonesia, 10/2020.

Source: Banking Regulation and Supervision Authority of Türkiye (BRSA), Financial Services Authority of Indonesia (OJK).

	Islamic Bank	*Conventional Bank*
Loan Amount	100.000	100.000
Term	60 months	60 months
Profit/Interest rate	1,52%	1,39%
Annual Cost Rate	20,97%	18,94%
Installment Amount	2.552	2.468
Total Repayment Amount	153.145	148.085

Figure 2.6 Credit Terms for Mortgage Financing, Islamic Bank versus Conventional Bank, Türkiye.

Source: The author's own based on the information from the banks' websites.

accounts. Therefore, murabaha financing results in creation of additional bank deposits. Moreover, investment based on musharakah or mudarabah also results in creation of new bank deposits (Siddiqi, 1992).

Zaman (2015a) asserts that the banking business is the creation of money and the giving of created money on loan to earn a profit, whether it comes in the form of interest or profit from mudarabah or musharakah shares (Zaman, 2015a). Anwar (2003) emphasizes that Islamic banks issue a credit to seek profit, just like their conventional counterparties. Islamic banks prefer lending money to entrepreneurs rather than becoming entrepreneurs. This motivates the Islamic banks to figure out the means to charge the time value of money. Murabaha financing, posing as a trader by engaging in a fictitious purchase, is one way to do that (Anwar, 2003). Murabaha is simply debt financing disguised in the form of a sale contract.

Chapra (1996) argues that money can tend to be more stable in an Islamic economy because there should be need-based consumption and productive investment instead of conspicuous consumption and speculative investment. Therefore, banks will avoid financing for speculative and unproductive purposes (Chapra, 1996). Werner (2005, 2009) argue that credit for production or productive credit creation is credit creation used for the creation of new goods and services, which increases GDP in the long term without inflation. There are two types of unproductive credit creation. The first one is in the form of consumptive credit, which increases GDP in the short term. This type also tends to drive inflation up by the extension of credit for the consumption but it does not lead to the creation of goods and services in the short term. Second type of unproductive credit creation is in the form of speculative credit which increases asset prices by the creation of credit for the use in asset or financial transactions (Werner, 2005, 2009). Beck et al. (2014) found that bank lending to enterprises drives the positive impact of financial development on economic growth. However, this is not valid for bank lending to households. Economic growth can be fostered by productive credit creation for the real sector's financing needs (Beck et al., 2014).

Siddiqi (1992) argues that money creation by Islamic banks is less expansionary than that of conventional banks because Islamic financing is linked to real productive activities, and Islamic banks' activities are more closely associated with the creation of additional wealth in the real sector (Siddiqi, 1992). Regarding this argument, the situation in Türkiye is illustrated in Figure 2.7. Consumer loans are a good proxy to check whether Islamic banks in Türkiye finance conspicuous consumption and speculative investment. Between January 2019 and September 2020, consumer loans (credit cards included) to total loans by Islamic banks has fluctuated around 13%. In September 2020, this ratio was 14.59% for Islamic banks, whereas it was 26.47% for conventional banks. In this period, housing loans consisted of more than 80% of consumer loans on average. It can be inferred that the case for Türkiye supports Siddiqi's (1992) argument.

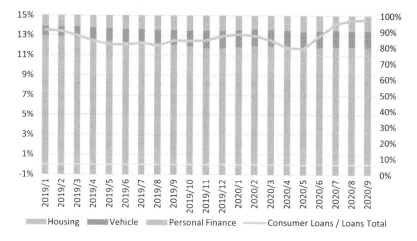

Figure 2.7 Consumer Loans Granted by Participation Banks in Türkiye, 2019/1–2020/9.
Source: BRSA.

As explained by Meera and Larbani (2009), at a certain time in an economy, X amount of money circulates with W amount of real things. When banks create Y amount of new money through lending, borrowers supposed to spend it to buy some of the real things. Therefore, the total amount of money in the economy increases (X + Y) while the amount of real things remains the same. As a result, the wealth is transferred from those who hold the initial X money to the borrowers of Y amount of loan, because of the fall in purchasing power of money.

Usmani (1998) supports the view that loans advanced by banks create artificial money:

> The supply of money through the loans advanced by the financial institutions does not normally match with the real goods and services produced in the society, because the loans create artificial money through which the amount of money supply is increased, and sometimes multiplied without creating real assets in the same quantity. This gap between the supply of money and production of real assets creates or fuels inflation.

It can be inferred that Usmani admits that Islamic banks create money but with real assets. However, this assumption reminds "Real Bills Doctrine," which states if banks lend only against the short-term commercial paper, the money supply will be automatically matched by real output. Therefore, inflationary over issue would be impossible provided the money is issued on loans made to finance real transactions (Humphrey, 1982). As an illustration, suppose a manufacturer sells $10,000 worth of goods to a customer and receives an invoice with payment due in 90 days. The customer has created a real bill that is not secured but represents tangible goods in the process. The manufacturer can sell the paper to a bank with a discounted value of $9,800. The bank monetizes the paper and later collects the bill at full value when the payment is due.[3]

The logic of the Real Bills doctrine is questioned by Javaid (2015), as he saw various flaws in details. For instance, any real asset may exchange many hands and, during each transaction, a financial intermediary may create credit money. Besides, as manufacturers generally finance their operations by borrowing loans from banks, they would add the debt servicing expense into the cost of goods, which adds to the selling price and makes inflation a vicious circle. Finally, profits of Islamic banks from murabaha financing would also produce a continuous rise in money and prices. Islamic banks are as inflationary as conventional banks because of their fractional reserve nature like conventional banks, not in terms of the nature of contracts, but in terms of the structure enabling them to expand the money supply (Javaid, 2015).

Islamic banks are creators of credit and money, like their conventional counterparts, which they have to compete with. They create credit and contribute to increasing debt levels in the debt-based financial system. Therefore, Islamic banks do not fit the risk-sharing and equity-based frame of Islamic finance. The main and most-debated alternative to credit creation of banks is 100% reserve requirement, and this is organized in various models under FRB.

5 Full (100%) Reserve Requirement

Full (or 100%) reserve banking is proposed in various forms as an alternative system to fractional reserve banking. Dixhoorn (2013) compares these proposals in four mainstream monetary plans – the Chicago plan, sovereign money, narrow banking, and limited purpose banking, which rest on the idea that money creation is centralized at an independent public institution (central bank) and deposit accounts become fully backed by central bank-issued money (Dixhoorn, 2013). FRB aims to eliminate commercial banks' ability to create money and establish economic stability by dividing commercial banks into deposit-keeping institutions and credit institutions so that banks first assume the role of a financial intermediary that collects money first then lends it (Tekdogan, 2020b).

Lainà (2015) presents a comprehensive mapping exercise of the history of FRB proposals, beginning with David Ricardo in the 19th century, continued during the Great Depression in the 1920s, and re-emerged after the global financial crisis. During this time, FRB was implemented in the UK the Bank Charter Act of 1844, which prohibited private money creation by requiring banks to fully-back banknotes with government-issued money. The US followed the same tradition in the National Acts of 1863 and 1864. However, all these efforts were futile since the prohibitions did not include bank deposits, which slowly became the dominant means of payment (Lainà, 2015).

The Chicago plan was first proposed by a group of economists at the University of Chicago as a radical reform of the monetary system by requiring reserves of 100% against all deposits subject to checks. The plan had some support among US politicians and economists almost adopted in the US (Hart, 1935). Phillips (1992) tells the history of the Chicago plan why it lost out to the alternative measures embodied in the Banking Act of 1935 (Phillips, 1992). Irving Fisher supported the Chicago Plan and highlighted some of its main advantages: large business cycles would be better controlled, bank runs would be eliminated, both government and private debt levels would be reduced substantially (Fisher, 1936). Benes and Kumhof (2012) tested these claims by embedding a comprehensive and calibrated banking system model in a dynamic stochastic general equilibrium model of the US economy and validated all four of Fisher's claims (Benes & Kumhof, 2012).

Sovereign money is an updated version of the Chicago plan by taking into account current banking practices shaped by technological advancement during the last century. This proposal is based on the idea that the state can conduct money creation more effectively and appropriately, and the payment system would be safer when banks' lending activity is separated (Dyson et al., 2016). The central bank will be the sole authority to create money and keep the growth of the money supply in line with the needs of a growing economy. Banks will only keep the records of accounts of their customers, whereas all the funds will be stored at the central bank (Sigurjonsson, 2015).[4]

Dixhoorn (2013) summarizes the arguments for and against FRB, while Dyson et al. (2011) address common critiques about FRB. The foremost ones are the probability of a shortage of credit and the risk of inflation because of allowing the state to issue money. Dow and Montagnoli (2015) thinks that FRB plan is unlikely to work, as new forms of money and new sources of credit would evolve outside the net, that is certain given the long history of financial innovation in the face of new regulatory restrictions (Dow & Montagnoli, 2015).

FRB is advocated by some Islamic economists as well. Askari and Krichene (2014) define Islamic finance as a two-tier financial system that consists of a 100% reserve depository and safekeeping banking system and a profit-loss sharing investment-banking system. Khan (1986) sees no significant difference between Islamic banking and FRB. However, the Islamic banking system further requires that loans and advances made by banks should be based on equity participation. Khan and Mirakhor (1989) argue that FRB would prevent the possibility of a banking crisis from interfering with the payments mechanism. Al-Jarhi (1980) includes FRB while setting the framework for a monetary and financial structure of an interest-free economy and suggests a gradual transformation to FRB accompanied by injection of additional resources to banks through central deposits. In order to fulfill the rules of Islamic economics that wealth redistribution must be justifiable, Al-Jarhi,

(2016) argues the central bank should enjoy full and direct control over the money supply by replacing the fractional reserve system with FRB. Chapra (1985) claims that FRB is one of the most important reforms to maintain continuous sanity in the economy. Zaman (2015a), referring to the Chicago plan, states that FRB is very much in line with Islamic principles since the power of money creation is supposed to belong solely to the government. Zaman (2015b) asserts that the way to FRB would be possible if Muslim leaders, Ulema, and intellectuals could understand the issues with the monetary system. Choudhury (2014) supports the Islamic transformation into a 100% reserve requirement monetary system with the gold-backed money as currency in relation to real economic transaction. This is one of the FRB plans, pure commodity standard, which opt for gold-backed money instead of fiat money. Tekdogan (2020a) regards FRB as an important step to achieve better functioning of waqf and zakat institutions and eliminating riba.

Hasan (2014) rates FRB impracticable for Islamic banking as he believes Islamic banks would hardly survive without credit creation. Hasan (2008) suggests that there is no point insisting on 100% reserve requirement if Islamic banks fulfill their part of the contract and put money to Shariah-compliant uses. He defends the credit creation of banks as it enables trade industry and commerce to run smoothly and he rather searches answer for what instruments the central banks could use for controlling credit creation in the case of Islamic banks. However, both of these studies do not elaborate the modus operandi of FRB proposals but only consider 100% reserve requirement.

The majority of Islamic economists, who confirm the money creation of Islamic banks, are in support of FRB. The argument that Islamic banks would not survive without credit creation brings up the question of whether if it is possible or not to establish an Islamic economic system with today's Islamic banks. If they don't serve the objectives of Islamic law, then why we insist on keeping them running? On the other hand, FRB proposals do not eliminate banks but they change the business of banking.

6 Conclusion

In this study, we clarified the money creation process of private banks and how and why Islamic banks are a part of this process. Then, we briefly explained the FRB system as the alternative of the fractional reserve system, which is the backbone of money creation process and the centerline of both conventional and Islamic banks. We showed that many Islamic economists are aware of the private money creation and they advocate full reserve requirement for banking system. However, we can argue that still many Islamic economists have a misconception about Islamic banks since they deny the fact that Islamic bank are also creators of money.

In some countries today, the required reserve ratio is zero. However, this does not eliminate the truth of the money multiplier and the fractional reserve system. Similarly, banks' use of different financing tools that do not include interest does not prevent the production of credit money. There are other factors that determine the money supply, such as depositors' preference to hold cash or deposit, customers' demand for loans and banks' loan supply. Without the need for Basel regulations, these factors restrict the money supply. For this reason, banks cannot reach an unlimited balance sheet size. The fractional reserve phenomenon existed before the emergence of central banks and the required reserve ratio policy. Banks continue to hold reserves in return for some of the deposits they keep, and this is called the fractional reserve system in the literature. In this respect, the claims that the fractional reserve system is not implemented in practice are wrong.

There are still a quite number of fiqh scholars who still do not know or understand the situation of money creation. Fiqh scholars who know and understand this phenomenon unfortunately set Islamic banks aside from this. It is not helping to deny the fact that Islamic banks create money. Some Islamic economists who confirm the money creation of Islamic banks and support FRB as the main alternative. Instead of denying the truth, we need to clarify whether it is necessary to put forward alternative ways to credit money production. And if necessary, we need to compare the pros and cons of these alternatives with the pros and cons of the current system. Otherwise, establishing an Islamic economic system would not go beyond a dream with the current Islamic financial transactions and instruments, which are different in form from conventional ones but the same in substance leading to the same economic results in essence.

The technology has been developing since the initiation of FRB proposals a century ago while the circulation of money happens electronically. Today's agenda regarding the financial system includes financial technologies, cryptocurrency, and digital currency while banking operations are carried out electronically. Sovereign money, one of the FRB proposals, is based on today's feasible setting for the implementation of FRB electronically. This can be harmonized with the idea of central bank digital currency that can make the transition to FRB much easier.

Islamic banks need to survive without credit creation; however, they are constrained by the requirements of the capitalist economy. So long as Islamic banks do not fit the risk-sharing and equity-based framework of Islamic finance and they do not serve the objectives of Islamic law, we should endeavor more to establish and develop Islamic financial institutions based on original Islamic values.

Notes

1 For instance, in Florence, the instability of the ratio between gold and silver made florin to be changed not in its weight but to be reckoned at a different value in units of account (see Usher, 1943).

2 The active ratio regulation announced by the Banking Regulation and Supervision Authority of Turkey (BRSA) on April 18, 2020, in order to ensure the most effective use of the resources held by the banks was put into practice on May 1,

2020, and then amendments were made in the regulation on April 30, May 29, August 10, and September 28. BRSA re-evaluated the active ratio regulation on November 24 within the framework of normalization steps and decided to abolish it as of December 31, 2020.

The formulation of the active ratio, which was announced in the decision dated April 18 and should not fall below 100% for deposit banks and 80% for participation banks, was as follows:

Active Ratio = [Loans + (Securities × 0.75) + (CBRT Swap × 0.5)]/[TL Deposit + (FX Deposit × 1.25)]

3 https://www.investopedia.com/terms/r/real-bill-doctrine.asp
4 For details see Dyson et al. (2016) and Jackson and Dyson (2012).

References

Al-Jarhi, M. (1980). A Monetary and Financial Structure for an Interest-Free Economy: Institutions, Mechanism & Policy. Retrieved from https://mpra.ub.uni-muenchen.de/66741/

Al-Jarhi, M. (2016). An economic theory of Islamic finance (No. 72698).

Anwar, M. (2003). Islamicity of Banking and Modes of Islamic Banking. *Arab Law Quarterly, 18*(1), 62–80. https://doi.org/10.1163/026805503773081735

Askari, H., & Krichene, N. (2014). Islamic finance: an alternative financial system for stability, equity, and growth. *PSL Quarterly Review, 67*(268), 9–54.

Beck, T., Büyükkarabacak, B., Rioja, F. K., & Valev, N. T. (2014). Who Gets the Credit? and Does It Matter? Household vs. Firm Lending Across Countries. *B.E. Journal of Macroeconomics, 12*(1). https://doi.org/10.1515/1935-1690.2262

Benes, J., & Kumhof, M. (2012). The Chicago Plan Revisited. *IMF Working Papers, 12*(202), 71. https://doi.org/10.5089/9781475505528.001

Chapra, M. U. (1985). *Towards a Just Monetary System.* Retrieved from http://ierc.sbu.ac.ir/

Chapra, M. U. (1996). Monetary Management in an Islamic Economy. *Islamic Economic Studies, 4*(1), 1–35.

Chick, V. (1992). The Evolution of the Banking System and the Theory of Saving, Investment and Interest. In P. Arestis & S. C. Dow (Eds.), *On Money, Method and Keynes* (pp. 193–205). https://doi.org/10.1007/978-1-349-21935-3_12

Choudhury, M. A. (2014). Micro Money and Real Economic Relationship in the 100 Percent Reserve Requirement Monetary System. *Islamic Banking and Finance Review, 1*(1), 25–36. https://doi.org/10.32350/ibfr.2014.01.02

Dixhoorn, C. Van. (2013). *Full Reserve Banking: An Analysis of Four Monetary Reform Plans.* Retrieved from http://sustainablefinancelab.nl/files/2013/07/Full-Reserve-Banking-Dixhoorn-SFL.pdf

Dow, S., & Montagnoli, A. (2015). A critique of full reserve banking. *Sheffield Economic Research Paper Series*, (2015008), 22.

Dyson, B., Greenham, T., Collins, J. R., & Werner, R. A. (2011). *Towards a Twenty-First Century Banking and Monetary System.*

Dyson, B., Hodgson, G., & Lerven, F. van. (2016). *Sovereign Money: An Introduction.* Retrieved from www.positivemoney.org

Fisher, I. (1936). 100% Money and the Public Debt. *Economic Forum, Spring*, 406–420.

Friedman, M. (1948). A Monetary and Fiscal Framework for Economic Stability. *The American Economic Review, 38*(3), 245–264. Retrieved from http://www.jstor.org/stable/1810624

26   *Ömer Faruk Tekdoğan*

Gorton, G. (1984). Private Clearinghouses and the Origins of Central Banking. *Federal Reserve Bank of Philadelphia Business Review*, pp. 3–12.

Graeber, D. (2011). *Debt the First 5,000 Years.* New York: Melville House Publishing.

Hagino, S., & Cavieres, L. (2013). OECD financial statistics for measuring the structure and size of the shadow banking system. *Proceedings of the Sixth IFC Conference on "Statistical Issues and Activities in a Changing Environment,"* 16–50. Retrieved from http://www.bis.org/ifc/publ/ifcb36b.pdf

Hart, A. G. (1935). The "Chicago Plan" of Banking Reform. *The Review of Economic Studies*, 2(2), 104–116.

Hasan, Z. (2008). Credit Creation and Control: An Unresolved Issue in Islamic Banking. *International Journal of Islamic and Middle Eastern Finance and Management*, 1(1), 69–81. https://doi.org/10.1108/17538390810864269

Hasan, Z. (2014). The Recent Turmoil and Monetary Policy in a Dual Financial System with Islamic Perspective. *Journal of Islamic Banking and Finance*, 31(4), 9–24.

Humphrey, T. M. (1982). The Real Bills Doctrine. *Economic Review of the Richmond Fed*, (Sep/Oct), 3–13.

Jackson, A., & Dyson, B. (2012). Modernising Money. In *Positive Money.* Positive Money.

Javaid, O. (2015). Methodology of Institutional Analysis and Its Implication for Contemporary Framework of Islamic Banks. *Humanomics*, 31(2), 183–200. https://doi.org/https://www.emerald.com/insight/content/doi/10.1108/H-07-2013-0051/full/html

Khan, M. S. (1986). *Islamic Interest-Free Banking: A Theoretical Analysis* (Vol. 33). Retrieved from http://www.jstor.org/stable/3866920

Khan, M. S., & Mirakhor, A. (1989). The Financial System and Monetary Policy in an Islamic Economy. *Journal of King Abdulaziz University-Islamic Economics*, 1, 39–57. https://doi.org/10.4197/islec.3-1.5

Lainà, P. (2015). Proposals for Full-Reserve Banking: A Historical Survey from David Ricardo to Martin Wolf. *Economic Thought*, 4(2), 1–19.

McLeay, M., Radia, A., Thomas, R., Mcleay, B. M., Radia, A., Thomas, R., ... Kumhof, M. (2014). Money Creation in the Modern Economy. *Bank of England Quarterly Bulletin*, 529(Q1), 57. Retrieved from https://www.bankofengland.co.uk/quarterly-bulletin/2014/q1/money-creation-in-the-modern-economy

Meera, A. K. M., & Larbani, M. (2009). Ownership Effects of Fractional Reserve Banking: An Islamic Perspective. *Humanomics*, 25(2), 101–116. https://doi.org/10.1108/08288660910964175

Menger, C. (2009). *On The Origins of Money.* https://doi.org/10.1017/CBO9781107415324.004

Ministry of Development. (2018). *Finansal Hizmetlerin Geliştirilmesi Özel İhtisas Komisyonu Raporu.* Retrieved from https://www.sbb.gov.tr/wp-content/uploads/2020/04/FinansalHizmetlerinGelistirilmesiOzelIhtisasKomisyonuRaporu.pdf

Mishkin, F. S. (2004). *The Economics of Money, Banking, and Financial Markets* (7th ed.). Addison-Wesley Series in Economics.

Obama's Remarks on the Economy. (2009). Retrieved from the New York Times website: https://www.nytimes.com/2009/04/14/us/politics/14obama-text.html

Phillips, R. J. (1992). *The 'Chicago Plan' and New Deal Banking Reform.* https://doi.org/10.20595/jjbf.19.0_3

Rochon, L.-P., & Rossi, S. (2013). Endogenous Money: The Evolutionary versus Revolutionary Views. *Review of Keynesian Economics*, *1*(2), 210–229. https://doi.org/10.4337/roke.2013.02.04

Siddiqi, M. N. (1992). Impact of Islamic Modes of Finance on Monetary Expansion. *Journal of King Abdulaziz University-Islamic Economics*, *4*(1), 37–46.

Sigurjonsson, F. (2015). *Monetary Reform: A Better Monetary System for Iceland*. Retrieved from https://eng.forsaetisraduneyti.is/media/Skyrslur/monetary-reform.pdf

Soddy, F. (1961). Wealth, Virtual Wealth and Debt: The Solution of the Economic Paradox. (3rd ed.). https://doi.org/10.2307/2224365

Song, I., & Oosthuizen, C. (2014). Islamic Banking Regulation and Supervision: Survey Results and Challenges. In *IMF Working Papers* (No. WP/14/220; Vol. 14). https://doi.org/10.5089/9781498380928.001

Tekdogan, O. F. (2020a). *İslam İktisadı Açısından Kaydi Para ve Kısmi Rezerv Bankacılığı*. İstanbul: İktisat Yayınları.

Tekdogan, O. F. (2020b). The Introduction of Waqf into Fractional and Full Reserve Banking Systems to Achieve Economic Stability. *Journal of Islamic Monetary Economics and Finance*, *6*(3), 531–554. https://doi.org/https://doi.org/10.21098/jimf.v6i3.1132

Tobin, J. (1967). Commercial Banks as Creators of Money. In D. Hester & J. Tobin (Eds.), *Financial Markets and Economic Activity* (pp. 1–11). Cowles Foundation at Yale University.

Usher, A. P. (1943). The Early History of Deposit Banking in Mediterranean Europe. In *Harvard University Press*. https://doi.org/10.2307/2226087

Usmani, M. T. (1998). *An Introduction to Islamic Finance*.

Werner, R. A. (2005). *New Paradigm in Macroeconomics*. https://doi.org/10.1057/9780230506077

Werner, R. A. (2009). Financial Crises in Japan during the 20th century. *Bankhistorisches Archiv*, *47*, 98–123.

Werner, R. A. (2014). Can Banks Individually Create Money out of Nothing? – The Theories and the Empirical Evidence. *International Review of Financial Analysis*, *36*(C), 1–19. https://doi.org/10.1016/j.irfa.2014.07.015

Zaman, A. (2015a). *Creation of Money and Islamic Banks* (pp. 1–19). Retrieved from https://www.researchgate.net/publication/286239351_English_Creation_of_Money_and_Islamic_Banks

Zaman, A. (2015b). *On the Nature of Modern Money*. Retrieved from http://ssrn.com/abstract=2535697

3 The Advantages of Islamic Banking and Financial Markets

Mabid Ali Al-Jarhi

1 Introduction

Islamic finance starts from rejecting interest-based lending. Such rejection appears to be religiously justified with varied degrees of emhasiz on Islam, Christianity, and Judaism. The abhorrence of interest is also found in Buddhism and Hinduism. However, the school of analytical Islamic economics has developed its economic rationale. The classical loan contract, upon which the financial system of market capitalism is founded, has been built on an interest rate flawed theory. The use of the rate of interest is marred with serious inefficiencies. This paper reviews the theoretical flaws underlying the classical loan contract and the inefficiencies surrounding interest rate use. Islamic finance alternatively provides finance in the form of money in return for equity or rights to share proportionately in future business profits and production. Finance is also offered as goods and services delivered in return for a commitment to repay their value at a future date or spot money in return for future commodities delivery. The paper goes further to explain the economic advantages of such a system. This paper addresses four questions: (1) Why all the fuss about the interest rate of interest? (2) Is Islamic finance, as an alternative to interest-based debt finance, viable and efficient? (3) How can Islamic finance be implied for the whole economy? (4) Given the theoretical flaws in interest rate theories and the inefficiencies surrounding the use of the rate of interest, what would be the shape of *Islamic monetary and financial markets* and how open market operations concerning relation to monetary managements and financial-market regulation are conducted?

2 Theoretical Flaws in Interest Rate Theories

The neoclassics developed a scheme for intertemporal choice for dated commodities. It was based on time preference, justifying a premium for present over future commodities. Due to its assumed perfections, the neoclassical model boils down to a barter model. Nonetheless, the neoclassics jumped from the context of commodities to money without realizing how big was such a jump. Along the way, they caused their interest rate theory irreparable

DOI: 10.4324/9781003377283-3

damage, which extended to similar alternative theories, e.g., the liquidity preference theory.

Böhm -Bawerk (1890) used the concept of time preference, initially developed by Carl Menger under impatience, as one of the justifications of conventional finance, i.e., selling present for future money at a premium. Then, he jumped outside his barter model to the monetary world, claiming that expressing the interest rate in terms of money (instead of commodities) depended on the monetary standard employed. Such jump belies Böhm-Bawerk belief in some imaginary mapping from the barter world of impatience or time preference to the monetary world of the rate of interest. Böhm -Bawerk (1890) justified interest by the presence of time preference and production taking time.

Time preference, as could be understood from Böhm-Bawerk, brings to mind the urgency of consumption. It can be a natural result of human mortality.[1] An individual's life can end at any moment. Under imperfect information, the present is admittedly more certain than the future. Such an idea is a direct reflection of costly information. Considering that the neoclassical model assumes perfect information, the neoclassical treatment of time preference is a serious mistake as it conflicts with perfect information.

At certain income levels, the homo ordinarius[2] finds that specific basic needs, like bread, rice, potatoes have a higher urgency than meat, fruit, and transport. As income rises, the relative urgency of basic needs changes in favor of other commodities, like meat, transportation, entertainment, etc.

Intuitively, given the level of real income, it would be axiomatic that each individual would have a different rate of time preference for each commodity. Besides, different individuals would have different rates of time preference for various commodities. In other words, individual and commodity heterogeneity concerning intertemporal preferences must be accepted.

Böhm-Bawerk relationship between the time spent producing a good and its time preference can be handled differently, taking the cue from Turkish black olives. They are cured in salt for a period that ranges from three to six months. The longer the period, the better taste. We can intuitively accept that better-tasting olives are more expensive given the olive quality itself. When ripe olives become ready to eat after six months, their taste may improve further by reducing saltiness. It would take even more time. Therefore, the best-tasting black olives command the highest price with having no bitter taste and lower sodium. Commanding a higher price would reflect the time involved in the production. However, we can consider each olive of a certain quality (taste plus other features) as a different commodity. It would help ignore the time spent in production. In other words, the time involved in producing commodities is fully reflected in their prices. We can therefore focus on time preference and ignore the other factor.

While Böhm-Bawerk's theory has been used by Fisher (1930) to construct a theory of intertemporal choice, and later by Keynes (1936) and the neoclassics in their theories of interest, we take a strong exception to its basic

30 *Mabid Ali Al-Jarhi*

premise. To justify a premium between the present and future consumption of a commodity, based on both factors, cannot be automatically used to justify a premium between the present and future money. What is required to accept such a jump from commodities to money is to treat money as an aggregate representing expenditures on commodities.

Market prices hardly reflect the rates of time preference for commodities. We can identify high-priced commodities with low rates of time preference and vice versa. Compare, e.g., the urgency of going from home to the airport in a regular, modestly priced car and to go to the same destination by a luxury car. While the price of the former is lower than that of the latter, the urgency of both is probably equal.

Aggregating the quantities purchased of a set of heterogeneous commodities (in terms of preference) multiplied by their prices gives the total expenditures over such commodities. Comparing such aggregate between two successive periods (t_1 and t_2) reflects several factors. They include changes in incomes, tastes, and technology. Furthermore, the relative amounts of each commodity reflect intertemporal allocation. Implicit in the two aggregates are the rates of time preference assigned by different individuals to different commodities. In other words, there is no way we can discover the commodity rates of time preference underlying the intertemporal choice. Similarly, we cannot sieve out a single rate of time preference that summarizes all or some of the commodity rates.

Therefore, we can contemplate the basis upon which interest rate theories relate their interest rate to some *social* rate of time preference. For the sake of argument, let us assume that we have one commodity as well as one individual. Suppose we added a few more individuals and a few more commodities while keeping the homogeneity of preferences and commodities. We would maintain one rate of time preference congruent with the homogenous preferences and commodities. Should we introduce money in such a fanciful economy, the price of one unit of present money would be equal to one unit of future money plus the rate of interest, which would be equal to the rate of time preference. Such a case mimics the neoclassical model; if we ignored that money should not exist to start within such a model; it would not be necessary unless the rate of time preference were treated under imperfect information.

Once we remove preferences and commodity homogeneity, there is no way to relate the interest rate on money to the set of the rates of time preference on commodities.

Therefore, it is flawed to hypothesize a social rate of time preference aggregated both over individuals and commodities and attach it to a quantity of money, representing perhaps expenditures on commodities and attach it to an amount quantity of money, representing perhaps expenditures on such commodities, is therefore flawed. Even if we were to consider money as an asset, we could not claim that the relationship between present and future quantity of money measures the same as between a combination of commodities goods available now and those available next period for purchasing using money. Given the commodity combination in question, they may be purchased for different amounts of money. Alternatively, the same amount of money can be used to purchase different combinations of commodities, each with a different weighted average of time preference. Therefore, there is no way to assign a unique rate of time preference to a certain sum of money. The neoclassical theory of loanable funds and Keynes liquidity preference theory have committed the same *faux pas*. The common mistake can be removed by identifying a well-defined mapping from a set of commodities, each with a unique rate of time preference ununiformly used by a set of individuals to a monetary aggregate. Some heroic assumptions regarding the homogeneity of commodities and individual preferences must be swallowed to allege such mapping. Such assumptions would be similar to the Sonnenschein Mantel Debreu (SMD) conditions necessary for a horizontal aggregation of individual demand curves into a market demand curve.[3] The above discussion leads to a single conclusion: no equilibrium rate of interest summarizing all individuals', viz, no equilibrium rate of interest summarizing all individuals' time preferences for all individuals and commodities can exist. This impossibility theory allows us to reject all interest rate theories. In other words, since it is impossible to identify the link between the rate of interest and the rates of time preference by *all individuals* for *all commodities*, the determination of an equilibrium rate of interest becomes impossible (Al-Jarhi 2023).

3 How Efficient Is Conventional Finance?

The use of the classical loan contract (trading present against future money at a premium) is prevalent in debt and pure risk trading,[4] a generally recognized source of destabilizing speculations that should have been abandoned at the outset from the configuration of any economic system. Yet, it has escaped the eyes of economists despite being the culprit behind many serious economic crises. Their adverse effects have been rather evident during the Great Depression of 1930 and the Great recession of 2008. However, policymakers' response focused on winding up their deregulation policies and switching to more regulation.

The conventional finance system earned its household acceptance through millennia of history. It has been practiced in Mesopotamia and ancient Egypt and continues to be adopted against the three revealed religions' teachings. The Jewish and Christian faithful managed to ignore or reinterpret their religious teachings with an eye on keeping the hardly unquestioned benefits of conventional finance. Muslims had persisted in avoiding Riba until the nineteenth century, when the Ottoman rule undertook heavy foreign borrowing to update the infrastructure. A renaissance had evolved in the mid-seventies of the last century when Islamic banks started to appear. However, they gradually followed the Judeo-Christian approach of developing ruses to mimic conventional finance while appearing on the surface to avoid interest.[5] It is associated with serious inefficiencies. The first is Samuelson-Friedman's inefficiency (Friedman 1969; Samuelson 1958). The payment of a positive (interest) rate of return on money, with the principal and return guaranteed, motivates traders to economize on the use of cash in transactions. The substitution of real resources for cash would reduce output below optimum.

The subject of interest can only be discussed in a monetary model containing information cost, triggering price search activities among traders. The second inefficiency, which we call the Hosios inefficiency, resulting from externalities in traders' search activities (Hosios 1990), appears. Price searchers discover that the extra information they acquire through their search is not salable. Therefore, they cannot recover their search cost, forcing them to limit their price search to levels below necessary to support producing and trading the optimum GDP. The conventional finance system focuses on pure intermediation between borrowers and lenders. Finance activities would be separate from commodity production and trading. There would be no way to address such inefficiency unless the commodity trading and financial activities were tied together. As will be seen below, this only can happen under Islamic finance.

The interest-based finance system provides no role for financial intermediaries to search for commodity prices and investment opportunities. This could enable them to substitute their search activities for those of households. When they sell the information they collect, all externalities are internalized. Households obtaining finance or investing through intermediaries would not be interested in searching. The ultimate result is to carry out most searching activities through information specialists. The trading volume would stay optimal, as no externalities remain to be internalized.

4 What Is Islamic Finance?

Islamic finance offers 20 investment and finance contracts to replace the classical loan contract. Finance modes encompass several forms. First and foremost, it provides partnership in product and profit, including Musharaka modes in agriculture,[6] industry, and services in addition to Mudaraba. Second, it includes Wakalah or agency finance. Third, it offers sale finance, including Bai' Bethaman Ajel (deferred-payment sale), Murabaha (markup sale), Salam, and Istisna'. The latter two modes offer payment against the future delivery of commodities. Fourth, it provides different types of Ijarah or leasing, including the sale of usufruct or the asset itself. Islamic finance also offers securitized financial instruments, including shares, Sukuk, fund shares, and syndicated finance. None of these modes offers present money against higher amounts of future money. Without exception, they deal with the real sector, as in product and profit partnership, or both the real and financial sector, as in the cases of sale finance and Ijarah. In other words, under Islamic finance, both the finance and real sectors are effectively interconnected.

5 The Islamic Finance Environment

Islamic finance can be offered in a purely Islamic economic environment or a mixed environment. Working in a mixed environment has its drawbacks, as it generally leads the regulator to focus on financial supervision while treating Islamic banks as conventional banks. The reason is twofold. First, like universal banks, Islamic banks provide both finance and investment services. Most host countries are not familiar with universal banking. They have inherited commercial banking from their colonialist masters. Second, the host countries wanted not to be involved in Shariah implementation. Shariah conformity has thus taken a back seat in the financial regulation of Islamic banks. Such an attitude encouraged convergence with conventional finance. Some regulators have established Shariah boards under their umbrellas to standardize financial products. However, such a step failed to attenuate convergence.

The host countries do not have an Islamic economic environment, as they all subscribe totally to market capitalism, the globally dominant economic system. Therefore, the discussion of Islamic banking operating in an Islamic environment would be strictly academic. An Islamic economic system must be briefly described. Then, the process of issuing and allocating money will be elaborated. A more detailed description could be found somewhere else (Al-Jarhi 1983).

5.1 Our Configuration of an Islamic Economic System

In an Islamic economic system, debt-based money is forsaken. Equity-based money would be instituted. All money would be issued in the form of investment accounts with banks, called Central Deposits or CDs, making such money available to fund users based on the 20 Islamic investment and finance contracts. A total reserve system would be applied, giving the central bank exclusive authority to issue money. The monetary authority and the Treasury and the Treasury can jointly outline the investment policy that is congruent with, and Treasury can jointly outline the investment policy that is congruent with the society's economic goals.

The monetary authority issues a money market tool named central deposit certificates, CDCs, to be sold to banks and the public. Its proceeds would be added to the CDs with banks. The instrument would be tradable in an open market with a rate of return, RCD, that is market-determined (unlike the rate of interest, which is an administered price). Such a rate would be used to anchor monetary policy and to estimate the real growth rate. The central bank would fine-tune monetary expansion against real growth through open market operations in the CDC market to reach absolute price stability. The government obtains its share in profit on the monetary base placed in invested CDs plus the commission that may be deducted by the central bank from the profit it receives on the CDCs proceeds placed in investment accounts. This revenue is the seigniorage of issuing money enjoyed by banks under fractional

34   *Mabid Ali Al-Jarhi*

reserves thanks to imposing total reserves. The government gets finance from banks to supplement its tax revenues and maintain a balanced budget.

6 The Financial Market under Islamic Finance

Under Islamic finance, the nature of financial instruments is radically changed. First, debt-trading instruments give way to equity-based instruments. Bonds and securitized debt would be eliminated and replaced by equity-based instruments like Sukuk, shares, investment certificates, and fund certificates. Investment certificates include securitized investments financed through Islamic investment and finance contracts. Second, Sukuk securitizes various income-earning assets whose titles and returns are effectively transferred to Sukuk holders. Pure risk-trading instruments (derivatives, including futures, and swaps) would disappear. The financial market directs itself to two purposes. First, to mobilize resources for investments. Second, to make the real sector more liquid through securitization.

Monetary policy can be carried out through open market operations in the CDC market when fine-tuning monetary expansion rate is required. Large changes in monetary expansion can better be reached through adding to or subtracting from CDs.

In a mixed economic environment, the government may wish to operate Islamic finance side-by-side with conventional finance without excluding the Islamic finance sector from monetary policy considerations. The monetary authority would issue equity-based money in proportion to Islamic finance assets' share in the total financial assets. The Islamic finance industry would be managed as above. It would be preferable to impose total reserves on the conventional finance sector. As Islamic finance's asset share rises, the share of equity money in the total money supply would increase correspondingly.

The gradual conversion to Islamic finance could bring extra income to the government that can be used in liquidating its outstanding bonds and treasury bills and leave a sizable amount every year to spend on tax reduction and public investment, especially in infrastructure, boosting the real rate of growth.

7 What Makes Islamic Finance a Viable Alternative?

7.1 *Efficiency*

- The absence of the rate of interest

Islamic finance would make the rate of interest redundant. The fictitious claim to an equilibrium interest rate is finally exposed. The financial system would maintain its theoretical coherence.

- The Absence of Inefficiencies related to debt-based money

Islamic finance abandons the classical loan contract. Finance would cease to be guaranteed by fund users, principal, and interest. The public and the central bank provide funds to the banking system based on profit and loss sharing, PLS, or Mudaraba. Under such an arrangement, there would be an incentive to substitute real resources for money in transactions. The Samuelson-Friedman's inefficiency would therefore be eliminated.

Islamic banks would become information specialists in commodity markets. They can offer their customers attractive deals when providing sale finance. Customers seeking bulk commodities would find it advantageous to make their purchases through Islamic banks. The result is less price search and less uninternalized externalities. Such a role of Islamic finance in commodity trading would significantly reduce the Hosios inefficiency.

- Risk-Sharing and Market Structure

Risk-sharing is an essential feature of the Islamic economic system. In the financial sector, households provide their funds to Islamic banks and financial institutions on a PLS basis for profit-and-loss sharing. Islamic banks and financial institutions supply funds to their users partly on PLS and partly on a sale-finance basis. Islamic finance is sometimes likened to a participatory sport than conventional finance, likened to spectators' sports (Al-Jarhi 2002).

- Relative predominance of risk-sharing in an economy

Kalemli-Ozcan et al. (2003) shows a positive and significant relationship between the degree of specialization and the amount of risk shared. Risk-sharing facilitated by a favorable legal environment, and a developed financial system is a direct causal determinant of industrial specialization. In other words, risk-sharing furthers specialization, thereby raising the efficiency of the economy as a whole. In an Islamic economic system, risk-sharing becomes prevalent through the financial market structure, producing more specialization and greater overall efficiency.

- Information Asymmetry and the Lemon Problem

Based on the classical loan contract, debt finance suffers from information asymmetry, reduced by costly monitoring. Complete monitoring of fund users would be so expensive that it would lead to prohibitively high lending costs. Equity finance in any system is often associated with the lemon problem, which exposes investors to losing ventures. The lemon problem can be handled by governance, feasibility studies for new projects, and financial analysis for existing projects.

Islamic banks carry out both investment and financing activities. Their ability to mix contracts free from information asymmetry with others suffering from information asymmetry eliminates information asymmetry from

36 *Mabid Ali Al-Jarhi*

their finance (Al-Jarhi 2002). They undertake investment professionally while observing proper governance, feasibility studies, and financial analysis. Their participation in investment projects would signal their due diligence and encourage individual investors to follow suit. Ultimately, the bank leadership in investment reduces information asymmetry and the lemon problem for the whole economy.

7.2 Stability

- Banks Stability

A conventional bank has liabilities that include demand, time, and saving deposits, which the bank guarantees. On the other hand, its assets are mostly debt instruments exposed to default risk. Such default can be expected at times of crisis. One bank's insolvency could cause a bank run, threatening the whole banking system.

An Islamic bank only guarantees demand deposits on the liability side. Meanwhile, saving and investment deposits are placed on a PLS basis. When a bank faces macroeconomic or bank-specific crises, investment depositors automatically share investment and default risk on the asset side (Khan 1986).

- Macroeconomic Stability

An integrated debt market in conventional finance has grown immensely in size and integration. Integrated debt markets are sources of both domestic financial instability and contagion.

In contrast, debt is created in Islamic finance by selling commodities on credit. Resulting debt instruments are negotiable only at face value. The absence of sudden and mass movements of funds and risk trading rules out instability and contagion.

- The dichotomy between the real and financial sector

Financial institutions in a conventional system are merely intermediaries between fund owners and fund users. The financial sector houses enormous financial assets that dwarf the real sector. As a source of instability and contagion, the financial sector moves the real sector into crises.

Islamic finance removes the dichotomy between financial and real activities. It leaves no room for excessive credit expansion, as each finance extended is automatically earmarked for specific uses.

Changes in the supply of money by policymakers would automatically translate into changes in excess demands and supplies of commodities, causing quantities of output produced to respond more quickly to market forces. In other words, markets are more likely to operate efficiently and smoothly. In the absence of debt and pure risk trading, no leakages to the financial sector would be possible. Changes in the money supply would be fully reflected in the commodity sector. This in itself is a significant improvement in the transmission mechanism. Therefore, it is interesting that Islamic finance supports market forces and mechanisms more than conventional finance.

7.3 Fund Mobilization

An unknown number of followers of religions that abhor interest (Hinduism, Buddhism, Judaism, Christianity, and Islam) consider it a religious duty to hold their funds outside the banking and financial sector, thereby placing their financial resources outside the development process. Islamic finance opens the door to mobilizing such resources, especially in many Islamic countries that would otherwise be kept idle. Islamic financial products would be both interest-free and ethical.[7] It makes Islamic finance even more effective resource mobilization to groups interested in both: the avoidance of interest and moral investment involvement.

* Adjustments to Policy Shocks

According to Al-Jarhi (2018), the prohibition of interest amounts precisely to the prohibition of nominal transactions, which involve money against nominal assets, encompassing debt instruments and rights to gambling payouts, both present nominal (monetary) values against future nominal (monetary) values. In other words, this amounts to the prohibition of debt and pure risk trading.

When the supply of money increases in an Islamic economy, spending increases directly and through more financing. In Islamic finance, both expenditure and finance are channeled exclusively through real transactions, i.e., money exchanged against commodities, allowing only one deferred counter value, if at all. Direct spending, therefore, means direct cash flows to the commodity sector. Financing would also boost both supply and demand. The quantity and price speeds of adjustment get full throttle, as no cash balances leak to nominal transactions. The transmission mechanism from monetary expansion to spending in the real sector is direct. In such an economy, adjustments are swift, and the market mechanism is fully supported.

In contrast, monetary expansion in a system with conventional finance transmits more slowly into the real sector. On the one hand, a substantial leak from monetary expansion flows into nominal transactions, viz, debt, and risk trading. The final effects on the commodity sector will not emerge until the payoff of gambling in the financial market reaches winners' pockets. Even in such cases, winners may decide to use their gambling payoff, postponing their commodity trade. The first effect of the financing directed to commodity sectors would go to the demand side first. Price speeds of adjustment would be higher, while quantity speeds of adjustments would lag. Inflation would be the ultimate result, even when the economy is below full employment.

38   *Mabid Ali Al-Jarhi*

Ultimately, we have slower adjustment speeds with conventional finance, biased toward price adjustments. The market mechanism would limb slowly to economic adjustment without ever settling down.

We can conclude that by prohibiting nominal transactions, Islamic finance boosts speeds of adjustment, as they would also be balanced between quantity and price speeds. The market mechanism is ultimately strengthened.

7.4 Systemic Integrity

Risk (business risk) is an essential ingredient of investment. In conventional finance, investment is financed through equity (stock market) or debt (borrowing from banks and issuing bonds). Banks accept only collateral risk. They always avoid bearing the risks of investment failure. Corporate bondholders follow the same rule, and their debt carries seniority over shareholders' rights. The result is that a few specialists, either entrepreneurs or shareholders, are left to be borne by a few specialists, either entrepreneurs or shareholders. Such a minority of risk bearers shoulder the brunt of investment failure. Although the per capita risk for society may be low, risk concentration on a small group could be unbearable. The commodity sector would be far removed from the finance sector, as each goes its way. In other words, the system would be disjoint.

In Islamic finance, banks and financial institutions advancing funds share risk with those receiving finance, including producers, traders, and the like. Islamic finance with proper corporate governance would allow investment-account holders to influence banks' investment decisions to share in the decision-making process by sitting on the boards of directors of firms receiving funds. Such change in banks' governance proposed by Al-Jarhi (2014) would extend risk and decision sharing to banks' asset and liability sides.

Therefore, we can notice that risk and decision-making are spread over a much larger number and a wider variety of concerned people. It allows for broader involvement in economic activities so that people will eventually feel they are partners rather than spectators.

The benefit of wider involvement goes beyond the mere feeling, adding to banks' stability. The finance sector would be closely tied to the commodity sector. It affords the economic system compactness and integrity between its different parts.

7.5 Equity

* Inequity associated with fractional reserves

Fractional reserves allow banks to use their available reserves to create more money, within the limits of the required reserve ratio. The lower the required reserve ratio, the higher the multiple of bank-created money relative to reserves. The central bank may find itself having to cater to reserve requirements of banks when they over extend their derived deposit creation.

The Advantages of Islamic Banking and Financial Markets   39

We consider this to be a source of inequity. It is universally recognized that moneyness depends on the general acceptability, which becomes especially critical with fiat money that has no intrinsic value. The public is therefore entitled to the seingorage resulting from the general acceptability they bestow on fiat money. Such seingorage must be fully yielded to government to spend for social benefit. Instead, it is imputed to banks' shareholders wealth. The obvious way to redress such injustice is to switch to total reserves. Replacing lending-based with equity-based money allows the central bank to become a partner in the process of finance, entitled to a share in the profit involved. This can be made directly available to government budget. It can be used to reduce taxation and/or provide a significant improvement to infrastructure. In both cases, economic growth would be boosted.[8]

- Income and wealth redistribution

By themselves, Islamic banks and financial institutions cannot reduce, let alone eradicate poverty. However, if given the right tools, they can contribute to society's efforts in that regard.

Islam prescribes a tax-subsidy approach to reducing poverty. A levy called Zakah is paid out by those whose wealth exceeds a certain minimum level in proportion to their property or income.

Zakah proceeds are earmarked for several uses, including income and wealth maintenance for the poor. Income maintenance is provided provisionally to the poor until wealth maintenance is restored. Zakah proceeds would be earmarked to finance micro-projects whose titles are given to the poor. Such a role in poverty reduction can be closely intertwined with economic development, as redistribution is mostly directed toward making the poor more productive, contributing to economic development.

Islamic banks can help by acting as custodians of Zakah proceeds and disbursement. Islamic banks are also mandated to have special accounts for the Zakah due on their shareholders' equity. They can even accept direct payments of Zakah and other donations on behalf of depositors and other donors. Banks can then use their Zakah funds to maintain the poor's income and wealth. By becoming the custodians of collected Zakah, they can allocate the received proceeds among the poor for income maintenance and use the rest to establish micro-projects; each would generate sufficient income to support one household. Transferring the titles to such projects to the poor implements wealth maintenance. Banks will charge for their services either directly or through compensation from the Treasury.

Conventional lending gives utmost attention to the ability to repay loans. To ascertain such ability, banks depend overwhelmingly on collaterals and guarantees. Thus, those already rich would have the most access to finance. In contrast, Islamic finance providing funds on an equity or profit-sharing basis would be more concerned with profitability and rates of return and less with collateral as the primary consideration. Sale finance seekers can offer the

40 *Mabid Ali Al-Jarhi*

financed commodities as collateral against future payments. Those who are not wealthy but either have worthy investment projects or seek financing for collateralizable commodities would have more access to finance.

7.6 Debt Sustainability

Conventional debt has specific characteristics that could place debtors in difficulties if circumstances do not allow them to repay in time. Interest is usually calculated on the outstanding debt balance, usually compounded annually and more often at shorter intervals. Debtors who fail to pay an installment on time are automatically considered delinquent, whether they have an excuse or not. They are often subjected to penalty rates of interest, which are higher than regular rates. It is not uncommon to find borrowers who have paid debt service that is many folds the original principal they borrowed. Credit cards and developing countries' debt are particularly symptomatic, as they continue to face debt problems that sometimes reach crisis levels. Debtors frequently seek debt relief through bankruptcy procedures. Developing countries appeal their cases with creditors clubs in London and Paris. Conventional debt generally lacks sustainability demonstrated during crises, when attention is usually directed to bail out lenders (banks) and not borrowers.

The debt created through Islamic finance has characteristics that make it sustainable. The total value of debt, which includes the spot value of commodities purchased on credit and an implicit markup, is set initially. When debtors face unavoidable circumstances that would make them temporarily insolvent, Shariah rules mandate that they are granted free rescheduling and grace periods to help them bring their finances back to order. No penalty fees can be levied in this case.

Due to the information asymmetry associated with conventional finance, moral hazard leads to using borrowed funds for non-prescribed purposes, leading to default. In contrast, the absence of information asymmetry and moral hazard from Islamic finance mandates that the advanced funds are used for their prescribed purpose through mixing and matching finance modes. Therefore, default resulting from improper use of funds would be most unlikely.

8 Islamic Finance in a Conventional System

The eight advantages of Islamic finance appear to be externalities that accrue to the economic system as a whole but do not accrue directly to any Islamic bank or financial institution in particular. Their external nature creates an incentive problem; Islamic bankers would not be sufficiently motivated to follow the Islamic finance paradigm to the letter. The incentive problem can be solved through a new Islamic banking regulatory approach (Al-Jarhi 2014).

Under the current configuration of conventional economics, Islamic bankers have to compete with conventional bankers who use the classical loan contract, which is more straightforward, requiring fewer procedures and less

The Advantages of Islamic Banking and Financial Markets   41

documentation than any of the 20 Islamic finance modes. Strict adherence to the Islamic finance paradigm would greatly benefit Islamic banks and financial institutions through its macroeconomic benefits. However, Islamic bankers being conventionally trained and working in a conventional environment, may still prefer to mimic traditional finance. Experience has shown that they can convince their Shariah boards to develop the necessary ruses for imitating.

Islamic banks keep their nominal brand name and mimic conventional finance to maintain their competitive position. It enables them to streamline procedures and documentation to conform to the pattern to which they have grown accustomed. Such mimicking has led to the deformation of Islamic finance as it increasingly converges to conventional finance. The insistence on keeping a nominal brand while the monetary authorities look the other way seriously affects stakeholders' interests.

The investment account holders would be subscribing to Islamic finance but, in reality, getting conventional finance. The rate of return on their investment accounts would hover around the rate of interest administered by the central bank, which would be much lower than the rate of return on investment in the respective economy. The economy would miss the eight advantages elaborated above while coping with conventional finance problems. Such convergence cannot be camouflaged for long. It will eventually become public, leading to suspicion and sarcasm that would ultimately destroy the industry's reputation.

9 Conclusions

Reform agenda for conventional finance is a dire need. Conventional finance has shown exposure to instability and contagion. The latest International Financial Crisis of 2008 was accompanied by widespread bank failure confronted by expensive bank bailouts, in addition to a severe recession that lingered for four years after the onset of the crisis. Some economists advanced reform proposals revolving around tighter regulation. Others suggested that capital movements should be curtailed.

Given the above analysis regarding Islamic finance, we can perceive that it prescribes the following institutional changes to contemporary market economies' problems the following *institutional* changes.

1   Replacing the classical loan contract with the 20 Islamic finance contracts,
2   Instituting an exclusive monopoly of the issuing of money through a government-owned central bank,
3   All issued money is to be placed in PLS investment accounts with banks so that the economy would switch from debt-based to equity-based money,
4   The central bank issues central investment certificates, to be held by banks and the public and traded in an open market as an interbank and monetary policy instrument,
5   Debt trading, as well as the use of all risk-trading contracts, is prohibited in financial markets,

42 *Mabid Ali Al-Jarhi*

6 Debtors would be granted free rescheduling in case of temporary illiquidity but penalized in case of delinquency.

The above prescription has been taken directly from the features that provide Islamic finance stability and make it less prone to crises.

Switching from interest-based finance to Islamic finance would serve three purposes simultaneously. First, the financial system would retain unfaulty theoretical foundations. Second, the serious inefficiencies caused by using the classical loan contract would be avoided. Third, the system would render real advantages to the macroeconomy and sizable seigniorage to the government, thereby improving growth prospects.

Notes

1 Mortals living in a world of perfect information should know when they die. Their future consumption can be planned under perfect foresight. Neoclassical economists ignored the consequences of their perfect model in this particular instance. Being mortal under prefect information would have similar consequences of immortality.

2 We use this term to describe a household who has bounded rationality and suffices not maximizes.

3 These conditions came about to deal with the problem of aggregation from individual to market demand. It was discovered by William Gorman in 1953 and came to be known as Sonnenschein-Mantel-Debreu [SMD]. The conditions have been independently developed by Sonnenschein, Mantel and Debreu.

4 Debt trade is defined as the purchase (sale) of a specific sum of future money for (in return of) a specific present sum of money, as in the case of buying (selling) a bond. Pure risk trading is defined as the purchase (sale) of an uncertain amount of future money (varying from zero to a positive value), which is the result of a gamble, for a specific amount of present money, as in the case of buying (selling) a lottery ticket.

5 The earliest ruse we know of was when Ancient (ethnically Arab) Jews found ways to fish on Saturdays. Since then, ruses continued to chip away from religious teachings everywhere. First, one does not violate religious teachings when charging interest to those outside his religion. Second, interest compensates lenders for inflation as well other rationalizations. Prophet Muhammad foretold his followers that Muslims would imitate Jewish and Christian was eventually.

6 Product partnership in agriculture includes Muzara'ah, Mugharassah and Mussaqah.

7 Being ethical results from Islamic finance obligation not to be involved in non-ethical investment activities, e.g., illegal weapons, alcohol, harming the environment, and the like.

8 A scenario of the application of our model was simulated to Turkey. We found that the resulting seigniorage reaches a multiple of government tax and non-tax revenue in few years.

References

Al-Jarhi, Mabid Ali. 1983. "A Monetary and Financial Structure for an Interest-Free Economy." Pp. 1–37 in *Money and Banking in Islam*. Center for Research in Islamic Economics, and Islamabad: Institute of Policy Studies.

Al-Jarhi, Mabid Ali. 2002. "A Comparison of Transactions in Conventional and Islamic Economies." Pp. 27–34 in *Theoretical Foundations of Islamic Economics*. International Institute of Islamic Thought (IIIT), Islamabad, Islamic Educational and Cultural Organization (ISESCO), Rabat, Islamic Research Institute, Islamabad, and Islamic Research and Training Institute, Jeddah.

Al-Jarhi, Mabid Ali. 2014. "Towards an Economic Theory of Islamic Finance Regulation." *Journal of Islamic Banking and Finance* 2(1):345–366. doi:10.1108/ IJIF-07–2017-0007.

Al-Jarhi, Mabid Ali. 2018. "Islamic Finance at Crossroads." *Intellectual Discourse* 26:431–462.

Al-Jarhi, Mabid Ali. 2023. *Economic Analysis: An Islamic Perspective-II (Forthcoming)*. Vol. II. First edition. Ankara/İstanbul: ASBÜ Yayınları ve TKBB Yayınları.

Böhm -Bawerk, Eugen von. 1890. *Capital and Interest: A Critical History of Economical Theory*. London: Macmillan and Co.

Fisher, Irving. 1930. *The Theory of Interest, As Determined by Impatience to Spend Income and Opportunity to Invest It*. London: The Macmillan Company.

Friedman, Milton. 1969. "The Optimum Quantity of Money." *Journal of Money, Credit and Banking Credit and Banking* 2(4):397–419.

Hosios, Arthur J. 1990. "On the Efficiency of Matching and Related Models of Search and Unemployment." *The Review of Economic Studies* 57(2):279. doi:10.2307/2297382.

Kalemli-Ozcan, Sebnem, Bent E. Sørensen, and Oved Yosha. 2003. "Risk Sharing and Industrial Specialization: Regional and International Evidence." *American Economic Review* 93(3):903–918. doi:10.1257/000282803322157151.

Keynes, John M. 1936. *The General Theory of Employment, Interest, and Money*. Cambridge: The Macmillan Company.

Khan, Mohsin S. 1986. "Islamic Interest-Free Banking Islamic A Theoretical Analysis." *Palgrave Macmillan Journals on Behalf of the International Monetary Fund* 33(1):1–27.

Samuelson, Paul A. 1958. "An Exact Consumption-Loan Model of Interest with or without the Social Contrivance of Money." *Journal of Political Economy* 66(6):467–482.

4 Suggestions for Banking Business Models of Islamic Banking

Current Issues and Practical Solutions for Future

Zeyneb Hafsa Orhan

1 Introduction

Islamic banking means providing banking services in line with Islamic ethos and rules. It is commonly agreed that the first Islamic banking experience was Mit Ghamr Savings Bank, established by Ahmed El-Najjar in Egypt in 1963. Even though the life span of the bank did not become so long since it was converted into Nasser Social Bank in 1972, the example of Mit Ghamr helped to the improvements of interest-free Islamic banking in both theory and practice. Currently, there are Islamic banks or windows – providing Islamic banking services under the roof of conventional banks – that exist almost all around the world. Even though it is not clearly known how many Islamic banks and windows exist in the world today, it is known that the assets of Islamic banking reached approximately 1,765 trillion dollars (IFSB, 2020).

Despite the wide spectrum of countries in which Islamic banks are established, the common business model – the way of doing business – for Islamic banks is this one; accepting deposits and making use of these deposits/funds as trade-based or partnership-based activities. This is, in fact, the traditional, intermediary business model. The prevalence of such a model among Islamic banks can be attributed to different reasons, such as the long heritage of this model in the banking sector in general or its simplicity. However, the current business model followed by Islamic banks is criticized due to different reasons, such as the lack of focus on profit-and-loss sharing (PLS) instruments planned to be the main element in Islamic banks and the weakness of socio-economic effects of Islamic banks in societies.

Having said that, there have been some changes in the banking business model since the liberalization process started in the 1980s. Such changes do arise more slowly and with a lesser content[1] in the Islamic banking sector. The details of these changes will be explained in more detail in the following sections.

In this context, the aim of this study is first to discuss the criticisms directed toward the banking business model in general, and the current business model of Islamic banks in particular, then to make suggestions regarding

DOI: 10.4324/9781003377283-4

the business model of Islamic banks by taking into account the related literature. The second section explains the method employed in this study. It is followed by the third section analyzing the topic based on the relevant literature. Finally, we end the article with the conclusion section.

This study is important due to the fact that the world is changing rapidly by the developments in technology and different events such as COVID-19. In such a dynamic atmosphere, it is important to keep the business model of Islamic banks also dynamic, efficient, and yet authentic.

2 Methodology

Between the options of qualitative and quantitative research methods commonly used in scientific research, this study uses the qualitative one since it depends on discussions, evaluations, and explanations rather than quantification and empirical analysis.

There are many different tools among qualitative research methods, such as in-depth interviews, field studies, etc. Instead of following one of these classical qualitative methods, this study follows a method whose steps are as follows:

- Conducting a literature review about the criticisms related to the business model of the banks and Islamic banks,
- Conducting a literature review about the suggestions for the business model of Islamic banks,
- Taking into account the criticisms and suggestions regarding the business model of Islamic banks, and making our suggestions.

As it can be understood from the above-mentioned points, the main tool used for the method of this study is the literature review, which requires a library search of the related books, articles, and documents. Critical evaluation of the collected material is another tool that will be utilized.

3 Analysis with Related Literature

This analysis section, which depends on the related literature, has four sub-sections; analysis of criticisms regarding banking business model, analysis of criticisms regarding Islamic banking business model, business model suggestions for Islamic banking, and our suggestions regarding the Islamic banking business model.

3.1 Analysis of Criticisms Regarding Banking Business Models

In this sub-section, changes in the banking business model and criticisms attributed to them will be evaluated due to the following events that happened during the last few decennia: liberalization, financialization, the financial crisis in 2008, developments in financial technologies (FinTech), and COVID-19.

By checking the examples of earlier banks such as Medici Bank (1397–1494) (De Roover, 1999), we can understand that the business model of banks has been more or less the same throughout centuries, i.e., to collect money in deposit accounts by offering lower interest rates and to give some parts (that is left over the reserved amount) of this money as credits with higher interest rates. Such a business model has been challenged since especially the liberalization period started in the 1980s. The main economic aspects of this period were less restriction on the movement of capital, and privatization. This period has made such changes also on the traditional intermediary banking business model. In that regard, Boyd and Gertler (1994) even asked whether the banks were dead. As a result of their empirical analysis, they concluded that, in contrast to the arguments, commercial banking is not declining in the USA (United States of America) but taking another shape, especially due to off-balance-sheet activities.[2] Similar results for the case of the USA were shared by Kaufman and Mote (1994). For Europe, Schmidt et al. (1999) used data for the period of 1982–1995 in order to understand the validity of the trend of disintermediation of banks meaning to shy away from their traditional intermediary role between savers and investors. The authors find that disintermediation is valid only for France but not in Germany and the UK (United Kingdom). However, it is found that another trend, which is securitization,[3] is valid for all of these three European countries.

The changes mentioned above in the banking business model were put under scrutiny, especially after the financial crisis in 2008. There have been many studies regarding the reasons and results of the crisis. The study of Helleiner (2011) summarizes the main reasons for the crisis as follows; the failure in market regulation, negative impacts of securitization mentioned above, and the prevalence of cheap credit, which led to a financial bubble. Foster and Magdoff (2009) list the main causes of the crisis as follows; the household debt bubble, the explosion of debt and speculation, monopoly-finance capital, and financialization which will be explained below. It can be noticed that similar reasons were mentioned by both of the studies. If one searches through similar studies, it can be realized that these are, more or less, the most commonly mentioned ones in the literature. Such reasons, together with others, started a crisis in the USA, which has spread to different parts of the world. The crisis did have a circular relationship with the banking sector, meaning that some new aspects of the banking business model were mentioned both as one of the reasons for the crisis, and also the business model with these new aspects was affected by the crisis in the end. Clerides (2014) explained the main reasons behind the banking crisis in Cyprus – a country affected by the crisis a lot in the Eurozone – as excessive lending, risk-taking, the bubble in real estate, expansion of banks overseas, and overconsumption by different economic actors. Some of these reasons were also mentioned in the case of the USA. Besides, an important aspect of the crisis in the USA is asserted as the activities of investment banks. Coppola (2014) asked whether investment banking is dead in the USA because the business model they had been following before the crisis was changed due to its negative impacts. The negative impacts were, among others, due to risky activities of the investment banks, such as securitization of mortgages. In this way, investment banks sold the mortgages to investors under the schemes of CDOs (collateralized debt obligations).

As it was mentioned above, financialization was one of the aspects of the financial crisis. What is meant by financialization is an increase in the numbers of the financial sector components compared to the real sector. In this way, financial markets, institutions, and instruments increase not only in numbers but also in importance. The above-mentioned liberalization and deregulation process paved the way for financialization. Furthermore, technological advancement is another auxiliary for financialization. Financialization has impacted economies, such as increments in debts and risk and shift of income distribution toward the financial sector. The main concern here is the impact of this process on the business model of the banking sector. For the case of Europe, Ayadi et al. (2011) listed the business model trends of the banks due to the financialization process as follows: diversification in terms of activities, securitization of loans, maturity transformation, wholesale, and money market funding, and use of credit derivatives. In order to check whether these trends have changed after the financial crisis, the authors collected data from 26 banks in Europe between 2006 and 2009 and concluded that there was a shift from wholesale and investment banking toward traditional retail banking due to the superiority of the latter one in profitability and being less risky at that period. For instance, Z-score was found to be 31 for retail banks while it was 6.8 for wholesale banks. On the other hand, ROA (return on assets) was 0.73% retail banks, whereas it was 0.08% for wholesale banks.

Depending on the above-mentioned literature, the main features of the changes in the banking business model due to the events of liberalization, the financial crisis in 2008, and the process of financialization can be listed as follows:

- Increase in off-balance-sheet activities
- Disintermediation
- Securitization
- Excessive lending
- Risk-taking, especially via products such as derivatives[4]
- Risky activities of investment banks
- The movement toward wholesale banking from retail banking.[5]

However, this new model has a tendency to lead to negative consequences during the crisis, and thus there have been criticisms toward that model. De La Torre (2011) summarizes four basic lessons that conventional banks need to learn regarding their business models after the crisis. These lessons are the potentiality of the business model of Islamic banking in terms of stabilizing credit growth, making investment depending on physical assets rather than synthetic products such as CDOs (collateralized debt obligations), using risk management tools, not for risk trading but risk mitigation, and not taking too much leverage. In a paper which was also written just after the crisis, Lenz (2011) points out the following problems regarding the banking business models; lack of connection with the real sector, leaning toward risky investment banking, and too much leverage, as also mentioned by De La Torre (Ibid.). Laeven and Valencia (2012) identified 147 systemic banking crises between 1970 and 2011. This is the period that can be called liberalization and financialization. Out of these 129 crises about which the authors have credit data, it is found that around 33% of them were preceded by a credit boom.

In sum, the criticism toward the current banking business model seems to concentrate on the following issues: excessive lending and credit booms, excessive risk-taking, especially through financially engineered synthetic products, and loss of connection between the financial and real sector.

After the changes in the business model of banks that arose due to liberalization in the 1980s, financialization in the following years, and financial crisis in 2008, another important impact on banks' business model came from technology in recent years. What is meant by technology here, especially the reflection of technology in the financial sector, is FinTech. Even though technology in general and FinTech, in particular, are attempted to be followed by banks, it is mentioned by many that FinTech will cause disruptive effects on current banking due to the appearance of non-bank institutions offering banking services and products, and competition coming from BigTech (such as Amazon, Apple, and Google) and FinTech companies (such as Stripe, Ripple, and Robinhood).[6] In that regard,

> The Economist suggests that unless incumbents (conventional banks) are successful in surfing the wave of innovation that FinTech has brought to their sector, banks could end up as mere deposit-taking utilities: If FinTech doesn't kill banks, it might instead sap the sector's profitability.
> (Consumer International, 2017, p. 18)

Besides e-wallets, the other disruptive areas can be listed as follows (Petralia et al., 2019):

- Maturity transformation through competition in lending,
- Payment services through new payment platforms (such as SnapCash, ApplePay, Google Pay, Alipay, and M-Pesa),
- Information processing through machine learning and AI (Artificial Intelligence),
- Liquidity provision and risk pooling.

Within this process, neo-banks with new business models were established, such as WingspanBank, ZUNO Bank, and Revolut. However, it is criticized that, for instance, ZUNO lost 130 million euros during a short period attributed to its business model focusing on collecting deposits more than giving credits (Ibid.). Revolut example, on the other hand, is criticized for concentrating on short-term growth without taking into account an equitable/just treatment to its workers (Ibid.).

Another business model that came into the scene via FinTech is open banking, meaning to share bank-related information with third parties. Europe has even published a regulation about it, which is called PSD2 (Payment Services Directive2). The criticisms in that regard depend on cyber risks and liability related issues under a potential failure (Ibid.). The possible effects of technology based banking models on crises are another issue to be concerned about.

A very recent event that is also expected to have important implications on banks' business models is COVID-19. One of the criticisms directed toward banks during this period is the insufficiency of model-risk-management (MRM) frameworks (Laurent et al., 2020). It is argued that banks are experiencing more model failures about which they need to improve by developing and applying short-term actions along with long-term plans (Ibid.). A related report of Deloitte (2020) lists that the pandemic showed banks the necessity to re-evaluate their willingness to take the financial risk and to shrink their credit risk appetite as the financial crisis in 2008 did.

Regarding more specific changes in different types of banking business models, the report of Deloitte (Ibid.) argues that retail banking will have some changes after COVID-19 such that banks' investment horizons will become shorter, and remote operating models will evolve. TCS (2020), on the other hand, expects that investment banking will undergo some important changes in terms of client engagement models (such as remote workplace setup), operations risk management (the dominance of machines will be seen here), and cloud adoption.

As it can be seen, the existing documents put a special focus on risk management processes about which technology seems to take over. The COVID-19 incident has been experienced recently, and it is not yet clear how the banking business model will take shape afterward.

3.2 Analysis of Criticisms Regarding Islamic Banking Business Model

The Medici Bank mentioned above was one of the earliest examples in banking which dates back to the 14th century. Despite this long-standing history, Muslims started to use banking at later times. In the Ottomans, for instance, the first bank was established in 1847. The main reason for the abstention of Muslims in establishing and using banks was riba (interest) ban in Islam besides some other economic injunctions such as the lack of gharar (extreme uncertainty), qimar (gambling), and cheating. When many Muslim communities did gain their independence from Western countries after the First World War, they felt the need for banking activities provided in compliance with their religion. With such a need, the idea of interest-free banking came into existence. Even though they were initially described as interest-free banking, their names were changed into Islamic banking after the 1970s due to the presence of other economics-related rules and regulations of Islam. The Mit Ghamr Savings Bank mentioned above, which was established in Egypt in 1963, is commonly accepted as the first Islamic banking example in the world. Since then, Islamic banks have expanded across the globe. Graph 4.1 shows the growth in asset size of Islamic banking worldwide from 2012 to 2019.

It can be seen from Graph 4.1 that the asset size of Islamic banking worldwide has increased almost constantly (except the year 2014) from 1.3 trillion dollars to 1.99 trillion dollars between 2012 and 2019. If it is considered that global banking assets were around 148 trillion dollars in 2018 (Statista, 2020), it can be realized that Islamic banking comprises nearly 1.2% of the global banking assets. That percentage cannot be considered much, but in some parts of the world, it reached to substantial amounts. For instance, according to the report of IFSB (2020), nearly half of the global Islamic banking assets (854 billion dollars) reside in the GCC (Gulf Cooperation Countries).

Besides its quantitative development, Islamic banking was planned and expected to answer the widely pronounced criticisms directed toward the banking business model with its qualitative aspects. In that regard, the business model of Islamic banks is especially seen as a panacea to the following problems:

- Excessive lending and credit booms (Ibrahim and Rizvi, 2018),
- Loss of connection between financial and real sector (Mirakhor and Krischene, 2009),

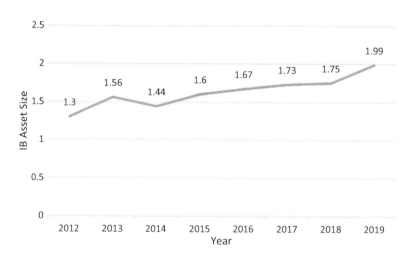

Graph 4.1 Growth in Islamic Banking Asset Size, 2012–2019 (trillion dollars). Source: Statista (2021). The graph is drawn by the author.

- Excessive risk-taking, especially through financially engineered synthetic products (Al-Zoubi and Maghyereh, 2007; Sorwar et al., 2016),
- Financial stability (Čihák and Hesse, 2010).

Islamic banks' planned equity-based structure rather than debt-based one is seen as an answer, especially for the first and second problems. What is meant by equity-based structure is that Islamic banks collect deposits not via interest-based time deposits but through partnership-based mudarabah (labor–capital partnership) on the asset side, and they do not directly give interest-based credits but provide financing through mudarabah and musharakah (capital–capital partnership) contracts on the liability side.[7] In both cases, Islamic banks have the potential (not guarantee) of earning profits and the difference between the taken profit and given profit would become the net earning of the banks. Injunctions of Islam regarding monetary transactions in general and the sale of debt, in particular, are seen to provide answers for the third problem. Together with the equity-based structure, risk-sharing instead of risk transfer is underlined. In fact, El Hawary et al. (2004) identify the idiosyncratic properties of Islamic banking and finance as follows; risk-sharing principle, connection to the real values, no exploitation, and no financing of sinful activities.

The main reason why it is argued that the theoretical background of the business model of Islamic banks should depend on equity-based, risk-sharing structures is the belief that such a structure would lead to allocative justice and efficiency. It is pronounced as "belief" here because such arguments are not always supported by empirical data or quantitative models. The aforementioned fourth point, financial stability, is expected to follow as a result of the use of the business model of Islamic banks based on equity and risk-sharing structures.[8] Such an argument has been empirically tested since especially the financial crisis of 2008. However, the results are yet to be conclusive. While some find a significant difference in favor of Islamic banks, some do not find such a difference. Trad et al. (2017) studied 78 Islamic banks from 12 countries for the period of 2004–2013. They found no statistical difference between Islamic and conventional banks in terms of riskiness and profitability. Al-Deehani et al. (2015) investigated 12 conventional and 13 Islamic banks from GCC for the period of 2001–2012. The results of GLM (multivariate general linear model) analysis showed that ROE (return on equity) decreased only 25% for conventional banks, whereas it dropped 67% for Islamic banks. Abdul Hamid and Azmi (2011) analyzed the performances of BIMB (Bank Islam Malaysia Berhad) and eight conventional banks in Malaysia for the period of 2000 and 2009. They also found that Islamic bank was far behind conventional banks in terms of ROE, but it was less risky. The number of studies can be increased, but this is not the main aim here. When similar studies are checked, it can be noticed that some find no difference, some explore the difference in some aspects and not in others. This primarily depends on the fact that the studied regions, number of banks, and periods vary from study to study.

52 *Zeyneb Hafsa Orhan*

However, in reality, things did not always go as planned and expected for the aforementioned business model of Islamic banks. Thus, there have been criticisms in that regard. One of the main criticisms is the lack of equity-based structures, especially on the liability side. Yousef (2004) explains such a deficiency and dominance of pre-agreed fixed return-based murabaha (mark-up-based sale) used by Islamic banks as "murabaha syndrome." The empirical proof for this argument can be shown from Turkey's experience, which is accepted as one of the growing powers in Islamic finance and banking. Orhan (2018) found that between 2005 and 2015, the preference of Islamic banks (so-called participation banks) in Turkey in terms of the use of funds depended on murabaha (60% share in total assets, and 99% share in credits). Chong and Liu (2009) show that only a small portion of Malaysian Islamic banks' financing is PLS-based. There are many reasons for the lack of profit-and loss-sharing contracts and dominance of debt-based ones in Islamic banks, such as risk, asymmetric information, lack of regulation, accounting system, and trust. But we will not go into detail about the reasons here.

The similarity between the business model of Islamic and conventional banks is another issue that is criticized. After underlining non-participatory financing practices as the norm, Khan (2010, p. 113) argues that "Islamic banking and finance is virtually indistinguishable from conventional banking and finance. What makes it Islamic is "Shariah arbitrage."" Similar criticism was mentioned by Ariff (2014), who argues that Islamic banks are busy with imitating conventional banking products with Shariah modifications.

Another commonly mentioned criticism toward the business model of Islamic banks is their lack or failure to deliver more socio-economic results. Asutay (2008, p. 1) argues that the quantitative development of Islamic banking and finance "… does not necessarily share the aspirations or the foundational claims of Islamic moral economy (IME), an authentic value system for human-centered economic development and social justice." Similar criticism is uttered by Tripp (2006).

3.3 Business Model Suggestions for Islamic Banking

Before continuing with our suggestions about the business model of Islamic banks, we would like to discuss some of the outstanding suggestions in the literature in that regard. This is important because we will benefit from such suggestions while formalizing ours.

As mentioned above, one of the criticisms regarding the business model of Islamic banking is its lack of socio-economic contributions. As a panacea for such a problem, Abdul Rahman (2007) underlines the importance of Islamic microfinance as a missing component of Islamic banking. In his suggested framework, Abdul Rahman argues that mudarabah can be one option in which "The entrepreneur will exercise full control over the business without interference from the Islamic bank but of course with monitoring" (Abdul

Rahman, Ibid., p. 47). However, the author himself confirms a possible problem area in this suggested model that since small enterprises are having difficulties in keeping proper accounts that can create problems in profit sharing calculations. Other products through which the author thinks an Islamic bank can conduct microfinance structures are musharakah, murabaha, ijarah (leasing), and qardh-ul hasan (interest-free loan). The second one is suggested especially for purchasing business equipment. Against the risk factor that can arise in these schemes, the author proposes a third-party guarantee or wakalah (agency) model used in takaful (Islamic insurance). Even though the wakalah system is explained in more detail by the author, the possible uses of all the aforementioned products, such as mudarabah, musharakah, are not discussed in detail, especially considering the issue of feasibility.

In parallel to the aforementioned suggestion of Abdul Rahman, Nor (2016) also discusses a proposal in order to improve the socio-economic side of Islamic banks. Her proposal is to depend on Islamic social banking. The difference of a social bank is its focus not only on financial outcomes but also on social ones. Some of the main features of such an Islamic social bank are listed as follows; avoiding excessive risk, linking between financial and real economic world, and involving in green projects. In attaining its goals, the author suggests that Islamic social banks can use musharakah, mudarabah, and either lending-based or equity-based crowdfunding. However, model details are not shared.

In fact, as the author herself also mentions, the idea of Nor (Ibid.) takes its roots in a well-known example, i.e., Mit Ghamr Savings Bank established in Egypt in 1963. The founder of the Mit Ghamr, Ahmed el-Najjar, took the example of savings banks in Germany and modeled it accordingly.

As it can be seen in Table 4.1, the business model of Mit Ghamr differentiates itself according to a social structure taken place on its liability side, i.e., social service fund comprised of voluntary donations of customers that would be transferred to the asset side in order to be used as an interest-free loan. But its applicability by Islamic banks today needs further elaboration.

A commonly suggested business model for Islamic banks is a similar one to "universal banking." What is meant by universal banking is briefly a banking model that provides different sets of services at once, such as retail banking, commercial banking, and investment banking services. In order to re-establish the aforementioned murabaha financing as a more sustainable solution,

Table 4.1 The Business Model of Mit Ghamr Savings Bank

Asset	Liability
Interest-free loan	Current Account
Partnership-based financing	Partnership-based investment account
	Social service fund

Source: Karaman (2017). Tabulated by the author.

54   *Zeyneb Hafsa Orhan*

Jatmiko (2017, p. 110) suggests a pricing mechanism depending on the real market rather than the financial market. The author argues that this can be attained by moving toward a more equity-based universal Islamic banking model in which

> ... the IB owns the share of a merchant (trader) either using mudarabah (non-voting rights) or musharakah (voting rights) mode of financing. While the merchant then trades its goods on the credit murabaha basis to the customers in the real sector of the economy and prices it according to both price elasticity of demand and that of supply mechanism, instead of a benchmark rate (such as LIBOR).

However, the feasibility of the model is not searched and discussed by the author.

Al-Jarhi (2004, p. 24), who is known for his general stress upon full-reserve system rather than fractional one, describes his suggested narrow banking as follows: "Investment deposits are given to banks on a profit-and-loss sharing basis. They are clearly associated with risk-taking, and they have specific maturities which, in principle, are not revocable." That is why some economists insisted on the total separation between demand and investment deposits by subjecting the former to 100% required reserves. Here, we will not go into discussions about the full-reserve system, but we can note that the arguments in that issue did not turn into any practical application so far.

3.4 Our Suggestions Regarding the Islamic Banking Business Model

As explained in the previous section, today, the most important factor affecting the business model of banking in general, and Islamic banking in particular, is technology or FinTech. It is expected that changes similar to the following ones might happen to the banking business models:

- The emergence of more non-bank institutions offering banking services,
- Increase in automatization, and decrease in labor in some segments of the business models of banking,
- Increase in online use by consumers, and decrease in physical facilities.

Thus, while making our suggestions regarding the business model of Islamic banks, we will especially take into account these elements.

3.4.1 Islamic Banking Models Having Connection with Crowdfunding Platforms

FinTech (financial technology) has been on the agenda recently. Some aspects of FinTech like Blockchain technology, cryptocurrencies, and AI FinTech are mentioned as the elements that can have significant effects on banking business models. We would like to construct our first suggestion on one of the developing aspects of FinTech, i.e., crowdfunding. As a very recent development in the financial arena dating back to the early 2000s, crowdfunding is briefly a method of raising funds through online structures. There can be three ways of raising funds via crowdfunding: in return for a gift or a share or as a donation.

Crowdfunding can be a good option for the business model of Islamic banks since the banks can provide funds for a wider group of society. Thus, the aforementioned criticisms directed toward Islamic banks regarding not being social or not providing microfinance options can be remedied to some extent by crowdfunding structures. Crowdfunding is mentioned as a supporter of the sharing economy, i.e., one of the main aspects attributed to Islamic economics and finance. In this way, crowdfunding as a FinTech element would not become a competitor to Islamic banks but a compliment.

The question to be asked here is how to construct a business model for Islamic banks that includes crowdfunding? Let us first share some existing examples in that regard. Alliance Islamic Bank Bhd. (The Star, 2019) has launched a social crowdfunding platform called SocioBiz in 2019. In order to launch the platform, Alliance Bank entered into a collaboration with an Islamic FinTech venture builder called Ethis Ventures Malaysia and some beneficiary partners. The model depends on four steps: applying to fundraise, starting crowdfunding, receiving funding, and applying for SIM (Social Impact Matching) Grant. The microfinance structure of such a model can raise the question of how Islamic banks can make money out of it. Examples in which Islamic banks can make money will be mentioned below, but there can always be some examples for Islamic banks about which they do not only concern money but also social output as this one.

While SocioBiz is more of a microfinance structure, crowdfunding applications can be integrated into the real estate sector. Ethis Crowd Indonesia is a good example in that regard. Ethis Crowd uses

> … a refined variation of Murabaha, which is the Istisna + Murabaha model, where the crowd orders houses and assets from the developer and makes progressive payments to contractors as these houses are built before selling them to Islamic Banks at a profit.
>
> (Ethis Crowd, 2019, p. 14)

As it is mentioned in the quotation, in that model, crowdfunding is integrated into istisna and murabaha contracts of Islamic banks. It can be thought whether this model can be costly since there are two intermediaries at once. In that regard, alternative schemes such as the existence of one subsidiary as a crowdfunding company can be thought of. However, the efficiency analysis of the alternative schemes requires further studies.

Another integrative approach is coming from Oman, where the Gulf's first crowdfunding platform called Waqf Blockchain was launched by Singaporean

Finterra in 2019. Islamic banks come to this picture by managing the assets raised by the platform. In the end, the profits would go to charity and/or investment (Unlock, 2019).

Even though it is not directly a crowdfunding platform, the Investment Account Platform (IAP) sponsored by Affin Islamic Bank is an example of an investment funding version of a crowdfunding platform. In the platform, funds are channeled from investors to finance viable ventures and projects. The model can be seen in Figure 4.1.

By taking into account these examples, we suggest that,

- The business model of Islamic banks can be improved by using crowdfunding platforms whose some parts can be allocated for social funding, and the rest can be used for investment purposes.
- The platforms are not required to be established by the banks directly. But outsourcing can be utilized, such as in the example of Oman.
- Islamic banks do not need to raise funds directly, but they can also be buyers of the products/services provided by the platforms in order to sell them later on, as in the example of Ethis Crowd. Or they can be the manager of the funds raised by the platforms.
- Islamic banks can establish IAPs among each other that are similar to crowdfunding platforms, as seen in Figure 4.1.

3.4.2 A Business Model Including P2P (Peer-to-Peer) Platforms and Smart PLS Contracts

P2P, one of the newest developments in FinTech, means matching investors with fund providers through online platforms. Similar to the logic of crowdfunding platforms, P2P platforms help one party meet with another party. Again as crowdfunding platforms, P2P platforms are quite compatible with partnership-based structures. Thus, there are some suggestions attempting

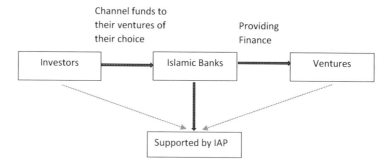

Figure 4.1 The Scheme of IAP.
Source: https://iaplatform.com/showIapInfo. Re-drawn by the author.

to connect P2P platforms with partnership-based Islamic finance contracts. Sa'ad et al. (2019) argue that especially musharakah investments are quite feasible for P2P financing. In the structure of the suggested musharakah smart contract, "... the peer-to-peer company will be appointed as an agent to facilitate the musharakah arrangement between the business owners and the investors" (Sa'ad et al., Ibid., p. 178). The authors list the steps of the aforementioned structure within five points. However, the feasibility is not entirely discussed.

Another Islamic Online P2P Lending Platform suggestion comes from Pişkin and Kuş (2019), who take mudarabah as the underlying contract. The whole process would have two main steps; the loan demand process and the investment process. In the first process, a borrower (the party who does not have the capital) would apply to the P2P lending platform based on mudarabah, and this application would be elaborated by an operator. In the second process, if the borrower's application is approved in the first process, investors would fund the borrower after requesting power of attorney.

Our suggestion in that regard, by taking into account the aforementioned suggestions, can be summarized as follows:

- Either collaborating with non-bank institutions or establishing separate banking lines for FinTech activities, including P2P, Islamic banks can establish P2P platforms.
- Islamic banks can be the founder of such platforms, and they may earn some income from advertisement, data sales, and being preferred investors to the project announcements. Investors can do businesses in either mudarabah or musharakah schemes through such platforms.
- In this way, the risk of involvement in partnerships would decrease for the banks since they would not directly become part of the partnerships. Instead, they would earn an intermediation fee.
- The applicability of each point, how much Islamic banks can earn from them, and the efficiency of each point can be analyzed further.

In order to decrease the risk further, Islamic banks can combine smart contracts with P2P activities. Another element developed by FinTech is smart contracts. Briefly,

> A smart contract is a self-executing contract with the terms of the agreement between buyer and seller being directly written into lines of code. The code and the agreements contained therein exist across a distributed, decentralized blockchain network. The code controls the execution, and transactions are trackable and irreversible.
>
> (Investopedia, n.d.)

One of the main aspects of FinTech is blockchain technology.[9] Thus, smart contracts are digital contracts that are decentralized and protected. The

58 *Zeyneb Hafsa Orhan*

contract would be put into life whenever its conditions are met, and it will not be materialized otherwise.

Smart contracts have several areas of use for banks in general. For instance, it can be used for credit card contracts. The main expected gain is cost reduction. Smart contracts can also have implications for Islamic banks. For instance, credit cards issued by Islamic banks can be structured according to smart contracts. As explained by Muneeza and Mustapha (2019), using blockchain smart contracts can ensure Islamic credit cards be used for buying prohibited items from Shariah non-compliant places such as casinos or places that sell mixed items such as food and alcohol at the same time.

But what we would like to underline here is the potential positive effect of smart contracts on an equity-based business model of Islamic banks. How can partnerships be integrated into smart contract structures? The peculiar aspect of Islamic finance, Shariah compliance, such as not buying prohibited items, can be programmed into the smart contract for any kind of financial transaction (Ibid.). In detail,

> This (the related rules of Shariah) can be automated or written into at the 'regulators' and all required 'parties' nodes that form part of the blockchain network. These nodes will then enable the system to validate transactions and append compliant blocks in the blockchain. In effect, the smart contract protocol can be utilized to set up any computer operation that is condition-driven so that transactions can only be possible after all required conditions for such transactions, including Shariah compliance, are accordingly satisfied.
>
> (Ibid., p. 77)

3.4.3 Business Model with Different Banking Structures

Today Islamic banks can organize themselves in different structures such as development banks as in the example of Islamic Development Bank, social banks (like Social Islami Bank Limited), investment banks (like European Islamic Investment Bank), etc. It is generally accepted that the most common type of Islamic bank is traditional commercial banks. What is meant by commercial banking is a banking structure in which deposits are accepted and then given as credits. Moreover, savings accounts are provided for individuals as well as businesses.

As in the aforementioned suggestion of constructing Islamic banks – or at least some parts of them – as social banks, some scholars such as Nor (Ibid.) argue that structuring Islamic banks differently from commercial banks can help them reflect their peculiarity more. In that regard, Boudjellal (2006) suggests that a non-banking financial intermediary called PLS banks can provide funds for long-term investment projects. The banks can do this by keeping equity stakes or buying sukuk (Islamic bonds) instruments. According to the author, these banks would resemble merchant banks in Great Britain or investment banks in the USA. By establishing Islamic investment banks, the author conceives that long-term investment needs would be matched, and newly starting businesses would get financing. The rest of the banks can be constructed as Islamic deposit banks. Thus, there can be two main types of Islamic banks in the system; Islamic investment banks and Islamic deposit (commercial) banks.

Besides, as was mentioned above, there are some suggestions about constructing universal Islamic banks.

In taking into account the suggestions such as establishing PLS, mudarabah Islamic banks, or universal Islamic banks, our proposal has the following points in that regard:

- Equity, PLS, or mudarabah prone Islamic investment banks can be established besides Islamic commercial banks. However, in order to do that, it needs to be investigated in detail what banks in a specific jurisdiction can do and cannot do according to banking laws.
- Also, potential issues and challenges that can arise due to the structure of investment banking need to be considered from the very beginning. Because investment banking in the USA shifted toward more risky activities leading them to suffer immensely during the crisis. Thus, what an Islamic investment bank can do and cannot do from the perspective of Shariah should be carefully evaluated at the outset.

A general structure of how such an Islamic investment bank can look like is illustrated in Figure 4.2.

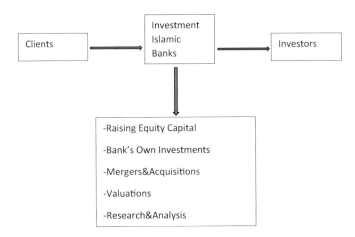

Figure 4.2 A Suggestion for an Islamic Investment Bank.
Source: It is graphed by the author.

60 *Zeyneb Hafsa Orhan*

Figure 4.2 is graphed using the general knowledge of what a typical investment bank does and what an Islamic investment bank can do, depending on the aforementioned points.

4 Conclusion

This study aims to make suggestions regarding the business model for Islamic banks. In simple words, the business model is defined as the way how a company is structured in order to generate value. Islamic banks are the institutions giving banking services in line with Islamic values, rules, and regulations.

In order to attain the aim of this study, first, discussions about the business model changes in banking since the 1970s due to the events of liberalization, financialization, financial crisis, FinTech developments, and COVID-19 were analyzed. In that regard, a list of changes has been provided by taking into account the related literature, such as dealing with more risky instruments, using off-balance-sheet items, and focusing on risk management processes.

Second, discussions about the business model of Islamic banks were analyzed. In that regard, the following points were focused on; lack of profit-and-loss-sharing instruments and deficiency in creating socio-economic output. In addition, suggestions made for the business model of Islamic banks were analyzed.

Third, considering all the information provided above, we made our unique suggestions in this respect. Our suggestions for the business model of Islamic banks comprise the following three issues:

- Islamic banking models having a connection with crowdfunding platforms,
- A business model including P2P platforms and smart PLS contracts,
- A business model with different banking structures, such as establishing Islamic investment banks.

As it can be noticed from these points, our suggestions are especially focusing on the recent developments in FinTech.

Therefore, the main policy implication for Islamic banks here can be that they need to focus more on FinTech developments. Giving the opportunity of establishing different types of Islamic banks, such as Islamic investment banks, can be another policy implication for the jurisdictions where Islamic banks operate.

Notes

1 What is meant by "lesser content" is that every kind of change in the conventional banking business model cannot necessarily happen in the Islamic banking sector due to the rules and ethics of Islam followed by Islamic banks.

Suggestions for Banking Business Models of Islamic Banking   61

2 As the name of it refers, off-balance-sheet activities are the ones including assets, debts and financing type of activities of the banks that are not included in their balance sheets. Such activities include operating type of leasing, joint ventures, and so on.
3 It means transforming the illiquid assets such as credit card debts into securities to be sold.
4 As the name suggests, derivative means a financial security which derives its value from an underlying asset such as a bond or a stock.
5 The main difference between retail and wholesale banking is that the first one concentrates on individual clients and small businesses whereas the second one deals with large clients such as government agencies, large corporations.
6 The effects of such competition require empirical testing to be (dis)proved. For instance, Petralia et al. (ibid.) finds that non-bank competition does not have significant effect on the decrease of interest margin, i.e. the main revenue source of banks.
7 Whether this can be provided in practice is another issue that will be discussed below.
8 Other aspects that can help to increase the stability can also be included such as the effect of zakah, charity, and alsm. But this is not directly the concern here.
9 "Blockchain is essentially a digital ledger or transactions that is duplicated and distributed across the entire network of computer systems on the blockchain. Each block in the chain contains a number of transactions, and every time a new transaction occurs on the blockchain, a record of that transaction is added to every participant's ledger." (Euromoney, n.d.)

References

Abdul Hamid, M., and Azmi, A. M. (2011). The Performance of Banking During 2000–2009: Bank Islam Malaysia Berhad and Conventional Banking in Malaysia, *International Journal of Economics and Management Sciences*, Vol. 1, No. 1, pp. 09–19.

Abdul Rahman, A. R. (2007). Islamic Microfinance: A Missing Component in Islamic Banking, *Kyoto Bulletin of Islamic Area Studies*, Vol. 1–2, pp. 38–53.

Al-Deehani, T. M., El-Sadi, H. M., and Al-Deehani, M. T., (2015). Performance of Islamic Banks and Conventional Banks before and during Economic Downturn, *Investment Management and Financial Innovations*, Vol. 12, No. 2-1, pp. 238–250.

Al-Jarhi, M. (2004). Remedy for Banking Crises: What Chicago and Islam in Common: A Comment, *Islamic Economic Studies*, Vol. 11, No. 2.

Al-Zoubi, H., and Maghyereh, A. I. (2007). Islamic Finance: A New Guide to Less Risky Investments, *International Journal of Theoretical and Applied Finance*, Vol. 10, No. 02, pp. 235–249.

Ariff, M. (2014). Whither Islamic Banking?, *The World Economy*, Vol. 37, No. 6, pp. 733–746.

Asutay, M. (2008). Islamic Banking and Finance: Social Failure, *New Horizon*, No. 169, pp. 1–3.

Ayadi, R., Arbak, E., and De Groen, W. P. (2011). Business Models in European Banking: A Pre-and Post-Crisis Screening, Center for European Policy Studies, Retrieved from https://ssrn.com/abstract=1945779 on 28.09.2020.

Boudjellal, M. (2006). Three Decades of Experimentation: Rethinking the Theory of Islamic Banking, *International Association for Islamic Economics, Review of Islamic Economics*, Vol. 10, No. 1, pp. 23–39.

62 Zeyneb Hafsa Orhan

Boyd, J. H., and Gertler, M. (1994). Are Banks Dead? Or Are the Reports Greatly Exaggerated?, *Quarterly Review, Federal Reserve Bank of Minneapolis*, Vol. 18 (Summer), pp. 2–23.

Chong, B., and Liu, M. (2009). Islamic Banking: Interest-free or Interest-based?, *Pacific-Basin Finance Journal*, Vol. 17, No. 1, pp. 125–144.

Čihák, M., and Hesse, H. (2010). Islamic Banks and Financial Stability: An Empirical Analysis, *Journal of Financial Services Research*, Vol. 38, pp. 95–113.

Clerides, S. (2014). The Collapse of the Cypriot Banking Systems: A 'Bird's Eye View, *Cyprus Economic Policy Review*, Vol. 8, No. 2, pp. 3–35.

Consumer International (2017). Banking on the Future: An Exploration of FinTech and the Consumer Interest, https://www.consumersinternational.org/media/154710/banking-on-the-future-full-report.pdf

Coppola, F. (2014). Is Investment Banking Dead?, *Forbes*, May 9. Retrieved from https://www.forbes.com/sites/francescoppola/2014/05/09/is-investment-banking-dead/#23c0793949e7 on 28.09.2020.

De La Torre, I. (2011). 4 Lessons that Western Banks Can Learn from Islamic Counterparts, *International Column*, 27 May–23 June, pp. 17–19.

De Roover, R. (1999). *The Rise and Decline of the Medici Bank: 1397–1494*, Beard Books.

Deloitte (2020). Retail Banking in the Age of Covid-19: Scenarios for Resilient Leaders. https://www2.deloitte.com/content/dam/Deloitte/global/Documents/Financial-Services/gx-fsi-retail-banking-in-the-age-of-covid-19.pdf

El Hawary, D., Grais, W., and Iqbal, Z. (2004). Regulating Islamic Financial Institutions: The Nature of the Regulated. *World Bank Policy Research Working Paper #3227*.

Ethis Crowd (2019). Ethis Islamic Crowdfunding Report, Volume 2. Retrieved from https://cdn2.hubspot.net/hubfs/2627399/Ethis%20Islamic%20Crowdfunding%20Report%20Vol.%202%20-%20May%202019.pdf on 2 October, 2020.

Euromoney (n.d.). What Is Blockchain? Retrieved from https://www.euromoney.com/learning/blockchain-explained/what-is-blockchain#:~:text=Blockchain%20is%20a%20system%20of,computer%20systems%20on%20the%20blockchain on 28.09.2020.

Foster, J. B., and Magdoff, F. (2009). *The Great Financial Crisis: Causes and Consequences*, New York: Monthly Review Press.

Helleiner, E. (2011). Understanding the 2007–2008 Global Financial Crisis: Lessons for Scholars of International Political Economy, *Annual Review of Political Science*, Vol. 14, pp. 67–87.

Ibrahim, M. H., and Rizvi, S. A. R. (2018). Bankl Lending, Deposits and Risk-Taking in Time of Crisis: A Panel Analysis of Islamic and Conventional Banks, *Emerging Markets Review*, Vol. 35, pp. 31–47.

IFSB (2020). Islamic Financial Services Industry Stability Report 2020.

Investment Account Platform (n.d.). What Is IAP? Retrieved from https://iaplatform.com/showIapInfo on 2 October, 2020.

Investopedia (n.d.). Smart Contracts. Retrieved from https://www.investopedia.com/terms/s/smart-contracts.asp#:~:text=A%20smart%20contract%20is%20a,a%20distributed%2C%20decentralized%20blockchain%20network 2 October 2020.

Jatmiko, W. (2017). Towards a Sustainable Islamic Banking System: Re-Embedding Murabaha Mode of Financing. *Indonesian Capital Market Review*, Vol. 9, pp. 101–116.

Karaman, H. (2017). *İslam düşüncesinde ekonomi, banka ve sigorta*, İz Yayıncılık, İstanbul.

Kaufman, G. G., and Mote, L. R. (1994). Is Banking a Declining Industry? A Historical Perspective, *Economic Perspectives*, Vol. 18, May, pp. 2–21.

Khan, F. (2010). How "Islamic" Is Islamic Banking?, *Journal of Economic Behavior & Organization*, Vol. 76, No. 3, pp. 805–820.

Laurent, M., Plantefeve, O., Tejada, M., and Van Weyenbrgh, F. (2020). Banking models after Covid-19: taking model-risk management to the next level, McKinsey&Company.

Laeven, L., and Valencia, F. (2012). Systemic Banking Crises Database: An Update, *International Monetary Fund Working Paper* WP/12/163.

Lenz, R. (2011). *Get Rid of Banks and Build Up a Modern Financial World!* Paper for the 17th Workshop on Alternative Economic Policy in Europe, Vienna/Austria, 16–18 September.

Mirakhor, A., and Krichene, N. (2009). Recent Crisis: Lessons for Islamic Finance, *New Horizon*, 01 October, 2009.

Muneeza, A., and Mustapha, Z. (2019). Blockchain and Its Shariah Compliant Structure, pp. 69–106, in *Halal Cryptocurrency Management*, Plagrave Macmillan.

Nor, S. M. (2016). Islamic Social Bank: An Adaptation of Islamic Banking?, *Journal Pengurusan*, Vol. 46, pp. 43–52.

Petralia, K., Philippon, T., Rice, T., and Véron, N. (2019). *Banking Disrupted? Financial Intermediation in an Era of Transformational Technology*. International Center for Monetary and Banking Studies, Geneva Reports on the World Economy, 22.

Orhan, Z. H. (2018). Business Model of Islamic Banks in Turkey, *Journal of Islamic Accounting and Business Research*, Vol. 9, No. 3, pp. 290–307.

Pişkin, M., and Kuş, M. C. (2019). Islamic Online P2P Lending Platform, *Procedia Computer Science*, Vol. 158, pp. 415–419.

Sa'ad, A. A., Ahmad, K., and Saleh, A. O. H. (2019). P2P Islamic FinTech Investment Innovation: A Proposal of Musharakah Smart Contract Model for SMEs Financing and Social Development, *Al-Shajarah: Journal of the International Institute of Islamic Thought and Civilization (ISTAC)*, Vol. October, pp. 169–184.

Schmidt, R. H., Hackethal, A., and Tyrell, M. (1999). Disintermediation and the Role of Banks in Europe: An International Comparison, *Journal of Financial Intermediation*, Vol. 8, No. 1–2, pp. 36–67.

Sorwar, G., Pappas, V., Pereira, J., and Nurullah, M. (2016). To Debt or not to Debt: Are Islamic Banks Less Risky than Conventional Banks?, *Journal of Economic Behavior & Organization*, Vol. 132, Supplement, pp. 113–126.

Statista (2021). *Value of Islamic Banking Assets Worldwide from 2012 to 2019.* Retrieved from https://www.statista.com/statistics/1090891/worldwide-growth-of-islamic-banking-assets/ on 29 January 2021.

Statista (2020). *Total Assets of Banks Worldwide from 2002 to 2018.* Retrieved from https://www.statista.com/statistics/421215/banks-assets-globally/ on 29 January 2021.

TCS (2020). *Repositioning Investment Banks: Driving Growth Post COVID-19.* Retrieved from https://www.tcs.com/content/dam/tcs/pdf/Industries/Banking%20and%20Financial%20Services/investment-banking-crisis-trends-resilience-strategy.pdf on 30.01.2021.

The Star (2019). *Alliance Islamic Bank Launches Social Crowdfunding Platform.* Retrieved from https://www.thestar.com.my/business/business-news/2019/05/17/alliance-islamic-bank-launches--social-crowdfunding-platform on 2 October, 2020.

Trad, N., Trabelsi, M. A., and Goux, J. F. (2017). Risk and Profitability of Islamic Banks: A Religious Deception or an Alternative Solution?, *European Research on Management and Business Economics*, Vol. 23, No. 1, pp. 40–45.

Tripp, C. (2006). *Islam and the Moral Economy: The Challenge of Capitalism.* Cambridge University Press.

Unlock (2019). *Oman Launches the First Blockchain Crowdfunding Islamic Waqf Platform.* Retrieved from https://www.unlock-bc.com/news/2019-09-18/oman-launches-the-first-blockchain-crowdfunding-islamic-waqf-platform on 2 October, 2020.

Yousef, T. M., 2004. The Murabaha Syndrome in Islamic Finance: Laws, Institutions and Politics. In: C. M. Henry & R. Wilson (Eds.), *The Politics of Islamic Finance.* Edinburg University Press, Edinburgh, pp. 63–80.

5 Financial Sustainability of Islamic Microfinance Institutions (MFIs)

Murat Yaş and Yi Chen

1 Introduction

According to the Global Findex Database, there are still an estimated 1.7 billion financially excluded adults worldwide, although 1.2 billion people have opened a financial account since 2011 (Demirguc-Kunt, Klapper, Singer, Ansar, & Hess, 2018). Therefore, the World Bank Group, private and public sector partners embraced measurable commitments to achieve Universal Financial Access by 2020 and help promote financial inclusion at the 2015 World Bank Group-IMF Spring Meetings. Even if achieving the target of ending poverty has been on the World Bank's agenda for a long time, more than 700 million people still live in extreme poverty and struggle to fulfill the most basic needs such as education, health, and access to clean water. In both cases, Microfinance Institutions (MFIs) play a very important role by providing financial services to households and micro-enterprises that are poor and excluded from traditional commercial banking services. Moreover, microenterprises require long-term access to financial services by MFIs in the early stages of their business activities to enhance the operational sophistication and catalyze their business growth. At this point, it is important to note that the financial sustainability of MFIs is essential for poverty alleviation and enhancing financial inclusion.

The World Bank announced that Indonesia has achieved to reduce the headcount ratio at $1.90 per day from 27.4% in 2006 to 4.6% in 2018. Despite having the world's one of the largest unbanked population with 95 million people, financial inclusion rose from 36% to 49%, with an increase of financial access for the poorest from 22% to 37% during the period of 2014–2017 (Demirguc-Kunt et al., 2018). Considering the important role of microfinance practices, the country particularly provides a compelling case differing from other countries by an outstanding achievement of effective microfinance techniques to alleviate poverty and enhance financial inclusion.

Over the last decades, MFIs in Indonesia have innovated various financial products and services to ensure better credit access by the poor. Thus, the country has probably the most remarkable diversity of both conventional and Islamic microfinance in comparison with other developing countries (Seibel &

DOI: 10.4324/9781003377283-5

66 *Murat Yaş and Yi Chen*

Table 5.1 Financial Institutions in Indonesia

Types		Total Institutions	Total Offices Network
Commercial Banks	Conventional	130	30,837
	Islamic	34	1937
Rural Banks	Conventional	1,526	5,936
	Islamic	162	631
Cooperatives	Conventional	NA	61,524–73,828★
	Islamic	7000★★	NA

Sources: OJK (2020), MoCMSME (2019)★, (Sakti, 2019)★★

Dwi Agung, 2006). In August 2020, there were 130 commercial banks with 30,837 offices and 1,526 rural banks with 5,936 offices (see Table 5.1). According to the Ministry of Cooperatives and Micro and Small Medium Enterprises (MoCMSMEs) of the Republic of Indonesia, there were between 61,524 and 73,828 formal savings and loan cooperatives under its supervision in 2019.

In Indonesia, the country with the largest Muslim population in the world, Islamic microfinance has evolved since 1991, consisting of Islamic commercial banks, commercial banking units, rural banks, and financial cooperatives (Seibel & Dwi Agung, 2006). In 2020, Islamic financial institutions in Indonesia comprised 34 Islamic commercial banks with 1,937 offices; 162 Islamic rural banks with 631 offices (see Table 5.1). Based on the estimations of Baitul Maal Wat Tamwil (BMT) associations, there were more than 7000 Islamic financial cooperatives under the supervision of MoCMSMEs and Otoritas Jasa Keuangan (OJK) (Sakti, 2019).

Depending on their licensing, regulation, and supervision, Indonesia has three categories of Islamic MFIs: formal, semi-formal, and informal. Islamic commercial banks and Islamic rural banks (BPRS) are formal Islamic MFIs that are regulated and supervised by OJK. BMT, Baitul Tamwil Muhammadiyah (BTM), and Baitul Qirad (BQ) are semi-formal Islamic microfinance cooperatives licensed under the supervision of MoCMSME (Masyita & Ahmed, 2013). There are also quasi-microfinance channeling groups, credit associations (ROSCAs), and rotating savings classified under the informal Islamic MFI category (Seibel & Dwi Agung, 2006).

BMT, an Islamic microfinance cooperative, stands for *Baitul Maal* and *Baitul Tamwil*. BMTs not only collect, manage, and distribute zakat, infaq, and sadaqah for improving social welfare but also act as financial intermediaries, manage savings and funding by providing financial services with the pursuit of profit. Therefore, BMTs have a crucial role in alleviating poverty in remote and rural areas while maintaining their cooperatives' operational and financial sustainability (Maulana & Akbar, 2019). Moreover, BMTs reduce the barriers to accessing formal financial services for micro and small enterprises and provide better access to credit for the poor, enabling them to pull themselves out of poverty (Beck, 2015; Hosen, 2006). Thus, BMTs have been key players to alleviate poverty in Indonesia over the last decades.

There is growing interest in the determinants of MFIs' financial sustainability, and this is reflected clearly in the literature. Luoto, McIntosh, and Wydick (2007) display that the introduction of a credit registry for MFIs helped decrease missed payments and delinquency. Many studies show that repayment under group lending is enhanced by trust coming from social conformity and reciprocity (Attanasio, Barr, Cardenas, Genicot, & Meghir, 2012; Cassar, Crowley, & Wydick, 2007; Feigenberg, Field, & Pande, 2010). Additionally, the religious intensity of the group leader and members improves repayment performance (Ashta & De Selva, 2012; D'Espallier, Guérin, & Mersland, 2011). Cost reduction is essential to ensure the financial sustainability of MFIs. Battilana and Dorado (2010) find that loan sizes, ages, and scale are the main drivers of the operating expense ratio of MFIs. Moreover, empirical evidence from Niger also showed that digital payments reduced costs to 25% (Aker, Boumnijel, McClelland, & Tierney, 2016). Cull, Demirgüç-kunt, and Morduch (2007) and Hermes et al. (2011) had international evidence on the trade-off between efficiency and outreach of MFIs. The studies which investigate the nexus between performance and regulatory involvement yields mixed results (Hartarska & Nadolnyak, 2007; Mersland & Øystein Strøm, 2009).

Parallel to the discussion on financial sustainability MFIs, BMTs' financial sustainability has recently become one of the central issues in microfinance literature (Hadisumarto & Ismail, 2010; Hamzah, Rusby, & Hamzah, 2013; Maulana & Akbar, 2019; Nasution, 2013; Wulandari, Kassim, Adhi Kasari Sulung, & Iwani Surya Putri, 2016). The microfinance ecosystem in Indonesia, with thousands of MFIs and distinguished microfinancing practices, provides a fertile ground to examine the determinants of MFIs' financial sustainability. Therefore, the growth of recently published studies on the sustainability of BMTs created a large body of literature. However, there are limited studies that conduct critical survey literature on BMTs' financial sustainability. Thus, this study attempts to fill the gap in the literature by offering a critical survey of the BMT literature over the past 15 years. We reviewed studies on the determinants of efficiency, profitability, and sustainability of BMTs to learn what challenges they face and how they manage to overcome these barriers from the recent literature.

To sum up, this study offers a critical survey of semi-formal Islamic MFIs in Indonesia, namely BMT literature over the past 15 years. It reviews studies on the financial sustainability of BMTs in Indonesia through investigating their challenges and how they managed to overcome these barriers. The literature so far suggests that human resources development, microfinance techniques, linkage programs, cost management, competitiveness, regulation and supervision, the funding structure, and management information systems (MIS) of BMTs are critical factors that determine the financial sustainability of BMTs. The most significant impact seems to come from linkage programs, the introduction of regulations, new technologies, and innovations in financial services and payment systems.

68 *Murat Yaş and Yi Chen*

2 Financial Sustainability of BMTs in Indonesia

2.1 Human Resources Management

It is established that the sustainability of BMTs is associated with human resource development (Seibel, 2015; Zuhria, 2012). Many studies highlight that there are many issues related to human resource management that BMTs need to address for achieving targeted social and financial performance (Hamzah et al., 2013; Husaeni & Dew, 2019; Rusydiana & Devi, 2013; Zuhria, 2012).

Numerous studies indicate that a lack of managerial skill in the employees is a fundamental barrier that worsens the financial sustainability of BMTs in Indonesia. Mustamir and Mawardi (2006) used the sample of BMTs in Pekanbaru documented that BMTs lack managerial skills in the employees, particularly in accounting, reporting, and administration. Moreover, Adnan, Widarjono, and Anto (2003) examined factors influencing the performance of the best BMTs in Indonesia. They found that the nexus between BMT performance and managers' level of education is positive. Several studies also note that unlike Islamic commercial banks and Islamic rural banks, human resources working in BMT are relatively less professional (Rusydiana & Devi, 2013; Maulana & Akbar, 2019).

In order to fill personnel-related gaps in human resource management, BMTs should develop and implement a plan through redeployment, retraining, and recruitment for required staff and management positions. Moreover, BMTs fail to attract highly skilled and educated employees due to paying a low salary and an unfavorable human resource recruitment system (Husaeni & Dew, 2019). Therefore, BMTs can provide employer-sponsored university education in return for mandatory service for the long-term. Additionally, BMTs can establish or expand training departments to include training in new products, accounting, administration, and overall staff capacity (Hamzah et al., 2013; Zuhria, 2012).

Various studies investigated the relationship between the salary of employees and the sustainability of BMTs in Indonesia, yet those studies yielded mixed results. Widiyanto and Ismail (2009) used a sample of 60 BMTs from 2002 to 2004 and explored that rise in salary affects the efficiency of BMTs adversely. However, Adnan et al. (2003) suggested a positive relation between salary and financial performance of BMT. On the other hand, Rusydiana and Devi (2013) argued that it is essential to have performance-based pay for employees since it can motivate them to work harder under penalty or bonus contracts.

2.2 Microfinancing Techniques

The financial sustainability of BMTs is positively associated with the profitability of the business of micro-enterprises. Thus, the selection process of micro-enterprises as BMT members is crucial to enhance the effectiveness of BMT financing, which enables all of the parties to enjoy the profit. BMTs must put special emphasis on the capability and experience of micro-entrepreneurs in running a business as well as the credibility and honesty to reduce the cases of adverse selection and moral hazards. BMTs usually visit the houses of applicants to know their economic or business feasibility before approving any financing (Effendi, 2013). Sometimes, financing successful micro-enterprises plays a key role in the sustainability of BMT financing (Hadisumarto & Ismail, 2009).

Although BMTs were not initially established for providing financial services to women, many BMTs have gradually embraced women as their primary beneficiaries. Microfinance mostly targets women since they show careful investment, disciplined spending, and better repayment (D'Espallier et al., 2011). Effendi (2013) interviewed women clients of BMTs in Pasuruan, East Java, and concluded that BMTs did not empower women as intended because they often did not have control over their acquired funds. Yet, they sometimes achieved to grow their business and generate additional income for families. Rahayu (2020) used four BMTs in Yogyakarta as a sample and found that even though women are BMTs' crucial clients, none of BMTs explicitly invoked women's empowerment in their organizational vision. The study shows that BMTs' objective to target women is not reducing gender inequality but rather motivated by pragmatic business considerations, particularly the self-sustainability paradigm. Similarly, Sutiyo, Pitono, Raharjanto, and Sinaga (2020) examined the microfinance performance of BMTs targeting women in Purbalingga to provide financial services. The study explored that women clients have a high repayment rate and asset growth, yet their poverty alleviation performance is low.

Many studies documented that asset quality is one of the most critical factors for the financial performance of BMTs in Indonesia (Indrawati, 2008; Mulyana & Supardi, 2008; Zahra & Wijayanti, 2019). The rate of repayment and business success of micro-enterprises determine the asset quality of BMTs. Therefore, BMTs evaluate the economic and business feasibility of their clients before providing microfinancing (Effendi, 2013). More precisely, BMTs require membership, credibility (honesty), business skills, business experience, and collateral to minimize the probability of default (Adnan & Ajija, 2015). In cases of facing difficulty to collect debts, BMTs often use a spiritual approach such as reminding Qur'an verses about debt as a religious obligation that needs to be fulfilled (Nasution, 2013).

Beck (2015) and Satar and Kassim (2020) showed that a high frequency of meetings between BMT employees and customers might significantly reduce non-performing financing. Some BMTs suffer from low repayment rates of their clients in remote and rural areas due to the low frequency of customers' meetings with BMT employees related to the high cost of transportation and time constraints (Effendi & Utami, 2016).

Several studies argued that implementing an incentive mechanism for good payment can improve asset quality (Bursztyn, Fiorin, Gottlieb, & Kanz, 2019; Hadisumarto & Ismail, 2010; Robinson, 2002). Many BMTs use some incentives such as giving mark-up or profit payment discount, souvenir, add their savings and enhance the ceiling of financing for clients with good payment records (Hadisumarto & Ismail, 2010). Such incentive mechanism contributes benefit to all parties, especially for maintaining the sustainability of BMTs' microfinancing and the business growth of micro-enterprises.

Many BMTs use group lending as a microfinancing technique, where liability for repayment is shared among members. In cases that liability for repayment is not shared among members, BMTs prefer to include Imam's wife and community leader in the group to put spiritual and psychological pressure on members and ensure a good repayment rate (Beck, 2015). Dusuki (2008) argued that adopting a group lending mechanism positively has important repercussions for transferring information between BMTs and members. Therefore, group lending can reduce cases of adverse selection and moral hazards.

2.3 Linkage Programs

Many researchers have emphasized the importance of linkage programs' role in the financial sustainability of BMTs since the early years of their activities. Numerous studies inspect linkage programs-financial sustainability relationship by investigating the impact of coordination between BMTs and those with different mandates such as commercial banks, rural banks, NGOs, social funds, and rural development projects on efficiency and profitability of BMTs (Hamada, 2010; Maulana & Akbar, 2019; Zuhria, 2012). However, there are still limited linkage programs despite the strategic need for coordination in human resource development, MIS, and access to external sources of funding. Although OJK and the Central Bank of Indonesia (BI) do not provide a regulatory framework for BMTs, they strongly urge commercial and rural banks in Indonesia to launch linkage programs with BMTs for the development of Islamic microfinance practices (Monetary Policy Report, 2009). Along the same line, Rusydiana and Devi (2013) explored that linkage programs between BMTs and BPRSs are a top priority for BMTs after conducting in-depth interviews with BMT practitioners.

Several studies are exploring the vital role of linkage programs on the human resource development of BMTs. Seibel and Dwi Agung (2006) highlighted that Permodalan Nasional Madani (PNM) put more emphasis on the human resource development of BMT in cooperation with PINBUK and ABSINDO. Rusydiana and Devi (2013) also argued that BMTs need to strengthen coordination with PINBUK in organizing training for BMTs' employees and managers. Adnan et al. (2003) found that among 47 BMTs in Java, 43 of them have good cooperation with other institutions, particularly with PINBUK and Dompet Dhuafa. This cooperation covers many aspects of management, including management training.

One of the most crucial functions of the linkage programs is the extension of financing to micro and small businesses. Unlike Islamic commercial and rural banks (BPRSs), BMTs are likely to know micro and small enterprises in rural and remote areas better than commercial banks. Moreover, many BMTs have remarkable expertise and experience in providing financial services to micro-entrepreneurs. Thus, a linkage program represents a win-win investment for all parties involved. In turn, BMTs that lack funds will be greatly helped by linkage programs enabling them to channel financing to micro and small enterprises (Hamada, 2010; Rusydiana & Devi, 2013; Sutiyo et al., 2020). Fitriasari (2019) investigated the impact of linkage programs on the financial sustainability of BMTs. The author found that linkage program funds have an essential role in the sustainability of BMT operations. Especially, small- and medium-scale BMTs cover almost half of their total liabilities through linkage programs. Moreover, PUSKOPSYAH, as an arm of ABSINDO, also plays as the lender of the last resort for local BMT members, where the funds usually come from member's fees. Bank Indonesia also initiated the establishment of apex institutions with the participation of PNM, Amanah Ventura, and Permodalan BMT as liquidity providers to BMTs.

Linkage programs have a significant role in improving MIS in BMTs too. To illustrate, PINBUK currently provides core banking software and mobile applications for BMTs. Many BMTs still record financial transactions manually (Hadisumarto & Ismail, 2009). Therefore, PINBUK's efforts to digitalize accounting entries, credit history and provide various payment services have significant implications for improving the cost efficiency of BMTs. Linkage programs also enable technology to transfer from commercial banks to BMTs in different regions of Indonesia (Seibel, 2015).

2.4 Cost Management

One of the main barriers preventing the financial sustainability of BMTs is that microfinance services are often very costly. This is also reflected in its high mark-up or profit rates that BMTs charge members. The high cost is related to several underlying reasons, such as labor costs, transportation costs, fixed asset costs, and funding costs. Today, it is well documented that there is a positive relationship between cost efficiency and BMTs' financial performance (Mawardi, 2005). Therefore, it is important to discuss what factors can drive cost efficiency in detail to ensure BMTs' financial sustainability.

In terms of efficiency, BMTs in Indonesia have difficulty in managing two categories of pressure: cost and revenue pressures. Thus, either members of BMTs absorb them by higher cost of financing or BMTs improve efficiency through the operational processes to reduce costs (Yeow, Chuen, Tan, & Chia, 2018). Many BMTs undergo high operating costs for providing financial services to unbanked poor in remote and rural areas. The cost of transportation, search costs to reach the poor, staff shortage, and low frequency of meetings often end up with low asset quality and cost inefficiency for BMTs (Effendi & Utami, 2016; Perdana & Maxwell, 2005).

BMTs in Indonesia could apply a fintech ecosystem such as a highly secure digital payment service that can reduce the geographic distance, costs, and protect members' privacy (Yeow et al., 2018). Moreover, many BMTs provide microfinance services to micro-entrepreneurs in a local business area (Pasar) to ensure a higher frequency of meetings with members and repayments. It decreases the cost of monitoring business activities, reduces transportation costs, and saves time for improving BMTs' cost-efficiency.

2.5 Competitive Positioning

Existing BMTs need to become more efficient and competitive to survive in the microfinance industry in Indonesia. Many studies argue that a high level of competition is one of the most important external challenges for BMTs in Indonesia (Indrawati, 2008; Mulyana & Supardi, 2008; Zahra & Wijayanti, 2019). Therefore, maintaining an adequate spread between the profit-sharing rate and financing rate as well as reasonable operational costs becomes critical to the sustainability and profitability of the BMTs in Indonesia.

One crucial question has been whether the high cost of microfinancing is justified or could negatively impact demand (Beck, 2015). Tambunan (2015) interviewed micro-enterprises and found that 14.2% of them do not access microfinancing due to high financing costs. Many BMTs prefer to charge high financing rates due to operational inefficiencies and, sometimes, even exploitive practices (Ledgerwood & White, 2006). Therefore, improving cost efficiency will gradually reduce microfinancing costs (Badranaya, 2017; Effendi, 2013). In addition to improving cost efficiency by BMTs, the Indonesian government can also lower the cost of financing by developing the physical infrastructure necessary in rural areas, which would reduce operational costs for BMTs (Ledgerwood & White, 2006).

The linkage programs play a significant role in turning competition into coordination where all parties can enjoy a profit. Therefore, BI attempts to reduce the high level of competition among Islamic commercial banks, Islamic rural banks (BPRS), and BMTs through a linkage program. BPRS and Islamic commercial banks can provide financial services to micro and small enterprises by channeling funds to BMTs (Seibel & Dwi Agung, 2006). Moreover, Islamic commercial banks and BPRS can benefit from BMTs' experience and expertise in financing micro and small enterprises in remote and rural areas, whereas BMTs can solve their lack of funding problem via linkage programs (Fitriasari, 2019; Rusydiana & Devi, 2013).

2.6 Regulation and Supervision

Currently, BMTs are subjected to the same regulation and supervisory policies as other non-financial cooperatives. Many scholars argue that the lack of tighter regulation and supervision for financial activities of BMTs has been a key challenge for their performance (Widiyanto & Ismail, 2009). Moreover, several studies claim that a large number of BMTs is already dormant or technically bankrupt due to lax controls of MoCMSME on BMTs (Seibel, 2015).

Financial Sustainability of Islamic Microfinance Institutions 73

There is a fierce debate on regulatory and supervisory issues of BMTs among practitioners, academicians, and regulators (Hamzah et al., 2013).

There was an increasing number of controversies surrounding BMTs in recent years. Many people have raised the question of whether BMTs have led to greater exploitation of the poor (Effendi, 2013; Sandberg, 2012). Therefore, many researchers recently investigated the financial sustainability of BMTs and their impact on poverty alleviation in Indonesia (Widiyanto & Ismail, 2009; Wulandari et al., 2016; Yuniar, 2015). Several economists highlighted the need for a system of prudential regulation, mandatory auditing, and effective supervision by an appropriate financial authority rather than MoCMSME (Seibel, 2015).

In 2013, Financial Services Authority (OJK) in Indonesia announced implementing various regulatory procedures and standards to change the perception that MFIs are risky financial cooperatives and improve BMTs' efficiency and performance (Yeow et al., 2018). According to the new "MFI Act," there are new restrictive barriers to entry; applicable capitalization, and licensing requirements. Moreover, BMTs need to meet capital requirements depending on the coverage area and submit financial reports quarterly to the OJK. Indonesia's new MFI Act went into effect on 8 January 2015. Moreover, BMTs must obtain prior approval from the OJK before merging or consolidating with other BMTs (KPMG Indonesia, 2015).

Although the new MFI act has a vital role in improving the financial soundness of BMTs in Indonesia, many researchers emphasized the need to leave room for the flexibility of BMTs activities. Meanwhile, the objective of OJK was turning semi-formal and informal MFIs into formal rural banks and commercial banks in the long term (Supervision and Regulation of Microfinance Institutions in Indonesia, 2016). However, several giant BMTs continue to channel a part of their funding to maintain non-financial business activities such as real estate business, car dealership, or financing their partner companies. Therefore, they continue to operate as BMTs to avoid OJK's tighter regulation and supervision.

OJK's new restrictions on BMTs' activities can reduce the profitability and efficiency of BMTs. Again, the motivation for putting restrictions on financial services provided by BMTs might be turning them into formal MFIs, either Islamic commercial banks or BPRS. However, tighter regulation on business and financial activities of BMTs can prevent ongoing innovation and development of BMT. Therefore, it can create potential negative implications for poverty alleviation and sustainability of BMTs in the long term (Ledgerwood & White, 2006).

2.7 The Funding Structure

Many studies recently documented that funding structure can determine the financial sustainability of BMTs (Hasbi, 2015; Lisa, 2016; Mulyana & Supardi, 2008). Therefore, with a target capital structure in mind, a BMT might need to develop a financing strategy that considers the range of funding options available, including Islamic deposits, minimum amounts for voluntary and compulsory savings, external sources of funding, linkage programs, mergers, and acquisitions.

Many researchers argued that adequate capital is a primary concern for BMTs to cover operational costs and bear the loss at the infancy stage (Mukhtar, 2014; Zahra & Wijayanti, 2019). After interviewing 44 BMTs, Adnan et al. (2003) explored that 29 BMTs feel that their capital is not adequate. Maulana and Akbar (2019) suggested that BMTs can raise initial capital through special cooperation with the government, non-government, private parties, and company social responsibility funds. Raising equity capital from the third parties will strengthen the capital of BMTs for expanding micro-financing activities and coverage areas that BMT employees actively work.

Mulyana and Supardi (2008) argued that there is a positive correlation between capital structure and the performance of MFIs in Indonesia. Hasbi (2015) used a sample of 152 BMTs from 12 provinces of Indonesia and concluded that a high debt-to-equity ratio positively affects the profitability of BMTs. Similarly, Lisa (2016) examined the impact of third-party funds on BMTs' profitability and found that external funding sources drive BMTs' profitability. Therefore, linkage programs play a crucial role in covering funding shortages of BMTs and ensuring the sustainability of providing financial services to micro and small entrepreneurs.

It had been a long time that BMTs did not have a last resort lender to manage liquidity risk. Therefore, many BMTs had difficulty managing asset-liability mismatch and reduce liquidity risk. However, PUSKOPSYAH started to act as the lender of the last resort for local BMT members. Moreover, the establishment of apex institutions with the participation of PNM, Amanah Ventura, and Permadolan BMT enables liquidity management to diminish the liquidity and credit risk of BMTs.

Membership fees, voluntary and compulsory savings from a large number of members also facilitate the collection of saving and Islamic deposit funds on a large scale. Even though membership fees can be considered an important barrier to financial inclusion, many BMTs charge a very small membership fee and compulsory savings to overcome an entry-cost barrier. Membership fees, voluntary and compulsory savings can play an essential role in decreasing the cost of funding and dependence on external sources of funding.

2.8 Management Information Systems

Recently, many qualitative and quantitative studies showed that BMTs have inadequate MIS infrastructures, and it negatively affects their financial performance (Hosen & Sa'roni, 2012; Iswanaji, 2019; Rusydiana & Devi, 2013). Therefore, BMTs should put more effort into ensuring that their MIS are closely aligned with their business strategies. Launching IT initiatives such as

Financial Sustainability of Islamic Microfinance Institutions 75

mobile banking, automated teller machines (ATMs), and digitalizing operational activities can reduce operating costs, attract more members and improve the sustainability of BMTs (Ledgerwood & White, 2006; Mukhtar, 2014).

Most of BMTs still rely on manual paper-based systems to record the history of financial transactions. In other words, field workers capture all disbursement of funds and collection of repayments manually on paper notebooks (Hadisumarto & Ismail, 2009; Yeow et al., 2018). Iswanaji (2019) used samples of 100 BMTs in Indonesia and found that the use of accounting information systems by BMTs positively affects the services of Islamic MFIs, both individual accountants and organizations. Therefore, many BMTs try to digitalize their financial statements to improve their MIS for higher security, accessibility, accuracy, and reliability of their financial indicators. Nevertheless, it takes long hours for field officers to enter all the paper-based transactions into standalone computer systems and increases operating costs of BMTs.

After continuous development of smartphone technology, a fall of prices, and the recent Covid-19 lockdown, a smartphone is not a luxurious but an essential and affordable item. According to Statista, the number of mobile internet users in Indonesia amounted to 73 million in 2015 and grew to 191 million in 2020. Therefore, developing robust and secure mobile applications plays a vital role in BMTs' reaching the poor in rural and urban areas (Iswanaji, 2019). Moreover, innovations in payment services via smartphones can reduce costs for both payee and payer, reduce risks, and increase privacy (Beck, 2015). Using information technologies such as mobile banking and mobile wallets can reduce operational costs and, consequently, diminish the rate of financing for micro and small enterprises (Vong & Song, 2015).

3 Conclusions and Policy Recommendations

In this study, we explore that the literature so far suggests that human resources development, microfinance techniques, linkage programs, cost management, competitiveness, regulation and supervision, the funding structure, and MIS of BMTs have a significant association with the financial sustainability and performance of BMTs. Therefore, MFIs, governments, regulatory and supervisory bodies, partners of MFIs such as NGOs, commercial and rural banks must pay special attention to each of these determinants to ensure the sustainability of MFIs.

There are crucial implications of this study for regulatory bodies and MFIs. It will be beneficial to summarize key lessons learned from the financial sustainability of BMTs in Indonesia. First, linkage programs often had a remarkable contribution to the sustainability of BMTs through the improvement of human resource management, getting access to external sources of funding, technology transfer, and turning stiff competition into coordination. Second, BMTs need a unique regulatory framework to improve their financial soundness, yet regulatory bodies should leave room for flexible and tailored microfinance practices to address the needs of the poor. Third, taking advantage of new technology and fintech to revolutionize microfinance practices has a vital role in ensuring the financial sustainability of BMTs by using digital delivery channels for financial services, mobile microfinance adoption, and mobile wallets.

In conclusion, this critical survey of literature would like to bring attention to microfinance studies, particularly the financial sustainability of BMTs in Indonesia. Although there are thousands of BMTs implementing distinguished microfinance practices, the number of research on BMTs' financial sustainability remained still limited. Moreover, few studies on this topic have been published in high-rank journals by reputable researchers despite the high growth rate of publications on poverty alleviation and microfinance practices in the world. Limited data availability and distinguished microfinance practices are important challenges for conducting empirical research on MFIs in Indonesia. Therefore, BMTs, OJK, MoCMSMEs, and Microfinance Associations such as ABSINDO and Perhimpunan BMT Indonesia can play a crucial role in facilitating academic research on BMTs through collecting and sharing a wide range of data MFIs in Indonesia.

References

Adnan, M. A., & Ajija, S. R. (2015). The effectiveness of Baitul Maal wat Tamwil in reducing poverty. *Humanomics*, *31*(2), 160–182. https://doi.org/10.1108/H-03-2012-0003

Adnan, M. A., Widarjono, A., & Anto, M. B. H. (2003). Study on factors influencing performance of the best BMT in Indonesia. *IQTISAD Journal of Islamic Economics*, *4*(1), 13–35. Retrieved from http://journal.uii.ac.id/index.php/Iqtisad/article/viewFile/363/279

Aker, J. C., Boumnijel, R., McClelland, A., & Tierney, N. (2016, October 1). Payment mechanisms and antipoverty programs: Evidence from a mobile money cash transfer experiment in Niger. *Economic Development and Cultural Change.* University of Chicago Press. https://doi.org/10.1086/687578

Ashta, A., & De Selva, R. D. S. (2012). Religious practice and microcredit: Literature review and research directions. *SSRN Electronic Journal.* https://doi.org/10.2139/ssrn.1600622

Attanasio, O., Barr, A., Cardenas, J. C., Genicot, G., & Meghir, C. (2012). Risk pooling, risk preferences, and social networks. *American Economic Journal: Applied Economics*, *4*(2), 134–167. https://doi.org/10.1257/app.4.2.134

Badranaya, D. (2017). Efficiency of Financing in Sharia Cooperatives. *ETIKONOMI*, *16*(2), 249–264. https://doi.org/10.15408/etk.v16i2.5437

Battilana, J., & Dorado, S. (2010). Building sustainable hybrid organizations: The case of commercial microfinance organizations. *Academy of Management Journal*, *53*(6), 1419–1440. https://doi.org/10.5465/amj.2010.57318391

Beck, T. (2015). Microfinance: A critical literature survey. *IEG Working Paper* (Vol. 2015/4). Retrieved from http:/www.worldbank.org/ieg

Bursztyn, L., Fiorin, S., Gottlieb, D., & Kanz, M. (2019). Moral incentives in credit card debt repayment: Evidence from a field experiment. *Journal of Political Economy*, *127*(4), 1641–1683. https://doi.org/10.1086/701605

Cassar, A., Crowley, L., & Wydick, B. (2007). The effect of social capital on group loan repayment: Evidence from field experiments. *The Economic Journal, 117*(517), F85–F106. https://doi.org/10.1111/j.1468-0297.2007.02016.x

Cull, R., Demirgüç-kunt, A., & Morduch, J. (2007). Financial performance and outreach: A global analysis of leading microbanks. *Economic Journal, 117*(517). https://doi.org/10.1111/j.1468-0297.2007.02017.x

D'Espallier, B., Guérin, I., & Mersland, R. (2011). Women and repayment in microfinance: A global analysis. *World Development, 39*(5), 758–772. https://doi.org/10.1016/j.worlddev.2010.10.008

Demirguc-Kunt, A., Klapper, L., Singer, D., Ansar, S., & Hess, J. (2018). *The global findex database 2017: Measuring financial inclusion and the fintech revolution.* Washington, DC: World Bank. https://doi.org/10.1596/978-1-4648-1259-0

Dusuki, W. A. (2008). Banking for the poor: The role of Islamic banking in microfinance initiatives. *Humanomics, 24*(1), 49–66. https://doi.org/10.1108/08288 660810851469

Effendi, J. (2013). *The role of Islamic microfinance in poverty alleviation and environmental awareness an Pasuruan, East Java, Indonesia.* Universitätsverlag Göttingen.

Effendi, J., & Utami, A. R. (2016). The effect of social capital on customer's repayment rate at Islamic microfinance institution. *Al-Iqtishad: Journal of Islamic Economics, 8*(2). https://doi.org/10.15408/aiq.v8i2.2631

Feigenberg, B., Field, E. M., & Pande, R. (2010). Building social capital through microfinance. *NBER working papers.* Retrieved from https://ideas.repec.org/p/nbr/nberwo/16018.html

Fitriasari, T. (2019). The effectiveness of linkage programs: Case study of BMTs in Indonesia. *International Journal of Business and Society, 20*(March 2016), 210–220.

Hadisumarto, W. bin M. C., & Ismail, A. G. B. (2009). Sustainability of BMT financing for developing micro-enterprises. *Munich Personal RePEc Archive, 7434*(7434), 1–31.

Hadisumarto, W. bin M. C., & Ismail, A. G. B. (2010). Improving the effectiveness of Islamic micro-financing: Learning from BMT experience. *Humanomics, 26*(1), 65–75. https://doi.org/10.1108/08288661011025002

Hamada, M. (2010). Commercialization of microfinance in Indonesia: The shortage of funds and the linkage program. *The Developing Economies, 48*(1), 156–176. https://doi.org/10.1111/j.1746-1049.2010.00102.x

Hamzah, D., Rusby, D. Z., & Hamzah, Z. (2013). Analysis problem of Baitul Maal Wat Tamwil (BMT) operation in Pekanbaru Indonesia using analytical network process (ANP) approach. *International Journal of Academic Research in Business and Social Sciences, 3*(8), 215–228. https://doi.org/10.6007/IJARBSS/v3-i8/138

Hartarska, V., & Nadolnyak, D. (2007). Do regulated microfinance institutions achieve better sustainability and outreach? Cross-country evidence. *Applied Economics, 39*(10), 1207–1222. https://doi.org/10.1080/00036840500461840

Hasbi, H. (2015). Islamic microfinance institution: The capital structure, growth, performance and value of firm in Indonesia. *Procedia - Social and Behavioral Sciences, 211*, 1073–1080. https://doi.org/10.1016/j.sbspro.2015.11.143

Hermes, N., Lensink, R., Meesters, A., Hermes, N., Lensink, R., & Meesters, A. (2011). Outreach and efficiency of microfinance institutions. *World Development, 39*(6), 938–948. Retrieved from https://econpapers.repec.org/RePEc:eee:wdevel:v:39:y:2011:i:6:p:938-948

Hosen, M. N. (2006). *Buku Saku Bank-ku Syariah.* Jakarta: Pusat Komunikasi Ekonomi Syariah.

Hosen, M. N., & Sa'roni, L. S. (2012). Determinant factors of the successful of Baitul Maal Wat Tamwil (Bmt). *International Journal of Academic Research in Economics and Management Sciences*, *1*(4), 36–55.

Husaeni, U. A., & Dew, T. K. (2019). The dynamics of the development of Baitul Maal Wa Tamwil in Indonesia with the swot analysis approach. *International Journal of Scientific & Technology Research*, *8*(08), 1678–1685.

Indrawati, H. (2008). Analisis Faktor-Faktor yang Mempengaruhi Kinerja Keuangan BMT: Studi pada BMT Sarana Kota Malang. *Jurnal Akuntansi*, *2*, 142–155.

Iswanaji, C. (2019). Analysis of accounting information system using hot fit model method in Indonesia Islamic micro financial institutions. *Applied Finance and Accounting*, *5*(2), 1. https://doi.org/10.11114/afa.v5i2.4172

KPMG Indonesia. (2015). *New Indonesian "Branchless Banking" and Microfinance Law – a catalyst for microfinance growth?* Jakarta. Retrieved from https://assets.kpmg/content/dam/kpmg/pdf/2016/07/id-ksa-financial-inclusion-indonesia.pdf

Ledgerwood, J., & White, V. (2006). *Transforming microfinance institutions.* The World Bank. https://doi.org/10.1596/978-0-8213-6615-8

Lisa, O. (2016). Analysis of effect of capital structure, company size and distribution of funds against third party financing and its implication on profitability (Studies in Islamic Cooperative Baitul Maal Tamwil in Indonesia). *International Journal of Finance and Accounting*, *5*(3), 158–164. https://doi.org/10.5923/j.ijfa.20160503.03

Luoto, J., McIntosh, C., & Wydick, B. (2007). Credit information systems in less developed countries: A test with microfinance in Guatemala. *Economic Development and Cultural Change*, *55*(2), 313–334. https://doi.org/10.1086/508714

Masyita, D., & Ahmed, H. (2013). Why is growth of Islamic microfinance lower than its conventional counterparts in Indonesia? *Islamic Economic Studies, The Islamic Research and Training Institute (IRTI)*, *21*, 35–62.

Maulana, M. I., & Akbar, N. (2019). The potential of Bait al-Mal wa Tamwil (BMT) in developing the border area of Indonesia – Malaysia. *Jurnal Ilmu Ekonomi Syariah (Journal of Islamic Economics)*, *11*(January), 97–116.

Mawardi, W. (2005). Analisis Faktor-Faktor yang Mempengaruhi Kinerja Keuangan di Bank Umum di Indonesia. *Jurnal Bisnis Strategi*, *1*(14), 83–93.

Mersland, R., & Øystein Strøm, R. (2009). Performance and governance in microfinance institutions. *Journal of Banking & Finance*, *33*(4), 662–669. Retrieved from https://econpapers.repec.org/RePEc:eee:jbfina:v:33:y:2009:i:4:p:662-669

Ministry of Cooperatives and Micro and Small Medium Enterprises (MoCMSMEs). (2019). Retrieved from https://ushirika.go.ke/cooperative-sector-statistics/

Monetary Policy Report Q1–2009. (2009). https://www.bi.go.id/en/publikasi/laporan/Documents/f60600d31f4c45c5bd9b6b2d4110efdaMPRQ209.pdf

Mukhtar, Y. (2014). Development Model of BMT(Baitul Maal wat Tamwil) in West Sumatra. *SSRN Electronic Journal*. https://doi.org/10.2139/ssrn.2392671

Mulyana, & Supardi. (2008). *Analisa Rasio Laporan Keuangan Lembaga Keuangan Syariah: BMT Mubarak Pasar Argosari.* Yogyakarta: STIE Nusa Megar Kencana.

Mustamir, & Mawardi. (2006). Problematika Penerapan Ekonomi Islam di Baitul Maal Wat Tamwil (BMT) Pekanbaru. *Jurnal Publik & Bisnis*, *4*(1), 27–35.

Nasution, A. C. (2013). Effiency of Baitul Maal Wa Tamwil (BMT): An effort towards Islamic wealth management in microfinance institution. In *The 5th Islamic Economics System Conference (iECONS 2013), "Sustainable development through the Islamic economics system"* (pp. 1–9).

OJK. (2020). *Indonesia banking statistics.* Retrieved from https://www.ojk.go.id/en/kanal/perbankan/data-dan-statistik/statistik-perbankan-indonesia/Documents/Pages/Indonesia-Banking-Statistic---January-2020/Indonesia Banking Statistic January 2020.pdf

Perdana, A. A., & Maxwell, J. (2005). Poverty targeting in Indonesia. In *Poverty targeting in Asia* (pp. 136–186). Edward Elgar Publishing. https://doi.org/10.4337/9781845424701.00010

Rahayu, N. S. (2020). The intersection of islamic microfinance and women's empowerment: A case study of baitul maal wat tamwil in indonesia. *International Journal of Financial Studies, 8*(2), 1–13. https://doi.org/10.3390/ijfs8020037

Robinson, M. S. (2002). *The microfinance revolution: Volume 2. Lessons from Indonesia.* World Bank Publications. Retrieved from https://ideas.repec.org/b/wbk/wbpubs/14254.html

Rusydiana, A. S., & Devi, A. (2013). Challenges in developing Baitul Maal wat Tamwiil (BMT) in Indonesia using analytic network process (ANP). *Business and Management Quarterly Review, 4*(2), 51–62.

Sakti, A. (2019, July). Towards an effective legal and regulatory framework for Islamic cooperatives (Baitul Maal wat-Tamwil/BMT) in Indonesia. *Insight Islamic Economy Bulletin,* 12–13. Retrieved from https://knks.go.id/storage/upload/1563795796-INSIGHT%20-%202nd%20Edition-compressed.pdf

Sandberg, J. (2012). Mega-interest on microcredit: Are lenders exploiting the poor? *Journal of Applied Philosophy, 29*(3), 169–185. https://doi.org/10.1111/j.1468-5930.2012.00560.x

Satar, N., & Kassim, S. (2020). Issues and challenges in financing the poor: Lessons learned from Islamic microfinance institutions. *EJIF - European Journal of Islamic Finance, 1*(15), 1–8. https://doi.org/10.5220/0010115501020108

Seibel, H. D. (2015). Notes Islamic microfinance in Indonesia : The challenge of institutional diversity. *Journal of Social Issues in Southeast Asia, 23*(1), 86–103. https://doi.org/10.1355/sj23-ld

Seibel, H. D., & Dwi Agung, W. (2006). Islamic microfinance in Indonesia. *Working Papers.* Retrieved from https://ideas.repec.org/p/zbw/uocaef/20062.html

Supervision and Regulation of Microfinance Institutions in Indonesia. (2016). In *OJK international seminar on microfinance & financial inclusion.*

Sutiyo, Pitono, A., Raharjanto, T., & Sinaga, J. B. B. (2020). Woman microfinance in Indonesia: Present status and future direction. *International Journal of Rural Management, 16*(1), 105–124. https://doi.org/10.1177/0973005219898922

Tambunan, T. (2015). *Financial inclusion, financial education, and financial regulation: A story from Indonesia.*

Vong, J., & Song, I. (2015). Microfinance and gender equality in Indonesia (Vol. 11, pp. 35–53). Singapore: Springer Singapore. https://doi.org/10.1007/978-981-287-347-7_4

Wulandari, P., Kassim, S., Adhi Kasari Sulung, L., & Iwani Surya Putri, N. (2016). Unique aspects of the Islamic microfinance financing process. *Humanomics, 32*(3), 230–247. https://doi.org/10.1108/H-09-2014-0062

Yeow, A., Chuen, D. L. K., Tan, R., & Chia, M. (2018). Indonesian Microfinance Institutions (MFI) move to technology – TBOP's prodigy experience. In *Handbook of blockchain, digital finance, and inclusion* (1st ed., Vol. 2, pp. 431–449). Elsevier. https://doi.org/10.1016/B978-0-12-812282-2.00017-6

Yuniar, G. N. (2015). Development of MSMEs (Micro, Small and Medium Enterprises) by Baitul Maal Wat Tamwil (BMT) as an instrument for poverty reduction. *Advances in Economics and Business*, *3*(2), 41–44. https://doi.org/10.13189/aeb.2015.030201

Zahra, M. H., & Wijayanti, P. (2019). Antecedent financial performance of Baitul Mal wat Tamwil (BMT): Study in BMT Binama Semarang. *Journal of Islamic Accounting and Finance Research*, *1*(1), 47. https://doi.org/10.21580/jiafr.2019.1.1.3729

Zuhria, A. (2012). *Baitul Mal Wa Tamwil Development in Indonesia*, (March), 1–14. https://www.academia.edu/4004609/Baitul_Mal_Wa_Tamwil_Development_in_Indonesia

6 Contemporary Issues in Takaful Sector and Possible Solutions

Hakan Aslan[1]

1 Introduction

The insurance business is more complicated than any other financial business activity in terms of Islamic law. In the classical fiqh literature, no such agreement can fit into a definition of insurance. However, there existed several applications which were acknowledged as mutual cooperation and indemnity in the Islamic history, such as *aqilah* (العاقلة) and *muawalah* (الموالاة), even though they were not accepted as insurance applications. Aqilah is defined as a group of people who share the blood-money (diyah) responsibility (Khan, 2003). If any person was killed from the tribe, the other person had to pay the blood money equivalent to 100 camels or 200 cows or 200 sheep or 1000 gold dinar (Bardakoğlu, 1994). The underlying logic of *aqilah* is to share the monetary burden among the tribesmen, which is similar to the insurance system. However, it did not have any commercial aim, but insurance does. Muawalah was another system for those who were not a member of any tribe or people who were newly converted to Islam. The main idea was similar to *aqilah* (Özen, 2013). Islamic scholars have tried to find answers to the question of whether insurance is permissible in Islam, considering those previous applications in Islamic history. The very first known opinion about insurance in Islam belongs to the Ibn Abidin. There are two known fatawa[1] from him about insurance. The first one was found in his book titled "*Mecmûatü'r-resâil*" and the second one was mentioned in the "*Reddü'l Muhtar*" in 1825 and 1836 respectively (Hacak, 2006). In 1870 when the great fire of Beyoglu occurred, people asked about fatwa on insurance whether it was allowed in Islam. At that time, Shaykh al-Islam granted permission for insurance contracts for Muslims had to protect their property which was given by Allah (Zerka & Neccar, 2009). There are three different opinions on insurance in Islam. The first opinion allows the insurance system with regards to the idea of insurance as developing social solidarity and cooperation. The second opinion does not conceive any kind of insurance business as permissible in Islam. The

---

1 A section of this chapter was adapted from the author's Ph.D. thesis, but enhancements have been made.

DOI: 10.4324/9781003377283-6

third opinion defends that cooperative and mutual insurance are acceptable in Islam, but commercial insurance is not. According to the third opinion, three main issues in the conventional insurance business make it incompatible with the Islamic law. Those issues are *gharar* (high uncertainty), *maysir* (gambling), and *riba* (interest). For this reason, it emerges in the recent Islamic financial development a new method of insurance – takaful.

The word "takaful" is derived from an Arabic root word "ka-fa-lah", which means "guarantee, bail, or an act of securing one's need" (E. R. A. E. Ali & Odierno, 2008, p. 3) and thus "ta-ka-ful" means guaranteeing each other. The word "insurance" also has a similar meaning in English, which is derived from the word "insure". "Insure" literally means a guarantee, or securing indemnity in case of loss, damage, or death. Similarly, the word "sigorta" is used for "insurance" in Turkish. This word is derived from "sicurta" an Italian word that means "guarantee".

Economically, takaful is an Islamic alternative to conventional insurance with the aim of mutual assistance. Fundamentally, takaful is a mutual guarantee or assurance built on the principle of al-Aqd, or contract, which is "provided by a group of people living in the same society against a defined-risk affecting one's life or tangible assets" (Ahmad & Auzzir, 2012, p. 2). In other words, it offers mutual protection of the properties by joint sharing the costs of losses that occurred to any of the members. From this point of view, Lahsasna (2016, p. 51) argues that takaful is a kind of mutual insurance that members are both insurers and the insured. Takaful is also known as cooperative insurance due to its nature (Billah, 2003a, p. 19). Billah (n.d.) expresses that Islamic insurance should be compliant with the principle of mutual cooperation.

Parallel to the development of the Islamic financial system, risk management alternatives to conventional insurance became an essential need in Islamic finance operations. The takaful system was developed as an alternative risk management method for insurance operations in the 1970s. Conventional insurance has the elements of gharar (high uncertainty), maysir (gambling), and riba (interest) since it is considered unlawful according to Islamic scholars. Takaful solves these issues by changing the insurance operations' contractual structure and separating collected contributions (insurance premiums) and shareholders' funds (SHFs). However, the practical implementation of takaful has diverged from its theoretical framework over time. It has been more than 40 years since the first takaful company started its operations, but many issues have still not been solved. This study reviews contemporary discussions on takaful studies and takaful operations, highlights issues in the takaful sector and attempts to offer proposals for these issues using qualitative techniques. In this study, the most problematic issues in the takaful sector have been discussed and categorized. Then, possible solutions are offered to those issues. Besides that, the wakalah–cooperative takaful model proposed and its operational framework explained, which is expected to solve several Shariah concerns discussed in the literature. This study is limited to only offering a conceptual framework. Further studies may investigate the practicality of this model and other proposed solutions for the takaful market.

In this study, first, we explained the theoretical framework of takaful and its contemporary practice to provide a better understanding of the takaful system. Second, we addressed and classified contemporary issues in the takaful sector in the light of recent takaful literature. Finally, we concluded the paper by offering possible solutions for the takaful sector's issues.

2 Theoretical Framework of Takaful

The word "takaful" literally means "mutual solidarity, joint guarantee" (Rahman & Redzuan, 2009, p. 19). Technically, takaful can be defined as "a group of people who agreed upon to collect a sum of money for the purpose of indemnifying each other against the risks that can occur in the future". Today, the term "takaful" is used for this system, an alternative way of insurance where elements of *riba*, *maysir*, and *gharar* are eliminated. The issue of interest occurs in the case of investment activities in the insurance business, whereas collected funds can be invested in Islamic financial products, and thus the issue of *riba* will be eliminated. Other main issues undermining the development of Islamic insurance are *gharar* and *maysir*. According to Islamic law, risk is not a property that can be traded in a sale transaction. However, in the conventional insurance contract, the product is not certain and thereby contains risks, and the insured does not know whether he will get the compensation or not at the end. This situation causes *maysir* (gambling) problems. Because the insured person invests a certain amount of money while expecting a larger amount in return under this kind of sale contract. This is how *maysir* may occur. Even if he is eligible for the compensation, there is no guaranteed amount or ratio to which he should be entitled. This situation induces the issue of uncertainty (*gharar*) inevitably. These kinds of problems will not be solved as long as the insurance is based on sale contracts. For this reason, it is under the takaful and ta'awun principle – a joint solidarity – that the Islamic insurance is developed and the tabarru' (contribution/donation) contract that funds are collected. These contribute significantly to the resolution of those issues that are both inevitable in conventional insurance and impermissible in Islamic insurance.

One of the earliest Islamic economists M. Nejatullah Sıddıki (1984) discussed different opinions of the Islamic scholars toward insurance when the concept of insurance was new to the Muslim society at his time. It is reported that some of the scholars considered the underlying philosophy of the insurance business as compliant with Islam. On the other hand, some scholars agreed with the adoption of insurance except for life insurance. Furthermore, some scholars regarded insurance as gambling by nature, and others perceived that insurance was inseparable from riba (interest) and gharar (excessive uncertainty) (Sıddıki, 1984, p. 87). Furthermore, it has been common to divide the opinions of scholars on insurance into three categories. The first group of scholars (e.g., Mohammad Abduh, Mustafa Ahmad Zarqa, Ahmad Taha Al-Sanusi, M. Nejatullah Siddiqi, Mohammad Muslehuddin) agrees that the conventional insurance practices are entirely permissible in Islam and there is not any element of riba (interest) in it (Billah, 1998, p. 410). The second group of scholars (e.g. Mohammad Abu Zahra, Abdurrahman Isa Ahmad Ibrahim, Muslim League Conference in 1965) acknowledges the non-life insurance practices but opposes life insurance due to the possibility of the existence of gharar and maysir. In addition, they claim that life insurance practices contravene the legacy and inheritance principles in terms of Islamic law. The third group (e.g. Mustafa Zaid, Abdullah al-Qalqeeli) expresses their open dissent of insurance and states that insurance contracts enclose elements of gharar, maysir, and riba (Billah, 1998, p. 411). The third opinion led Muslims to find an alternative way to manage risks: takaful.

Contrary to popular opinions, Islam, in fact, encourages risk management, and it does not contradict with the belief of the foreordination/destiny of Muslims. There are several examples in the early Islamic history as well as practices of Prophet (peace be upon him), which encourage mutual risk-sharing (Htay et al., 2012, p. 4). It is widely accepted that the most important factor of risk management in Islam is mutuality, where risk sharing is preferred over risk transfer which is a common practice of conventional insurance systems.

The first takaful company, Islamic Insurance Company, was established in 1979 in Sudan, followed by Saudi Arabia, which established the Islamic Arab Insurance Co. Besides Muslim countries, Switzerland and Luxembourg were the prominent countries in Europe regarding inaugurating takaful companies, where their takaful companies were founded in 1981 and 1983, respectively (Billah, 2003b, p. 5). Meanwhile, the Fiqh Academy of the Organization of Islamic Cooperation (OIC) has also given the fatwa[2] that declared the commercial insurance to be null and advocated the cooperative insurance as an alternative (Bhatty & Nisar, 2016, p. 6). There were very few countries offering takaful until 2000s, but the number of countries offering takaful business has increased rapidly (IFSB & WBG, 2017, p. 10), not to mention the developments of the supervisory and the regulatory framework of the takaful accompanying the business practices. Meanwhile, there are 323 takaful operators (TOs) worldwide, and the global takaful assets have reached USD 62 billion with a 16% growth rate in 2020. Iran, Saudi Arabia, and Malaysia have the biggest asset sizes with USD 20, 17, and 12 billion, respectively. However, compared to the total Islamic financial assets, around USD 3.4 trillion, the takaful market only accounted for less than 2% of the total Islamic finance assets (Refinitiv, 2021).

From a regulatory point of view, Malaysia is the first country where a comprehensive takaful regulation (Takaful Act[3]) was issued in 1984 (Bhatty & Nisar, 2016, p. 6). Afterward, Sudan, Saudi Arabia, Pakistan, Bahrain, and UAE followed Malaysia in terms of developing regulations on takaful. This rapid growth has initiated the establishment of international standard-setting and regulatory bodies namely, Accounting Auditing Organization for Islamic Financial Institutions (AAOIFI) and the Islamic Financial Services Board (IFSB). AAOIFI has aimed at developing accounting, auditing, Shariah, and governance standards for IFIs. There are two directly related shariah standards set by AAOIFI regarding insurance. One of them is called Islamic Insurance Standard (No. 26), and the other one is called Islamic Reinsurance Standard (No. 41) (AAOIFI, 2015). Furthermore, there are four financial accounting standards (FAS) for takaful companies set by AAOIFI, namely FAS 12, 13, 15, and 19. Standards developed by IFSB are more technical, contrary to shariah principles. These standards mainly focused on issues such as governance, risk management, retakaful, solvency requirements, and supervisory review for takaful undertakings. At least 50% of the member countries have implemented these standards and more than 40% of the members have even entirely implemented each of the standards (IFSB, 2019). Regulations and standards developed by AAOIFI and IFSB have flexible implementation approaches, which means that the standards set by those authorities are not mandatory at the beginning. When member countries start to endorse these standards, they will become mandatory at regulatory and supervisory authorities' sole discretion (COMCEC, 2019).

There are two main divisions in takaful operations based on their operational structures in actual practice. According to their principal agreement, takaful entities can operate on either a commercial or mutual base. The commercial-based insurance system is the most commonly applied method globally. While, there are several cooperative/mutual structures which are adopted in countries like Saudi Arabia and Sudan (Frenz & Soualhi, 2010, pp. 128–129).

There are different models of takaful based on its contractual structure, such as wakalah, mudarabah, hybrid (combination of wakalah and mudarabah), cooperative, waqf-wakalah. Among these models, the hybrid takaful model is the most practiced model worldwide. Figure 6.1 shows the modus operandi of the takaful hybrid takaful model. We explained this model first because it is the most common model in the market, and second, it consists of mudarabah and wakalah contracts.

The operational procedures of the hybrid model, as shown in Figure 6.1, can be explained as follows:

1 Participants sign a contract and give contribution based on tabarru'. These contributions are collected as a takaful fund and treated as ta'awun (mutual cooperation) against certain risks.
2 The TO manages the takaful fund on behalf of participants as an agent and charges the *wakalah* (agency) fee in return of its management service of the takaful fund. This fee is usually applied at a certain percentage of the contribution which is determined by statistical and actuarial calculations.
3 The TO manages some part of the takaful fund as either an investment fund manager or a *mudarib* (profit sharing partner). In this phase, the TO

generates the income on a profit and loss sharing basis. The profit/loss sharing ratio must be determined at the first step, when participants join the takaful fund. The SHF, which is owned by shareholders, represents SHFs in the figure. In this model, the TO has two sources of income.

4   The TO manages the cash reserves, distributes the shares to the retakaful operator and pays compensations to the participants in the case of any claims.

5   If there is any surplus in this account after the claims, reserves, and other payments are deducted, it will be distributed to the takaful fund. According to the contract, this surplus may be shared among participants, used as charity, kept as a reserve or reflected as a discount for the participants.

6   In the case of any deficit in this fund, the TO gives qard al-hasan (interest-free loan) from SHF to the fund to maintain technical operations. When the fund has the surplus, the TO takes its qard back by instalments or as a lump sum, which is depended on the operational results.

7   Lastly, participants receive their shares from the surplus (if any) at the end of the contract term, if it is prescribed in the contract beforehand. There is also another benefit in the family takaful along with compensation rights. Family takaful funds, generally separated into two funds, namely personal investment fund and risk fund. Personal investments reflect the other benefits besides compensation.

Wakalah, mudarabah, and the hybrid models are the fundamental models in the takaful sector. Earlier, takaful operations started with mudarabah model where there is no wakalah fee applied. It is numbered as the second step in Figure 6.1. Mudarabah model was not practiced for long, due to difficulty to determine mudarabah income for the takaful operator. Later on, they switched to wakalah model where mudarabah profit is not available. This model is still practiced in some of the GCC countries. However, TOs changed to hybrid model to have mudarabah return for investment operations while charging wakalah fee for insurance operations. This is the most practiced model by the takaful sector (Aslan, 2021).

There are also some modifications that can be implemented to those operational models. However, these modifications are not allowed in most countries according to the shariah standards of the AAOIFI. Modified models offer a share from surplus to the TO. This model is practiced in Malaysia. Shariah basis for this model is explained as; if a TO performs well, it may deserve to be rewarded with a share from surplus. This share is considered as a performance fee which is defined as jualah in Islamic commercial law.

Eventually, there were always various kinds of practices/customs among Muslim societies, similar to insurance such as aqilah, muwalah, and nihd.[4] However, modern insurance practice was a new concept in the Muslim world that occurred in the late 19th century. Scholarly debates between the 1960s and 1970s caused a pursuit for an alternative insurance model, which led practitioners and scholars to the takaful. Since the first debates about insurance

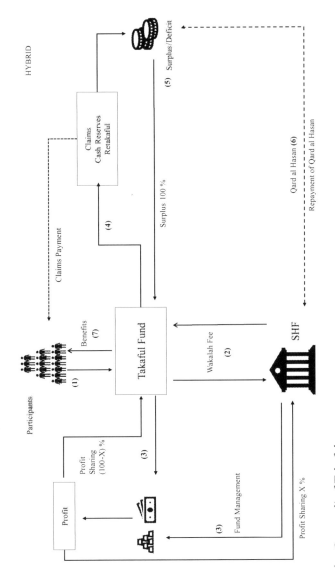

Figure 6.1 Modus Operandi of Takaful.
Sources: E. R. A. E. Ali and Odierno (2008) and Frenz and Soualhi (2010).

from an Islamic perspective discussion did not entirely settle, we will discuss the details about the issues in the takaful sector in the following section.

3 Contemporary Issues in Takaful

The theoretical framework of the takaful industry has been presented in the previous section. Nonetheless, several difficulties and issues have hampered the further development of the takaful industry in the world. These challenges have been mentioned in several reports. For example, the report of CIBAFI (2018) shows the contemporary status of the takaful market from the view of the professionals by conducting a survey which is delivered among 24 countries. According to practitioners, issues of awareness, lack of Islamic financial products, deficiencies in the regulatory and supervisory environment, lacking trained talents for the sector, Shariah specific problems are the main challenges that takaful industry has been facing. These similar issues also have been indicated in other sources as well (COMCEC, 2019, pp. 55–58; Habib, 2018, p. 177; World Bank & IDGB, 2016, pp. 111–113). In the meantime, there are other challenges and factors that affect the demand of the customers such as awareness, knowledge, compatibility of shariah issues and ease of use. Although all of these problems are interrelated to each other, they can be categorized as follows:

1. *Regulation and Supervision*: Developing an appropriate regulatory and supervisory framework is the primary step to be taken by governments to provide trustworthy, resilient, and secure takaful ecosystems. In most countries, regulatory development is lacking, although the TOs have started their operations. Furthermore, in some countries, governments are unwilling to develop regulations according to the needs of the takaful sector (COMCEC, 2019), which, in fact, should have been tailor-made (CIBAFI, 2018) considering their specific requirements incurred by the nature of the Islamic jurisdiction. Otherwise, the insurance sector will be more unfavorable for the TOs. Additionally, governments should consider international standard-setting bodies' requirements while developing regulations (Habib, 2018).

2. *Awareness and Public Perception*: Previous studies have shown the deficiency of the awareness of customers about takaful and its salient features in most countries. Along with awareness, perceptions is another crucial issue from the customer perspective (Habib, 2018). For this reason, TOs should offer idiosyncratic products that differentiate themselves from their conventional counterparts (CIBAFI, 2018). TOs should show that they value the substance over the form for takaful operations. Therewithal, they must promote takaful more to affect public awareness positively.

3. *Shariah Specific Needs*: TOs need to implement Shariah supervision and regulation. Lacking Shariah supervision causes trust issues among customers. Shariah governance framework will increase trust on the takaful ecosystem. Meanwhile, lacking shariah regulation comes with accounting problems where TOs have salient products and funds which should be reported

peculiarly. For example, takaful funds are owned by participants and it has to be treated differently.

4. *Investment and Retakaful Needs*: TOs only invest in products which is in line with shariah principles. However, it is difficult to find adequate financial products to invest in (COMCEC, 2019; World Bank & IDGB, 2016). Especially, less volatile, fixed-income products such as sukuks play an essential role in general takaful operations. Also, TOs need retakaful operators considering their risk carrying capacity. Like insurance companies, takaful companies need entities to share their risks. Retakaful is the alternative for reinsurance. Developing takaful ecosystem requires retakaful operators.

5. *Trained Human Resources*: Due to previous problems, there is a big gap in skilled talents in the takaful industry (COMCEC, 2019). As it has been presented earlier, countries whose takaful markets are more developed usually have more research and development outputs. Without enough talents involved, it is difficult to discover problems in practice and develop proper policy recommendations.

As pointed above, a general summary has been made on the main challenges of the development of the takaful industry in the world. The following discussions will emphasize the attempts to solve these issues and explicitly point out problems in the takaful model.

Although the majority of the Islamic scholars were initially against life insurance, the takaful system was later considered lawful and uncontradicted with the bequest and inheritance rules in the Islamic commercial law (Billah, 1993). It is noticeable that the early family takaful practices mostly followed the bequest and inheritance laws, with clear distinctions between the family takaful and the life insurance (Billah, 1997). However, the current family takaful practices allow policyholders to nominee a sole beneficiary for their savings fund, which is a controversial issue with regards to the bequest and inheritance laws in Shariah (Elatrash & Soualhi, 2016). Contemporary secular laws allow the nomination of the sole beneficiary in life insurance. But there are specific rules on the distribution of inheritance in Shariah. Thus, sole beneficiary nomination contradicts with these specific rules. Shalim (2016) discusses some opinions toward life insurance from the Islamic jurisprudence perspective and deduces some rules and principles regarding operational, governance, accounting practices of family takaful to maintain its operations in line of Shariah.

As mentioned in the previous section, the income of a TO in the mudarabah model is contingent upon investment profits. That is, the TO ought to cover operational expenses from the underwriting surplus, which makes the mudarabah model risky and recondite in regards to its consequences for the TO. In addition, there is a contradiction between the spirit of tabarru' (donation) and that of a mudarabah contract (profit sharing) (Bhatty & Nisar, 2016, p. 10). This kind of issues has paved the way for the development of the wakalah model.

According to the pure wakalah model, TOs are not allowed to get a share from the surplus. This issue affects the pricing mechanisms of the TOs and harms competitiveness in the market, which is argued by professionals (Bouheraoua & Ahmad, 2011, p. 16). The pure wakalah model has been animadverted on the shortfall of incentive mechanisms (Htay et al., 2012, p. 16). It is also criticized for insufficiency in meeting the expectations of the shareholders' expectations of a substantial return from their provided capital (Bhatty & Nisar, 2016, p. 10). The Malaysians modified by adding incentive fees from the underwriting surplus to facilitate the implementation of this model, which is considered as a reward for successful underwriting operations (Frenz & Soualhi, 2010, pp. 139–140). It is noticeable that the modified model practices are not allowed according to the standards of the AAOIFI. However, there are applications of a hybrid model, which is a combination of wakalah and mudarabah models, allowing the TOs to increase its source of income into two channels, which is allowed by the AAOIFI.

In regard to Shariah and legal compliance, the ownership issue arises, providing that takaful fund is not a separated entity. Besides, the application of qard al-hasan causes injustice issues among takaful participants (Frenz & Soualhi, 2010, p. 144). For example, in the first year, the takaful fund borrows qard al-hasan from the SHF. In the subsequent years, the TO will take the loan back on behalf of the participants if there is a surplus. However, as owners of the takaful fund, the participants may change over time, typically in the general takaful. As to overcome these problems, more attempts have been explored and accomplished. As a result, it is believed by some scholars that the waqf model is able to be a resolution of this kind of issue.

The issue of the ownership of the takaful fund has been widely discussed among Shariah scholars and there are contentious opinions regarding it. The idea of implementing waqf into the insurance business ensued from the ownership issue of the takaful fund, where it has been seeking more legal basis from a shariah perspective (Frenz & Soualhi, 2010, pp. 144–145). However, there is an opposing opinion toward the discrepancy of implementation of waqf in insurance practice. Khorshid (2004) highlights several reasons and attempts to answer why the waqf cannot be implemented in the insurance business. Nana (2016, pp. 86–87), disputes those objections from Shariah scholars regarding the waqf implementation in takaful business and provides several answers to those opinions. Meanwhile, he pinpoints various practical challenges in implementing the waqf takaful model. Concisely, those challenges are possible regulatory conflicts of the establishment of waqf for takaful, finding retakaful for waqf takaful model, tax issues, and so on. For example, waqf should be administrated by different kinds of authorities in Malaysia rather than its current procedures (M. M. Ali, 2016, p. 468). Meanwhile, Jalil and Rahman (2015) assert that the wakalah-waqf structured takaful model is more Shariah friendly because there is no issue regarding conditional tabarru' or hibah (grant/donation).

Htay and Salman (2013b) discuss the Shariah and ethical issues in the modified mudarabah model. This model is the modified version of the pure mudarabah model. However, it seems that this model is not in practice anymore to the best of our knowledge. Meanwhile, they criticize the modified waka-lah model from the Shariah and ethical perspectives in another study (Htay & Salman, 2013a). They discuss the agency problem and the Shariah issues and argue that the performance fee may bring the agency problem.

Soualhi (2010) addresses the surplus distribution issue from the Shariah perspective, and he analyses rulings on surplus distribution for TOs in several countries. He concludes that the surplus belongs neither to the participants nor to the TO. In this way, he justifies the share of the surplus among the TO and participants. He also adds that the distribution ratio should be in line with the principles of Islamic finance and be equitable.

Abozaid (2016) critically evaluates takaful models and attempts to seek bet-ter takaful models. He proposes an ibaha structure for the takaful fund instead of tabarru'. Ibaha means making something free or allowable (Brill, 2020). According to this model, the ownership of the takaful fund will still stay with the participants contrary to tabarru' which actually means disengagement. Abozaid (2016) argues that his proposal will solve ownership issue in the takaful practice in terms of Shariah. Also, he attempts to set some parameters for a proper takaful model. Mohammad Mahbubi Ali (2016) tries to examine takaful models and then he suggests the musharakah ta'awuniyah (cooper-ative partnership) model to be the best example of the practice in terms of Islamic principles. Besides, he indicates the importance of business feasibility examination before implementing this model.

Eventually, takaful practices consist of several issues and discussions in the literature which has not been resolved. We attempted to offer several propos-als to solve these issues in the takaful sector mentioned above. Specifically, this study offers a new takaful operational model which may solve the prob-lems discussed above.

4 Proposals for the Issues in Takaful

Theoretical foundations of takaful were developed in the 1970s. Since then, it has been widely practiced among Muslim countries with different struc-tures. Although the theoretical framework of takaful is structured seamlessly, several issues from different perspectives have been discussed in the literature. These issues can be categorized as follows in Table 6.1:

4.1 Proposal for Shariah Issues

There have been several issues pointed in the above section. First, shariah issues are discussed in the literature widely. Once, the takaful's contractual structure is always considered tabarru'. However, participants expect bene-fits after performing the tabarru' that makes this contract bilateral, which is similar to its conventional counterpart. This discussion furthers criticism on ownership of the takaful fund. If this collected fund is hibah, how can par-ticipants be the owner at the same time? For this reason, takaful contract and

92 Hakan Aslan

Table 6.1 Categorization of Issues in Takaful

Shariah	Development	Marketing
Ownership of the Takaful fund	Human Resource	Awareness
Shariah Governance Framework	Regulation & Supervision	Public Perception
Surplus Sharing	Retakaful	Digital Adaptation
Qard Guaranteeing	Investment Tools	
Contract Type		

Source: Author's own.

ownership structure should be defined well to avoid criticism. This issue can be solved using the wakalah–cooperative model, which is explained below. There will be no issue either on ownership or contract. However, this model needs further investigation to its applicability in the current market practice.

Sharing surplus with TO is also criticized by scholars and not allowed by AAOIFI due to ownership issues. Technically sharing surplus may benefit the TO's marketing and pricing mechanisms. It can increase competition for customers' sake. On the other hand, using different models may not be needed to share the surplus. However, it is argued that surplus should be shared among participants. TOs should avoid taking a share from it. Soualhi (2016) discussed this issue in detail in his study. We can argue that cooperative structure fits these arguments, which de facto makes surplus only owned or shared among participants.

Guaranteeing qard al-hasan is a critical point of takaful practice. In theory, TO may ask for extra contributions to the risk fund from participants, but this is not practiced and, in some cases, not allowed by market regulators. Guaranteeing qard al-hasan makes takaful similar to conventional insurance. Takaful is promoted as a risk-sharing model for insurance. Guaranteeing qard al-hasan makes takaful as risk transfer type of insurance. TO needs to use better pricing methods to avoid such practices. Besides, cooperative models can be implemented. Figure 6.2 shows operational steps for the wakalah–cooperative model.

According to this model, several issues which have been discussed in the earlier section can be solved. We can elaborate how it may affect as follows:

1 Participants cooperative fund aims to help cooperative members in case of any certain risks occur. This structure ends shariah discussion on tabarru' and hibah issues.
2 The TO manages the takaful fund on behalf of the cooperative as an agent and charges the *wakalah* (agency) fee in return for its management service of the takaful fund. *Wakalah* fee will be charged for insurance operation management by TO. This fee is usually applied at a certain percentage of the contribution which is determined by statistical and actuarial calculations. Typically, cooperative insurance companies are

Contemporary Issues in Takaful Sector and Possible Solutions 93

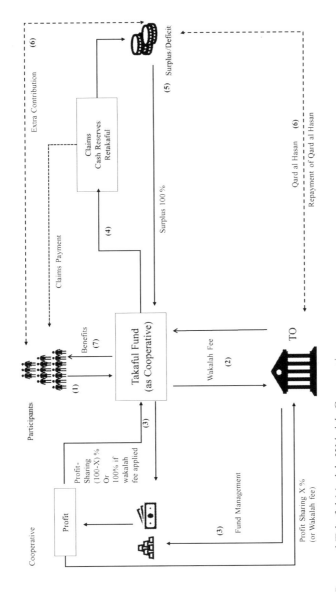

Figure 6.2 Proposed Takaful Model: *Wakalah*–Cooperative.
Source: Author's own.

managed by cooperative members. This situation can lead to mismanagement or failure in terms of professionalism. For this reason, the cooperative fund needs a profit-oriented manager to operate its operations professionally, which will be a TO in this model. Cooperative management, which will be among members and insurance operations operated by TO, should be separated from takaful management to solve the conflict-of-interest problem. Current takaful models do not give a place for takaful fund members in the takaful fund decisions. Everything is managed and decided by TO practically. In this model, the takaful fund will be structured as a cooperative to solve the legal entity issue of the takaful fund by including participants in the decision-making process. Current practice allows TO to decide on behalf of participants. Contrary to this, participants play a substantial role in the operational management of the takaful fund.

3   The TO manages some of the takaful fund as either an investment fund manager or a *mudarib* (profit sharing partner). In this phase, the TO generates the income on a profit and loss sharing basis. The profit/loss sharing ratio must be determined at the first step when participants join the takaful fund. Besides, that cooperative can decide to give two layers (the first one of insurance operation services and the second layer for investment management) *wakalah* fee instead of profit sharing. In this case, TO only charges a determined fee; all profit/loss will go to takaful fund. However, this application may affect the essence of the takaful and ta'awun spirit.

4   The TO manages the cash reserves, distributes the shares to the retakaful operator, and pays compensations to the participants in the case of any claims. Retakaful should be the last option if the calculated risk is able to be handled by takaful fund. This model will be more practical to be practiced if each type of insurance has its own cooperative – for example, car cooperatives, house cooperatives, etc. In this way, as long as there is no catastrophic risk, retakaful may not be needed.

5   If there is any surplus in this account after the claims, reserves, and other payments are deducted, it will be added back to the takaful fund owned by participants. According to the contract, this surplus may be shared among participants, kept as a reserve, or reflected as a participant discount. However, considering this structure as cooperative, the surplus will be kept as long as a cooperative member is unwilling to leave the fund/membership. If the cooperative members are willing to leave, his share can be given back to him if he has any.

6   In the case of any deficit in this fund, members/participants will theoretically give an extra contribution to the fund. This is an unwanted situation in practice. However, this situation can be prevented in two ways. First, contributions should be collected with considerations of some extra reserve at the beginning. Second, TO may give qard al-hasan (interest-free loan) to the fund to maintain technical operations. When

the fund has the surplus, the TO takes its qard back by instalments or as a lump sum, which is dependent on the operational results. However, the qard option should be considered only in very urgent situations. Otherwise, this may lead takaful to form a risk transfer mechanism, which is highly criticized in current practice.

Lastly, there will be another benefit in the family takaful along with compensation rights. Family takaful funds, generally separated into two funds, namely personal investment fund and risk fund. Risk fund works as similar to general takaful operations. The risk fund is used in case of fatal injury or death. However, life insurance operations were criticized by some scholars in the past, this is more similar version of the historical example of Aqilah, which is allowed by the Prophet (peace be upon him). At the same time, a personal investment fund works for each person separately for their own investment choices. Collected funds utilized long-termed Islamic profit and loss shared investment tools.

As elaborated above, the wakalah-cooperative model may solve shariah issues regarding the takaful model. Besides that, shariah governance frameworks are not well established in some countries. This problem can cause distrust of the TO regarding *Sharia* sensitivity. Also, TO may not be concerned about *Shariah* issues as much as participants; for this reason, a qualified *Shariah* governance framework is essential for the takaful market.

4.2 Development of Takaful

Regulatory and supervisory issues are the main obstacle for the development of takaful market. Regulators and supervisors have to consider market needs while developing rules and regulations. Better regulations and supervision system means positive growth for the takaful system. Without proper regulation and supervision, customers will not prefer takaful products due to problems related to governance mechanisms.

Developing a takaful system also requires retakaful operators, which is another essential need for a takaful ecosystem. Retakaful is the risk–sharing body of the TOs. Without retakaful operators, TOs either need to rely on conventional reinsurance companies or hold the risks only on the takaful fund, where the second option is not likely. For this reason, retakaful operators is a must for a takaful ecosystem.

Qualified human sources are essential to maintain takaful operations, especially in the markets where takaful has just started to emerge. For this reason, qualified training and education centers need to collaborate with market practitioners and authorities. The essence of Islamic finance should be taught to takaful market practitioners to keep takaful operations unique. Otherwise, the takaful system may converge to the conventional insurance system.

The takaful market is not limited to risk management operations. There are also financial activities attached to maintain takaful products and services.

Significantly, family takaful businesses heavily rely on financial investment products. For this reason, feasible Islamic investment products play an essential role in the development of the takaful system. Short-term investment tools are vital for general takaful operations, while family TOs require long-term investment tools. While developing short-term investment tools, professionals must avoid using the back doors of the Shariah, such as organized tawarruq and bai inah-based investment tools (wash sale type operations).

4.3 Marketing Issues

Once takaful practice is well established, TOs and academic institutions collaborate to increase awareness regarding takaful services and products. Islamic financial literacy is very low compared to financial literacy. Takaful literacy is even lower. The stakeholders of the takaful ecosystem should collaborate to develop awareness about takaful products and services. For example, Malaysia is making efforts to raise awareness among Islamic financial participants by using Friday khutbas (Aslan & Avcı, 2021). Opening new training and education centers for Islamic financial literacy will help to increase awareness toward takaful products and services. Not only increasing awareness but also misperception regarding takaful has to be handled to increase the marketing potential of the takaful products.

Recently, digital transformation has had a rejuvenating effect on financial services. For this reason, TO needs to adopt new ways to enrich their customers. Also, Gen-Z is the future customer for the takaful companies. Gen-Z is more adaptive to technology, and they prefer to handle everything online. TO's need to design their products based on future customers' needs using new technological approaches (Aslan & Avcı, 2021). Insurance agencies will be old-school in a decade. TOs should smoothen their marketing activities by enabling customers to use mobile apps and websites for the management of their takaful services.

5 Conclusion

Takaful seems to be the best Islamic insurance alternative to conventional insurance. The takaful system has been developed and practiced since the 1980s. Although, there have been several issues addressed in the literature regarding Shariah, these issues arise mainly from differences between theory and practice. Practitioners need to converge to the theoretical framework of takaful while theorists develop better practices with the least possible issues and difficulties.

In this study, we attempted to emphasize the main issues that the takaful market has encountered. We categorized these issues to provide a better understanding along with offering possible solutions for the future. Wakalah-cooperative model can solve shariah issues, which has been addressed, in takaful operations. However, it might be challenging to implement because adjusting some regulations and going beyond the status quo needs some effort. Besides, developing human resources, increasing awareness, and adapting technological advancement to business operations may help develop and market takaful properly. The proposals that have been discussed above can be helpful for policymakers and market players to improve their takaful practices.

Notes

1 Fatawa is the plural from of the word fatwa, which means a formal ruling or interpretation on a point of Islamic law given by a qualified legal scholar (known as a mufti). See: https://www.britannica.com/topic/fatwa.
2 Please see for details: Resolution no: 9 (p. 13), https://zulkiflihasan.files.wordpress.com/2009/12/majma-fiqh.pdf.
3 Please see: https://www.bnm.gov.my/documents/20124/792371/booklet.en.pdf
4 The concept of nihd means sharing expenses. According to this concept, each member of a travel group contributes some funds and/or food to cover their needs during a journey. See for details: Ali, M. M. (2016). Takaful Models: Their Evolution and Future Direction. *Islam and Civilisational Renewal*, p. 470.

References

AAOIFI. (2015). *Shari'ah Standards*. Accounting and Auditing Organization for Islamic Financial Institutions.

Abozaid, A. (2016). Critical Shari'ah Review of Takaful Structures: Toward a Better Model. In S. N. Ali & S. Nisar (Eds.), *Takaful and Islamic Cooperative Finance: Challenges and Opportunities* (1st ed., pp. 93–111). Edward Elgar.

Ahmad, R., & Auzzir, Z. A. (2012). *Takaful* (1st ed.). Pearson.

Ali, E. R. A. E., & Odierno, H. S. P. (2008). *Essential Guide to Takaful (Islamic Insurance)* (1st ed.). CERT Publication.

Ali, M. M. (2016). Takaful Models: Their Evolution and Future Direction. *Islam and Civilisational Renewal*, 7(4), 457–473.

Aslan, H. (2021). *Factors Affecting the Development of Takaful (Islamic Insurance) System in Turkey: A Mixed Method Study* [Marmara University, Istanbul, Turkey]. http://dspace.marmara.edu.tr/handle/11424/216805

Aslan, H., & Avcı, E. (2021). Can Turkey Implement Malaysian Takaful Know-How into Turkish Market? A Qualitative Inquiry. *International Journal of Islamic Economics and Finance Studies*, 7(1), 1–30. https://doi.org/10.25272/ijisef.816143

Bardakoğlu, A. (1994). Diyet. In *Türkiye Diyanet Vakfı Islam Ansiklopedisi (DİA)* (pp. 473–479). Türkiye Diyanet Vakfı. http://www.islamansiklopedisi.info/dia/pdf/c09/c090327.pdf

Bhatty, A., & Nisar, S. (2016). Takaful Journey: The Past, Present and Future. In S. N. Ali & S. Nisar (Eds.), *Takaful and Islamic Cooperative Finance: Challenges and Opportunities* (1st ed., pp. 3–21). Edward Elgar.

Billah, M. M. (n.d.). *Development & Applications of Islamic Insurance (Takaful)*. Retrieved February 14, 2017, from https://tr.scribd.com/document/326011011/Islamic-insurance-pdf

Billah, M. M. (1993). Life Insurance? An Islamic View. *Arab Law Quarterly*, 8(4), 315–324. http://www.jstor.org/stable/3381725

98 *Hakan Aslan*

Billah, M. M. (1997). A Model of Life Insurance in the Contemporary Islamic Economy. *Arab Law Quarterly, 12*(3), 287–306. www.jstor.org/stable/3381844

Billah, M. M. (1998). Islamic Insurance: Its Origins and Development. *Arab Law Quarterly, 13*(4), 386–422. http://www.jstor.org/stable/3382093

Billah, M. M. (2003a). *Islamic and Modern Insurance Principles and Practices* (1st ed.). Ilmiah Publishers.

Billah, M. M. (2003b). *Islamic Insurance [Takaful]* (First). Ilmiah Publishers.

Bouheraoua, S., & Ahmad, M. A. J. (2011). Takaaful Operation : Appraisal of the Existing Models and Exploration of a Possible Alternative, the Wadi'ah Model. *Revue Des Sciences Économiques et de Gestion, 11*, 11–26. http://www.univ-ecosetif.com/revueeco/Cahiers_fichiers/revue-11-2011/13.pdf

Brill. (2020). *Ibaha. Encyclopaedia of Islam* (2nd ed.) https://referenceworks.brillonline.com/entries/encyclopaedia-of-islam-2/ibaha-SIM_3015?s.num=9

CIBAFI. (2018). *CIBAFI Global Takaful Survey: Risk Perception, Growth Drivers and the Impact of Technology.* http://cibafi.org/Files/L1/Content/CI1343-GTSReport2018.pdf

COMCEC. (2019). *Improving the Takaful Sector in Islamic Countries.*

Elatrash, S. R. J., & Soualhi, Y. (2016). The Practice of Takāful Benefit (Nomination) in the Contecy of IFSA 2013: A Critical Appraisal. *ISRA International Journal of Islamic Finance, 8*(1), 197–202.

Frenz, T., & Soualhi, Y. (2010). *Takaful and Retakaful: Principles and Practices* (2nd ed.). Munich RE.

Habib, S. F. (2018). *Fundamentals of Islamic Finance and Banking* (1st ed.). John Wiley & Sons.

Hacak, H. (2006). İslâm Hukukunda Sigorta ve Fıkıh Bilginlerinin Sigortaya Yaklaşımının Genel Bir Değerlendirmesi. *M.Ü.İlahiyat Fakültesi Dergisi, 30*, 21–50.

Htay, S. N. N., Arif, M., Soualhi, Y., Zaharin, H. R., & Shaugee, I. (2012). *Accounting, Auditing and Governance for Takaful Operations.* John Wiley & Sons. https://doi.org/10.1002/9781119198970

Htay, S. N. N., & Salman, S. A. (2013a). Shari'ah and Ethical Issues in the Practice of Modified Wakalah Model in Family Takaful. *International Journal of Business and Social Science, 4*(12), 128–132. https://doi.org/10.7763/IJTEF.2013.V4.313

Htay, S. N. N., & Salman, S. A. (2013b). Shari'ah and Ethical Issues in the Practice of the Modified Mudharabah Family Takaful Model in Malaysia. *International Journal of Trade, Economics and Finance, 4*(6), 340–342. https://doi.org/10.7763/IJTEF.2013.V4.313

IFSB. (2019). *Islamic Financial Services Industry Stability Report 2019.*

IFSB, & WBG. (2017). *Realizing the Value Proposition of the Takaful Industry for a Stable and Inclusive Financial System.*

Jalil, M. F. A., & Rahman, Z. A. (2015). Hibah, Tabarru' and Waqf Application in Takaful. In W. M. Z. Noordin, A. F. H. A. Razak, M. M. Ahmad, L. R. Lieu, & N. Nor (Eds.), *WIEF-UiTM Occasional Papers* (2nd ed., p. 161). WIEF-UiTM.

Khan, M. A. (2003). Islamic Economics and Finance : A Glossary. In *Routhledge* (2nd ed.). Routledge.

Khorshid, A. (2004). *Islamic Insurance: A Modern Approach to Islamic Banking* (1st ed.). RoutledgeCurzon.

Lahsasna, A. (2016). *Risk and Takaful Planning* (1st ed.). IBFIM.

Nana, A. (2016). A Proposed Marriage Between Endowments, Mutual Insurance and Institution of Agency in Islamic Law: An Introduction to the Waqf-Wakalah

Model of Takaful. In S. N. Ali & S. Nisar (Eds.), *Takaful and Islamic Cooperative Finance: Challenges and Opportunities* (1st ed., pp. 62–92). Edward Elgar.

Özen, Ş. (2013). Velâ. In *Türkiye Diyanet Vakfı İslam Ansiklopedisi (DIA)* (pp. 11–15). Türkiye Diyanet Vakfı.

Rahman, Z. A., & Redzuan, H. (2009). *Takaful the 21st Century Insurance Innovation* (1st ed.). McGraw-Hill.

Refinitiv. (2021). *Islamic Finance Development Report 2021.*

Shalim, K. M. Z. H. (2016). Revisiting Life Insurance in Islamic Law. *Turkish Journal of Islamic Economics*, *3*(2), 39–62. https://doi.org/10.15238/TUJISE.2014.3.2.39-62

Sıddıki, M. N. (1984). *İslâm Ekonomi Düşüncesi: Çağdaş Eserler Üzerine Bir Araştırma* (1st ed.). Bir Yayıncılık.

Soualhi, Y. (2010). Shari'Ah Inspection of Surplus Distribution in Takaful Operations. *IIUM Journal of Economics and Management*, *18*(2), 197–220.

Soualhi, Y. (2016). Surplus Distribution in Current Takāful Operations : A Critical Sharīʿah Perspective. *Arab Law Quarterly*, *30*(August), 1–21. https://doi.org/10.1163/15730255-12341323

World Bank, & IDGB. (2016). *Global Report on Islamic Finance: Islamic Finance: A Catalyst for Shared Prosperity.* https://doi.org/10.1596/978-1-4648-0926-2

Zerka, M. A., & Neccar, A. M. (2009). *İslam Düşüncesinde Ekonomi, Banka ve Sigorta* (H. Karaman (trans.); 2nd ed.). İz Yayıncılık.

7 Issues in Technology

An Analysis of the Potential Role of Fintech in Reshaping the Islamic Financial System

Mohammad Ghaith Mahaini

1 Introduction

The fourth industrial revolution, as well as the financial crises in 2008, set the foundation for fintech to disrupt the financial system. Technologies have enabled financial institutions to improve their services. It has also found new service providers that offer financial services in a completely new way. As a result, the Islamic financial system has the chance to evolve and develop. This paper utilizes qualitative and descriptive approaches in reviewing the potential role fintech can have in reshaping the Islamic financial framework. It analyzes the position of fintech in the Islamic financial framework and discusses the different categories of fintech solutions that could disrupt the Islamic finance industry. The study also highlighted the main issues hindering the proliferation of Islamic fintech. Namely, regulatory and legal issues, Shariah compliance issues, the lack of talents and knowledge centers, difficulties to access proper funding, and the availability of the required infrastructure. This paper recommends policymakers support startups that offer Islamic fintech-based financial services by providing balanced guidelines and improving the required infrastructure, such as uninterrupted access to the internet. Additionally, this paper suggests that fintech seems to be the new change agent for the financial industry. This might very well be a means of empowerment of a true Islamic financial system. Through further developing fintech, Islamic finance has a viable chance to break away from being a mere replica of conventional interest-based banking.

Islamic financial technology, otherwise known as "Islamic fintech" is a new term that has been subject to intense discussions by academicians and industry players alike. It is often mentioned in the context of innovating new financial services that can disrupt or replace existing services by relying on new technologies that came about after the fourth industrial revolution. This section discusses this revolution and the new norm that it has created. It then presents the definitions of both fintech and Islamic fintech in order to clarify their concepts. Lastly, this section also illustrates the methodology used in this paper.

DOI: 10.4324/9781003377283-7

1.1 The Fourth Industrial Revolution and the New Norm

The fourth industrial revolution refers to combining and moving the different everyday aspects of life into the digital realm in order to improve their speed, efficiency, and convenience (Haqqi, 2020, p. 209). Thus, it brought forward a new reality. A new world where technology completely disrupts well-established industries and economic sectors. As a result, things that were previously seemingly impossible are now the norm. New technology-intense companies have reshaped entire industries. For example, Uber, which is perhaps the biggest transportation company in the world, virtually owns no cars because it is merely a digital platform. The same goes for the hospitality industry, where Airbnb, which can be considered the largest host in the world, virtually owns no rooms. In other words, as put by Schwab (2016, p. 12), the latest industrial revolution has ventured into a new world where virtual and physical systems of manufacturing cooperate with one another in a way flexible enough to allow the creation of new operating models. Similarly, the financial sector was not isolated from new fundamental changes at the industry level as well.

The sense of urgency for change in the financial sector was exacerbated in the aftermath of the global financial crisis in 2008 (Abojeib & Habib, 2019; Haddad & Hornuf, 2019; Serbulova, 2021). This urgency for change seems to be driven by different motives. First, it calls for a more ethical and socially responsible financial system whereby values and ethics are essential factors to consider, not merely the financial outcome (Benedikter, 2012). Second comes the urgent need for financial institutions to cut costs (Serbulova, 2021). The third motive can be attributed to the lower levels of trust of the public toward traditional financial institutions (Haddad & Hornuf, 2019; Serbulova, 2021). This issue left the door wide open for new financial intermediaries to form and present potential sound alternatives for the current conventional financial institutions. The fourth and, perhaps, the most impactful reason is the technological advances in cybersecurity, mobile communications (Serbulova, 2021), and the foundation of the blockchain (Abojeib & Habib, 2019), which can be considered a spillover effect from the industrial revolution. The invention of blockchain technology has been so crucial that some even consider blockchain technology to be the current driver of the fourth industrial revolution (Kuo Chuen, 2017).

1.2 The Definition of Financial Technology (Fintech)

Financial technology, otherwise known as fintech, is defined by the World Economic Forum as "companies that provide or facilitate financial services by using technology" (World Economic Forum, 2015). However, Rabbani, Khan, & Thalassinos (2020) define fintech as "the fusion of information technology and finance for providing the financial services at an affordable cost with a seamless user experience". However, the most commonly used definition of fintech is perhaps the one provided by the Financial Stability Board and adopted by the Basel Committee on Banking Supervision (BCBS) (Rupeika-Apoga & Eleftherios, 2020). It states that fintech is: "technologically enabled financial innovation that could result in new business models, applications, processes or products with an associated material effect on financial markets and institutions and the provision of financial services" (Financial Stability Board, 2019). From the mentioned definitions, it can be inferred that fintech is concerned with providing an innovative solution for a financial need using modern technology.

Based on recent reports, fintech companies are no longer the exception but rather the norm in many markets (Ernst & Young, 2019). Ernst and Young report published in 2019 strongly suggested that around 68% of consumers are willing to consider a financial services product offered by a non-financial services company. The report also recommends increasing leverage of communication firms whereby 45% of consumers are more open to consider receiving a financial service from their communication service provider. This serves as evidence that financial institutions are no longer the only main go-to option for financial services. This is also applicable to Islamic financial institutions.

1.3 The Definition of Islamic Fintech

Islamic fintech is defined by Mustafa et al. (2020) as "any fintech catering to the needs of the Islamic financial institutions and is designed to as per the principles laid down by Shariah". However, the suggested definition limits the scope of Islamic fintech to services provided to Islamic financial institutions only. There might be fintech-based solutions that do not contradict the Shariah requirements that can be provided by entities other than the Islamic financial institutions such as telecommunication providers and startups. Said entities may not fulfill the legal and operational requirements to be considered financial institutions and, by default, would be excluded from the said definition. As such, for the remainder of this paper, Islamic fintech is used to describe any modern technology-based solution to financial needs that is offered in a way that does not contradict Shariah.

1.4 Methodology and Research Design

This paper utilizes a qualitative and descriptive approach in reviewing the potential role Islamic fintech can have in reshaping the Islamic financial system. It also aims at analyzing the position of fintech in the Islamic financial framework. Further, this paper discusses the challenges that Islamic fintech faces and their possible solutions. To achieve that, the author applied content analysis on a number of research papers in order to pinpoint the most commonly discussed issues and challenges facing the application of Islamic fintech around the globe. Since this paper highlights the issues in the application of fintech, which is rather technical in nature, the paper also analyzed several recent industry reports that discuss both fintech and Islamic fintech across different industries and jurisdictions. This neutral approach between academic and industry aspects is one of the distinguishing aspects of this paper. Finally, it is essential to mention that this paper is concerned with fintech solutions that facilitate offering financial services. Since cryptocurrencies, in and of themselves, are not a technology that provides financial services, the discussion about them is only limited to using them in other fintech solutions, particularly decentralized finance (DeFi).

The remainder of this paper is designed as follows: the following section discusses the position of fintech within the Islamic financial system. Section 3 details possible Fintech-based solutions that could reshape the Islamic financial system. Section 4 then analyzes the issues and possible solutions in the application of fintech in the Islamic financial system, while the last section includes the conclusion and policy recommendations.

2 Islamic Fintech within the Framework of the Islamic Financial System

The Islamic financial system has traditionally been based on three main components: Islamic capital market, Islamic banks, and Islamic insurance (Takaful) operators. The main objective of the first two pillars is to mobilize funds from surplus units to deficit units in the economy, while the aim of the takaful industry is to act as a safety net to absorb shocks due to covered perils. The regulators also offer a comprehensive oversight over the entire system.

The Islamic finance industry has been facing plenty of global and regional challenges for the last few years. Among which is the trade war between the United States and China, the political crisis engulfing various countries in the Middle East, the fluctuations in oil prices as well as the ongoing COVID-19 pandemic. Nonetheless, reports indicate that the Islamic financial services industry grew by 10.7% in 2020, with a total valuation of around USD 2.7 trillion (Islamic Financial Services Board, 2021). The Islamic banking industry has the largest share of the total Islamic finance industry, followed by the Islamic capital markets with 68.2%, 30.9%, and 0.9% for the Islamic banking sector, Islamic capital markets, and Takaful, respectively (Islamic Financial Services Board, 2021).

Islamic fintech has penetrated different aspects of each of the three pillars of the Islamic financial system. The transaction volume of Islamic fintech within the 57 Organisation of Islamic Cooperation (OIC) countries in 2020 amounted to a whopping USD 49 billion as per The Global Islamic Fintech Report. The report also forecasted the said amount to reach USD 128 billion by 2025 with a compound annual growth rate (CAGR) of 21%, which is higher than the 15% CAGR for the conventional fintech companies during the same period (Ahmed & Basit, 2021, p. 4).

Generally, the penetration of fintech takes two various forms. The first is when a traditional Islamic financial institution adopts new Islamic fintech-based solutions in order to maintain its market share. Examples of this

104 *Mohammad Ghaith Mahaini*

can be clearly seen in Malaysia, where Islamic banks offer new types of services such as e-wallets, for example. In fact, the first e-wallet to be launched in Malaysia was established by Maybank, one of the largest banks in the country (Abdullah, Redzuan, & Daud, 2020, p. 67).

The second form is when a new startup company is established to challenge the existing corporations by offering Islamic fintech-based services such as financing. This can be done either directly, such as in Islamic peer-to-peer crowdfunding, or indirectly through means such as Islamic digital and open banking services. As of early 2021, there are approximately 241 Islamic fintech startups operating worldwide (Ahmed & Basit, 2021, p. 4).

Within the evolving new form of the Islamic financial system, Takaful has also been challenged by Takaful technology (TakaTech) which can be considered as a sub-set of Islamic Fintech. A regulatory sandbox refers to a framework under which innovators have the chance to experiment with fintech solutions for a limited span of time under a relaxed regulatory boundaries (Haqqi, 2020, p. 216). Sandboxes established to foster Islamic fintech have reportedly been witnessing more TakaTech startup concepts (Salim, Abojeib, & Baharom, 2020, p. 9). Nevertheless, TakaTech startups are still trailing behind in numbers compared to the total number of Islamic fintech startups covering other areas (Ahmed & Basit, 2021).

Finally, the advances in cybersecurity and other related technologies allow regulators to address the new realities of the evolving financial sector in

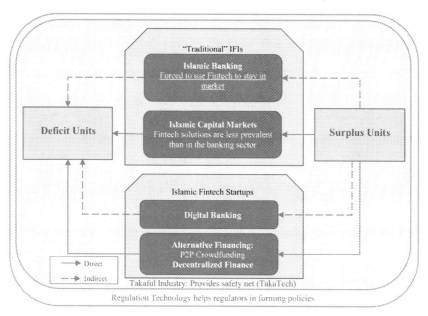

Figure 7.1 Islamic Fintech within the Framework of the Islamic Financial System.
Source: Author's own.

a better way. Serving as the governor of the financial sector, central banks can rely on regulation technology (RegTech) which is a sub-set of financial technology in order to enhance the efficiency and transparency in policies and regulations (UK Government Chief Scientific Adviser, 2015). Figure 7.1 illustrates the position of Islamic fintech and its sub-sets within the framework of the Islamic financial system.

As such, Islamic fintech has penetrated every aspect of the Islamic financial system. In some cases, it serves as a natural development of existing entities, while in other cases, it takes a form of a disruptive force through new startups that challenge the norm and offer better services than the existing institutions. That said, it is essential to mention that there are other fintech solutions that do not cater to the primary function of the financial system framework discussed above, i.e., mobilizing funds. Instead, they cater to supportive features. Examples of the said solutions are payment systems, digital banking, as well as peer-to-peer networks, and smart contracts. The following section illustrates some of the most commonly referred to Islamic financial technologies that could possibly reshape the industry.

3 Possible Fintech–Based Solutions that Could Reshape the Islamic Financial System

As discussed earlier, Islamic fintech can offer plenty of viable and innovative solutions for better Shariah-compliant financial services worldwide. There are numerous technologies that can be applied for that purpose. Each technology carries features and characteristics that address a specific issue either by improving the current traditional solutions or coming up with a completely new innovative solution. As such, the most logically plausible categorization of fintech technologies should be based on their different value propositions. Therefore, fintech solutions can be classified into three main categories: The first is the Islamic fintech solutions that challenge the core function of traditional Islamic banking. The second is the Islamic fintech solutions that challenge secondary financial services. The third category consists of both TakaTech and RegTech as supportive technologies for the Islamic financial framework.

3.1 Islamic Fintech Solutions that Challenge the Core Function of Traditional Islamic Banking

This category concerns Islamic fintech that completely disrupts the way traditional banking, including Islamic banking, operates. It offers other innovative and modern solutions to either alter or remove the role of intermediation that has historically been the cornerstone of the financial system.

Alternative finance refers to online digital finance activities that operate outside of the traditional banks and capital markets (*The 2nd Global Alternative*

Finance Market Benchmarking Report, 2021, p. 30). Alternative finance is, in essence, one of the main fintech solutions that promote financial disintermediation, which may be better for the achievement of the Shariah objectives (Irfan & Ahmed, 2019). Examples of alternative finance include peer-to-peer finance and crowdfunding. However, there are other examples of alternative finance that are pretty controversial from the perspective of Shariah, such as invoice discounting and cryptocurrencies (Anca, 2019).

Peer-to-peer financing and crowdfunding are disruptive fintech solutions that can eliminate the need for a bank as an intermediary between borrowers and lenders. Instead, they get matched on a website and, thus, disappear from banks' balance sheets (Oseni & Ali, 2019, p. 179). In crowdfunding, money is raised to finance certain projects by matching them with small investors (Anca, 2019).

As of February 2021, 76 different startups have been established that can be considered as alternative finance Islamic fintech companies among which, 44 startups cater for raising funds using peer-to-peer financing or crowdfunding (Ahmed & Basit, 2021).

Lastly, DeFi is another innovative financial technology-based solution that disrupts traditional financial intermediation. DeFi has the potential to build an alternate financial system that is more decentralized, creative, transparent, cross-border, and interoperable (Chen & Bellavitis, 2020). In essence, DeFi is a technology built using smart contracts, which, in turn, is facilitated by blockchain technology. Smart contracts are programs that would automatically get executed when a specific set of pre-coded conditions within the program are satisfied (Murray, Kuban, Josefy, & Anderson, 2008). On the other hand, blockchain is a log of transactions that is based on decentralizing and encrypting information in a way that makes it possible to manage the records while achieving trust amongst the parties involved (Anca, 2019). To put things in perspective, the total market capitalization of DeFi tokens was around USD 189 billion at the time of writing this paper ("Top DeFi Tokens by Market Capitalization," 2021).

At its core, the application of DeFi requires public smart contract platform such as the Ethereum blockchain (Zetzsche, Arner, & Buckley, 2020). This means that there is a need to depend on cryptocurrencies to facilitate taking advantage of the potential of DeFi. This is probably why there has been virtually no discussion about DeFi within the scope of the Islamic finance industry. The Shariah discussion of cryptocurrencies is still in its infant stage. Not to mention the Shariah discussion of using cryptocurrencies in smart contracts for financing purposes. The fluctuations in the prices of cryptocurrencies and the accusations of anti-money-laundering (AML) breaches are impacting the reputation of this industry from the first hand (Chen & Bellavitis, 2020) and affecting the Shariah judgment on the other. Therefore, the focus of Islamic fintech developers under this category has been primarily on Islamic crowdfunding.

As such, if the new technologies mentioned above are offered in a Shariah compliant manner, they have the potential to outcompete the intermediation role of traditional Islamic banks between surplus and deficient units. This is due to the advantages that these new technologies offer such as efficiency, cost reduction, speed, and convenience for all parties involved. This might render Islamic banks the more costly and inefficient alternative for both depositors and users of fund.

3.2 Islamic Fintech Solutions that Challenge Secondary Financial Services

This category caters to Islamic fintech, which disrupts financial services that are not related to financial intermediation. As a result, those fintech solutions can be applied by startups and the Islamic banks themselves as well. Islamic banks need to adopt suitable fintech solutions to stay competitive in the market and to reduce costs. There are numerous fintech solutions that can be discussed under this category. Examples are digital banking, payment systems, and wealth management solutions.

Digital banking has emerged due to the urgent need for cutting costs and improving synergy. Digital banking can take the form of mobile banking or online banking, whereby the bank does not have a physical presence in the form of offices and branches. Instead, the bank extends all its services via the internet using a mobile application and an online website. This form of banking allows for massive savings in overhead costs, especially reducing the number of employees needed (UK Government Chief Scientific Adviser, 2015). There have been some attempts to establish Islamic digital banks, such as the case of Tayyab in Kazakhstan and Niyah in the UK, which was later acquired by Wahed, a Saudi Aramco baked company, in late 2020 (Ahmed & Basit, 2021).

On the other hand, payment systems are probably the most sought-after fintech service nowadays. It is expected that payment systems such as non-banking payment cards, e-wallets, remittances, and foreign exchange service providers will experience the most growth in 2021 in terms of the number of new startups (Ahmed & Basit, 2021). One of the payment systems that has been gaining ground worldwide and especially in South East Asia, is the application of e-wallets as an effort to achieve a cashless society. An e-wallet is a payment system that facilitates settling financial transactions using different payment methods such as debit cards, pre-paid cards, credit cards, and even bank accounts. Using e-wallets improves security, convenience, speed, and seamlessness when performing electronic and digital payments (Abdullah et al., 2020). E-wallets application is bolstered by the development of smartphones and the improved penetration of mobile telecommunication services even in rural and less developed areas. It is reported that COVID-19 was a catalyst to boost the dependence on e-wallets as the preferred payment method in countries like Malaysia (*The 2nd Global Alternative Finance Market Benchmarking Report*, 2021, p. 101). E-wallet service providers offer a number of features, including: online payments to facilitate online shopping, point-of-sale integration, and QR codes to enable contactless payments, in addition, peer-to-peer payments, which facilitate transferring money to others (Alam,

108 *Mohammad Ghaith Mahaini*

Gupta, & Zameni, 2019). Islamic fintech startups specializing in payment systems mainly operate within the Middle East and North Africa, followed by Southeast Asia with 17 and 9 startups, respectively.

Wealth management is yet another avenue for fintech to disrupt the norms. With the urgency to bring down costs, wealth management firms are expected to automate or outsource operations in the middle and back-end offices (PwC, 2017). The new form of digital wealth management companies uses new technologies such as big data analysis, artificial intelligence (AI), Blockchain technology, and robotics to compete with the traditional wealth management companies (Alam et al., 2019). Nevertheless, there is an array of new services that have emerged with the proliferation of financial technology. Namely, robotic advisory, robotic retirement planning, micro-investing, digital brokerage, technology-based tools of investment, and fintech software applications for portfolio and financial services management (Fintechnews Singapore, 2018). The new form of wealth management companies that utilize what is now called WealthTech is typically able to waive the management fee entirely and only charge a minimal monthly subscription fee (Alam et al., 2019, p. 43). This is primarily due to their cost-efficiency. By early 2021, there has been a total of 32 Islamic wealth management companies. Surprisingly, most of the said companies operate in non-Muslim majority countries in Europe and North America (Ahmed & Basit, 2021).

3.3 Fintech Solutions as Supportive Technologies for the Islamic Financial Framework

This category focuses on the most critical technologies that support the financial industry rather than offering financial solutions in and of themselves. In particular, those technologies are TakaTech which is short for Takaful technology, and RegTech, which is short for regulation technology.

TakaTech or Takaful technology is the Shariah-compliant equivalent of InsurTech. It refers to the types of fintech solutions targeted at Takaful services. TakaTech aims at utilizing new technologies to improve the efficiency of providing Shariah complaint insurance coverages in order to reduce transaction costs. Among the possible services the new generation of TakaTech can provide are ultra-customized coverages, social Takaful, dynamic pricing as well as offering enhanced brokerage via deep learning and AI (Alam et al., 2019, p. 44). Therefore, Takaful participants can choose the exact coverages that suits their needs rather than a preprinted Takaful certificate. This will help in saving the money otherwise spent on unneeded coverages and would grant the users the chance to adjust the contribution paid based on the coverages chosen. Deep learning can utilize the online shopping behavior of the potential Takaful customers in order to suggest better coverages and products.

Additionally, there have been suggestions to establish a new model for Takaful using blockchain technology (Mohamed & Ali, 2018, p. 149) and smart contracts (Alam et al., 2019, p. 130). Moreover, among the possible application of TakaTech is utilizing AI and neural network to recommend the proper mix of takaful policies (Alam et al., 2019, p. 44).

Although TakaTech has been among the top three dominant fintech sectors in Malaysia (Salim et al., 2020), TekaTech is yet to achieve the interest and diversity that the other fintech solutions have received. This issue is not only limited to Takaful operators. In a survey done by PwC, almost a third of the surveyed insurance companies do not deal with InsurTech at all, even though three in four insurers believe that some part of their business is at risk of disruption (PwC, 2016). Nevertheless, it is reported that there are almost 12 insurance-related startups offering different forms of services to the overall insurance and takaful industry (Ahmed & Basit, 2021).

On the other hand, RegTech as a term was first mentioned in a report by the UK government chief scientific advisor in the year 2015, which targets observing the regulatory requirements (UK Government Chief Scientific Adviser, 2015). Generally, RegTech refers to the dependence on information technology for the purpose of regulatory monitoring, reporting, and compliance (Douglas, Barberis, & Buckley, 2017). With the rapid growth of fintech, there is a dire need for the regulatory authorities to cope with the change to avoid fintech from becoming a tool for money laundering, terrorism financing, and fraudulent activities. As such, RegTech is brought to regulators through a group of firms that make use of cloud computing, big data analytics, blockchain, and other technologies to bridge the gap with the financial institutions (Alam et al., 2019, p. 46). In essence, RegTech helps regulators in discharging their regulatory responsibilities more diligently and effectively (Mohamed & Ali, 2018, p. 26). Additionally, concerns about privacy, trust, and cybersecurity are among the most notable motives of governments and regulators to embrace RegTech (Douglas et al., 2017). As such, promoting RegTech would probably help the entire financial industry as it serves as a modern way to instill checks and balances between the different stakeholders and, therefore, promote better trust within the general public.

RegTech is still in its infantry stage in the Muslim world. Still, there have been remarkable improvements in regulating different fintech services in the last few years. A recent survey shows that almost 54% of Islamic fintech companies are directly or indirectly regulated. While around 22% still operate unregulated (Ahmed & Basit, 2021).

The importance of RegTech is to highlight the issues of Islamic fintech. Those issues need to be handled and appropriately addressed to maximize its benefits and minimize its risks. The following section explores a number of said issues and their possible solutions.

4 Issues and Possible Solutions in the Application of Fintech in the Islamic Financial System

Like any new concept, fintech faces many issues that challenge its potential in reshaping the Islamic finance industry. Those issues stem mainly from the

110   *Mohammad Ghaith Mahaini*

innovative nature of this new sector, which makes it susceptible to corrections and errors. The literature tackling Islamic fintech has discussed various issues which can broadly be summarized into five main categories, namely: regulatory and legal issues, the compliance with Shariah requirements, the lack of talents and knowledge centers, difficulties in attaining proper funding, and the issues in the infrastructure. This section discusses the aforementioned issues and their possible solutions.

4.1 Regulatory and Legal Issues

The most frequently mentioned challenge that fintech faces, in general, is regulatory and legal issues (Abojeib & Habib, 2019; Alam et al., 2019; Firmansyah & Anwar, 2019; Haddad & Hornuf, 2019; Haqqi, 2020; Hasan, Hassan, & Aliyu, 2020; Mohamed & Ali, 2018; Muryanto, Kharisma, & Ciptorukmi Nugraheni, 2021; Rabbani et al., 2020; Rusydiana, 2018). This issue is manifested in many different ways. On the first hand, many aspects of fintech are yet to be regulated. This could create loopholes in the financial system for fraudulent activities. On the other hand, too much regulation can cripple the growth and innovation in fintech startups (Alam et al., 2019). Complicated permit procedures can hinder the proliferation of Islamic fintech (Muryanto et al., 2021). Further, the lack of proper regulation might also impede the mass acceptance of the general public. When a service or a company is regulated, governed, and monitored by the relevant authorities, people might become more inclined to test that service. Moreover, the lack of proper governance and unified reporting standards make it hard for stakeholders to evaluate and compare fintech providers with each other (Hasan et al., 2020). Finally, concerns about privacy are also stemming, in large part, from the lack of proper regulation. It is also due to the decentralized and transparent nature of many fintech solutions. There is a trade-off between privacy and transparency (Abojeib & Habib, 2019). Too much transparency might infringe on the users' rights for privacy and data protection.

As a result, proper due care must be given by the regulators in the Muslim world in order for fintech to flourish and make a difference in the Islamic finance industry. The balance between the extremes: over-regulation and under-regulation, is much needed. A number of regulators from Muslim and non-Muslim majority countries are adopting the idea of Sandboxes to solve this conundrum. Examples include the United States and the UK (Haqqi, 2020), Malaysia (Salim et al., 2020), and Qatar (Qatar Fintech Hub, 2021). Sandboxes allow the fintech startups to enjoy some exceptions in order to perform a sort of controlled experiments for their disruptive ideas under the watch of the relevant regulators.

4.2 Compliance with Shariah Requirements

Compliance with Shariah of both the fintech companies as well as the enabling technologies is yet to be completely assured. While there is a strict oversight over the traditional Islamic financial institutions, Islamic fintech startups are not. This situation opens the door wide for Shariah compliance issues that might cause the general public to refuse to try this new sector's promising services. In fact, Hasan et al. (2020) considered Shariah compliance to be one of the significant challenges for the growth of Islamic fintech. Indeed, Shariah compatibility remains a unique challenge for the Islamic fintech industry (Salim et al., 2020).

Shariah compliance concerns can be raised over many fintech-based services. Examples of this can include e-wallet operators who potentially deposit or even invest part of the users' money with conventional banks. Additionally, crowdfunding platforms do not have to follow any Shariah standards in their operations because they are not financial institutions. With no external nor internal Shariah audit required, there is a higher chance for a Shariah breach to occur.

Additionally, a broad range of the core enabling technologies the fintech depends on are controversial in the eyes of Shariah. As mentioned above, DeFi depends on cryptocurrencies and smart contracts. Both of which are under debate. The first debate is as to whether cryptocurrencies can be considered currencies or not. Some scholars view that Bitcoin and other cryptocurrencies to be Shariah non-compliant (Hasan et al., 2020). The second debate is the Shariah compliance of smart contracts when the true identities of the contracting parties are not identified in person. Furthermore, with regards to cryptocurrency trading, if the private key was kept with a third-party, i.e., through a custodial wallet, traders can buy or sell cryptocurrencies with no assurance that the transactions are taking place in reality. This opens the door wide open for many Shariah issues with regards to contract execution even if the cryptocurrency is considered Shariah compliant. There are numerous other examples of potential Shariah issues that might arise from fintech companies as well as the enabling technologies. The discussion of which is beyond the scope of this research.

Still, there are some promising improvements in this aspect. More studies focus on offering Shariah analysis of the different fintech concepts, which will pave the way for a more unified Shariah position that, in turn, assure the general public. Still, the need for a form of Shariah standards that is inclusive and unrestrictive is still a dire need. Similar to the need for proper and balanced regulation, there should be in place some sort of Shariah oversight committee for the entire fintech community in each country. This will serve as a second and much-needed layer of assurance for the Islamic fintech stakeholders that this sector is offering a viable and trustworthy value proposition.

4.3 The Lack of Talents and Knowledge Centers

Shortages in talents seem to be a major issue facing the growth of Islamic fintech. Likewise, educational centers need to produce viable researches about the topic along with trained personnel to be able to bring results (Rabbani et al., 2020). The main problem with Islamic fintech talent development is that, in order to form a strong team, the startup needs to accumulate financial, legal, Shariah, and technical IT expertise under one roof. Still, doing so is relatively costly and can be beyond the financial capability of the startup. Since Islamic fintech is quite a new topic, specialized human expertise is high in demand and can be pretty costly (Abojeib & Habib, 2019).

Luckily, there might be many of viable solutions for this issue. Perhaps the most challenging yet most promising solution is to develop training programs and university specializations that focus on Islamic fintech and cover the fundamental knowledge for interested students. Another solution is by providing Shariah, legal and financial consultancy through the concept of a regulatory Sandbox discussed above. This can help bring down the startup funding requirement and promote creativity. Another possible solution is to outsource secondary tasks to third parties while the main team of the startup can focus only on the aspects they specialize in. The selection of the proper solution should be based on its practicality in addressing the talent scarcity issue on a case-by-case basis. After all, startups operate under different circumstances and there is no one size fits all solution.

4.4 Difficulties in Attaining Proper Funding

Since most fintech ideas are disruptive and out-of-the-box, convincing capital providers is also a challenge. The high capital requirements of some financial services constitute a barrier of entry for many innovative small startups. In fact, it is reported that one of the biggest hindrances for InsuTech has been the high capital barrier (PwC, 2016). Further, the nascent nature of Islamic fintech makes it harder for investors to ensure the future value of their potential investments and if the concept is worth investing in. Additionally, the previously mentioned issues of regulation, Shariah compliance, and talents availability are also bringing the total risk even higher for investors.

To address this issue, Islamic financial institutions can step in to help incubate fintech ideas. This is a win–win deal for both the IFI and the talented innovators. From the first hand, the IFI will make sure to maintain and grow its market share by being the innovative force in the industry. From the second hand, those who come up with innovative ideas can have access to the capital needed. There is also no need to attain legal approvals since the IFI already provides that.

Relatedly, the central banks provide a space for new innovative ideas to develop. This can be done by granting seed capital and offering limited approval to test the ideas in the real life. This form is already being used in countries like Malaysia and Qatar.

Finally, addressing the different issues of fintech development can also help bring down the level of risks and might, therefore, make investors more open to fund Islamic fintech projects.

4.5 The Availability of the Required Infrastructure

Although the infrastructure is quite established in many Muslim countries, other nations lack the basic infrastructure to facilitate the proliferation of fintech services such as electricity and access to a stable and uninterrupted internet connection. This is a major concern since one of the objectives of fintech is to promote financial inclusion even with the unbanked population. Estimates indicate that nearly two billion people have limited to no access to essential financial services (Demirgüç-Kunt and Singer, 2017). In fact, the underdevelopment of fintech infrastructure limits the understanding of its capabilities and hinders its progression (Hasan et al., 2020). Haddad and Hornuf (2019) suggest that the number of secure Internet servers, mobile telephone subscriptions has a positive impact on the development of fintech. Solving this issue requires government support.

To solve this issue, governments can open the door for local investors to become partners in developing the needed infrastructure through partial or full privatization as the case may require. Further, International institutions can help fund infrastructure projects related to internet access and electricity. Example of these institutions can be the Islamic development bank (IsDB).

If all other alternatives were exhausted, governments can resort to open the door for foreign investors to take up this task. Still these countries should be careful to protect their sovereignty and national interests when granting these rights to external parties.

5 Conclusion and Policy Recommendations

This study has illustrated how Islamic fintech can be implemented within the framework of the Islamic financial system. Fintech can help improve the services rendered by traditional Islamic banks and can also be applied by new startups that operate in a non-traditional, more efficient, and more inclusive way. The main objectives of fintech should be to increase efficiency, foster trust, and reduce costs. Some estimates have suggested that fintech technologies such as blockchain can help financial institutions save at least USD 20 billion in cross-border payment, regulatory, and settlement costs (Fanning & Centers, 2016).

This study resulted that fintech and its enabling technologies can be broadly categorized into three main categories. The first is the fintech that challenges the intermediation role of Islamic banks, such as alternative finance and DeFi. The second category includes fintech solutions that can handle secondary financial services such as digital banking, payment systems, and wealth management systems. The third category comprises supportive technologies for the Islamic financial framework. This category includes RegTech and TakaTech solutions.

The newness of Islamic fintech brings in many issues and challenges that need to be addressed. The most notable issue is the legal and regulatory challenges where not enough regulations would open the door for fraud while too strict regulation might impede creativeness. The second issue is the potential Shariah non-compliance of some fintech startups and some enabling technologies. The third issue is the lack of proper talent, research, and capacity-building programs to feed this talent-hungry industry. There are also other issues, such as the lack of proper funding and infrastructure needed for the proliferation of Islamic fintech solutions.

This research illustrates the importance of further research regarding the Shariah compliance of the enabling technologies of Islamic fintech. Additionally, the different fintech startups need to be taken as independent case studies to analyze their Shariah compliance. This would help improve the Shariah compliance of fintech startups from the first hand and increase public awareness from the other. Universities also have a major role to play. Capacity-building programs that can develop the much-needed talents for this growing industry are also essential.

This study recommends policymakers and regulators promoting financial technology within their jurisdictions. This can be achieved by providing the necessary infrastructure such as affordable uninterrupted internet access and electricity for the general public from the first hand, and nurturing innovative fintech ideas on the other hand. Fostering fintech startups can be achieved by organizing fintech competitions, providing tax exemptions for the first few years, and easing licensing requirements.

Fintech seems to be the new catalyst of the financial industry. Such a change agent might very well be a means of empowerment of a true Islamic financial system. Islamic finance has a viable chance to break away from being a mere replica of conventional interest-based finance.

References

Abdullah, N., Redzuan, F., & Daud, N. A. (2020). E-wallet: Factors influencing user acceptance towards cashless society in Malaysia among public universities. *Indonesian Journal of Electrical Engineering and Computer Science, 20*(1), 67–74. https://doi.org/10.11591/ijeecs.v20.i1.pp67-74

Abojeib, M., & Habib, F. (2019). Blockchain for Islamic social responsibility institutions. In *FinTech as a Disruptive Technology for Financial Institutions* (pp. 221–240). IGI Global. https://doi.org/10.4018/978-1-5225-7805-5.ch010

Ahmed, T., & Basit, A. H. (2021). *Global Islamic Fintech Report 2021. Global Islamic Fintech Report 2021.* Retrieved from https://cdn.salaamgateway.com/special-coverage/islamic-fintech-2021/Global-Islamic-Fintech-Report-2021-Executive-Summary.pdf

Alam, N., Gupta, L., & Zameni, A. (2019). *Fintech In Islamic Finance: Digitalizaltion, Development, and Disruption.* Cham: Springer. https://doi.org/10.4324/9781351025584-8

Anca, C. de. (2019). Fintech in Islamic Finance: From collaborative finance to community-based finance. In *Fintech in Islamic Finance: Theory and Practice* (pp. 47–63).

Benedikter, R. (2012). *Social Banking and Social Finance: Building Stones Towards A Sustainable Post-Crisis Financial System?* Retrieved September 26, 2021, from https://www.europeanfinancialreview.com/social-banking-and-social-finance-building-stones-towards-a-sustainable-post-crisis-financial-system/

Chen, Y., & Bellavitis, C. (2020). Blockchain disruption and decentralized finance: The rise of decentralized business models. *Journal of Business Venturing Insights, 13*(June 2020). https://doi.org/10.1016/j.jbvi.2019.e00151

Douglas, W. A., Barberis, J., & Buckley, R. P. (2017). FinTech, RegTech, and the reconceptualization of financial regulation. *Northwestern Journal of International Law & Business, 37*(3). https://doi.org/10.1177/0027950111411368

Ernst & Young. (2019). *Global FinTech Adoption Index 2019. Ernst & Young.* Retrieved from https://www.ey.com/en_gl/ey-global-fintech-adoption-index

Fanning, K., & Centers, D. P. (2016). Blockchain and its coming impact on financial services. *The Journal of Corporate Accounting and Finance,* 11–15. https://doi.org/10.1002/jcaf

Financial Stability Board. (2019). *FinTech and Market Structure in Financial Services: Market Developments and Potential Financial Stability Implications.* Financial Stability Board. Retrieved from https://www.fsb.org/wp-content/uploads/P140219.pdf

Fintechnews Singapore. (2018). *What Is Wealthtech? An Introduction.*

Firmansyah, E. A., & Anwar, M. (2019). Islamic financial technology (Fintech): Its challenges and prospect. *Atlantis Press, 216*(Assdg 2018), 52–58.

Haddad, C., & Hornuf, L. (2019). The emergence of the global fintech market: Economic and technological determinants. *Small Business Economics, 53*(1), 81–105. https://doi.org/10.1007/s11187-018-9991-x

Haqqi, A. R. A. (2020). Strengthening Islamic finance in South-East Asia through innovation of Islamic FinTech in Brunei Darussalam. In *Economics, Business, and Islamic Finance in ASEAN Economics Community* (pp. 202–226). IGI Global. https://doi.org/10.4018/978-1-7998-2257-8.ch010

Hasan, R., Hassan, M. K., & Aliyu, S. (2020). Fintech and Islamic finance: Literature review and research agenda. *International Journal of Islamic Economics and Finance (IJIEF), 3*(1), 75–94. https://doi.org/10.18196/ijief.2122

Irfan, H., & Ahmed, D. (2019). Fintech: The opportunity for Islamic finance. In Oseni, U.A., & Ali, S.N. (Eds.). *Fintech in Islamic Finance: Theory and Practice* (pp. 19–30). Routledge. https://doi.org/10.4324/9781351025584.

Islamic Financial Services Board. (2021). *Islamic Financial Services Industry Stability Report 2021.* Kuala Lumpur.

Kuo Chuen, D. L. (2017). Fintech Tsunami: Blockchain as the Driver of the Fourth Industrial Revolution. *SSRN Electronic Journal.* https://doi.org/10.2139/ssrn.2998093

Mohamed, H., & Ali, H. (2018). *Blockchain, Fintech, and Islamic Finance: Building the Future in the New Islamic Digital Economy.* Boston/Berlin: Walter de Gruyter Inc. https://doi.org/10.1515/9781547400966

Murray, A., Kuban, S., Josefy, M., & Anderson, J. (2008). Contracting in the smart era: the implications of blockchain and decentralized autonomous organizations for contracting and corporate governance. *Academy of Management Perspectives.* https://doi.org/10.5465/amp.2018.0066

Muryanto, Y. T., Kharisma, D. B., & Ciptorukmi Nugraheni, A. S. (2021). Prospects and challenges of Islamic fintech in Indonesia: A legal viewpoint.

International Journal of Law and Management, ahead-of-print. https://doi.org/10.1108/IJLMA-07-2021-0162

Oseni, U. A., & Ali, S. N. (2019). *Fintech in Islamic Finance: Theory and Practice. Fintech in Islamic Finance: Theory and Practice.*

PwC. (2016). *Opportunities Await: How InsurTech Is Reshaping Insurance.* Retrieved from https://www.pwc.com/gx/en/financial-services/assets/fintech-insurance-report.pdf%0Apapers3://publication/uuid/4BFC8642-CE86-46A9-8D40-F2854DCFFF6A

PwC. (2017). *Asset & Wealth Management Revolution: Embracing Exponential Change.*

Qatar Fintech Hub. (2021). *From Qatar to the World: A Report on the State of Fintech in Qatar.*

Rabbani, M. R., Khan, S., & Thalassinos, E. I. (2020). FinTech, Blockchain and Islamic finance: An extensive literature review. *International Journal of Economics and Business Administration, 8*(2), 65–86. https://doi.org/10.35808/ijeba/444

Rupeika-Apoga, R., & Eleftherios. (2020). Ideas for a regulatory definition of FinTech. *International Journal of Economics and Business Administration, VIII*(Issue 2), 136–154. https://doi.org/10.35808/ijeba/448

Rusydiana, A. S. (2018). Developing Islamic financial technology in Indonesia. *Hasanuddin Economics and Business Review, 2*(2), 143–152. https://doi.org/10.26487/hebr.v

Salim, K., Abojeib, M., & Baharom, A. (2020). *Islamic Fintech in Malaysia: Reality & Outlook.* Kuala Lumpur.

Schwab, K. (2016). *The Fourth Industrial Revolution.* Geneva: World Economic Forum.

Serbulova, N. (2021). Fintech as a transformation driver of global financial markets. *EDP Sciences, 273.* https://doi.org/10.1051/e3sconf/202127308097

The 2nd Global Alternative Finance Market Benchmarking Report. (2021). *Cambridge Centre for Alternative Finance.* Cambridge.

Top DeFi Tokens by Market Capitalization. (2021). Retrieved November 9, 2021, from https://coinmarketcap.com/view/defi/

UK Government Chief Scientific Adviser. (2015). *FinTech Futures. Government Office for Science.* Retrieved from https://assets.publishing.service.gov.uk/government/uploads/system/uploads/attachment_data/file/413095/gs-15-3-fintech-futures.pdf

World Economic Forum. (2015). *The Future of Fintech: A Paradigm Shift in Small Business Finance. Global Agenda Council on the Future of Financing & Capital.* Retrieved from http://www3.weforum.org/docs/IP/2015/FS/GAC15_The_Future_of_FinTech_Paradigm_Shift_Small_Business_Finance_report_2015.pdf

Zetzsche, D. A., Arner, D. W., & Buckley, R. P. (2020). Decentralized finance. *Journal of Financial Regulation, 6*(2), 172–203. https://doi.org/10.1093/jfr/fjaa010

8 Morality of Finance

An Islamic Economics Approach

Harun Şencal and İsa Yılmaz

1 Introduction

Shariah, as the core of Islamic governance, "represented and was constituted by a moral law" in the pre-modern Muslim societies; hence locating the legal as a mere "instrument of the moral, not the other way around" (Hallaq, 2012, p. 10). Furthermore, such morality determines the secondary domains such as law, education, economy, and political governance (Hallaq, 2012) and establishes and shapes the relationships and institutions within the societies (Asutay, 2012b). This is because the economy and other domains were embedded within the society in the pre-modern period (Polanyi, 2001).

However, as institutional logic that shapes a society change, societies transform accordingly. Following "the great transformation," as Polanyi (2001) calls it, after the 18th century, the state and corporate structures (i.e., the capitalist market system) have become the dominant institutional logics shaping the societies as well as the domains within the society such as law and education (Thornton & Ocasio, 2008). As a result, the vices of pre-modern societies have become the virtues of modern societies.

This chapter, first, critically evaluates the three core concepts of the morality of Islam in relation to finance, namely indebtedness, accumulation, and interest and explores their role in the global financial crisis of 2008. Second, the study traces the emergence and development of Islamic finance within the global financial system and discusses the role of instrumental morality in the convergence of the products and services (provided by the Islamic financial institutions (IFIs)) toward conventional institutions. Furthermore, the study discusses whether the IFIs have been successful in terms of offering a solution to the moral problems arising due to the operations of the conventional financial sector, with particular attention to the core principles explored in the first part. Lastly, the study examines the current trends in Malaysia, Turkey, and the Islamic Development Bank (IsDB) to envisage the future direction of Islamic finance.

In the next section, we approach these three concepts in the light of Islamic economics, and then, in the third section, we evaluate the global financial crisis of 2008 based on these moral concepts. In the fourth section, we examine

DOI: 10.4324/9781003377283-8

the Islamic financial sector and its location within the global economy. In the fifth section, we explore the success and failure of IFIs in terms of offering a solution to the moral problems arising due to the operations of the conventional financial sector. In the last section, we present concluding remarks and a way forward considering the prospects.

2 Core Moral Principles of Islam Related to Finance

In this section, we present the three core principles of the morality of Islam in relation to finance, namely indebtedness, accumulation, and interest. Although there are many important principles, due to space limitations, we evaluate only three principles that also played a crucial role in the global financial crisis of 2008.

2.1 Indebtedness

Islam does not prohibit borrowing (Al-Baqarah, 2/282) yet discourages it as this is evident in the supplication of Prophet Muhammad (peace be upon him): "O Allah, I seek refuge with you from all sins, and from being in debt" since debt might lead to telling a lie or breaking a promise (Sahih al-Bukhari, 2397). Besides such individual-level misbehaviors, debt can also cause social problems among community members (Sipon et al., 2014). The discouragement from debt was not limited to verbal warnings but also articulated by the refrainment of the Prophet from offering funeral prayers for Muslims until their debts are paid off (Sahih al-Bukhari, 2295).

In pre-modern Muslim societies, religion rather than the capitalist market system shaped the relationships and institutions (Thornton & Ocasio, 2008). Hence, "Indebtedness," even though allowed, is considered and perceived by Muslims as a vice that one should avoid as much as possible. However, in the modern market system, debt lies at the heart of the economy. Hence it is a reasonable act, if not a virtue (Lazzarato, 2012). We may consider debt, particularly with the purpose of consumption, as a colonization process. Spatial colonization, which had taken place during the 19th century, provided capitalism with unexplored lands for extension of the markets spatially, hence, sustaining the never-ending production process. However, in contemporary periods, capitalism – more or less – has reached every corner of the world, thus exhausting the spatial extension limits. From a capitalist perspective, particularly following the rise of neoliberalism after the 1970s, this brings us to a new colonization process, namely temporal colonization. Through the expansion of the credit, both at the individual (thanks to the banking system) and state level (thanks to the International Monetary Fund (IMF) and the World Bank (WB)), actors are indebted with the expectation of future welfare in exchange of submission to the demands of the lenders. These demands trap the individuals within the capitalist market system as a worker to earn money to repay the debts

Morality of Finance: An Islamic Economics Approach   119

and oblige the states to comply with neoliberal policies as a precondition of the IMF and the WB.

2.2 Accumulation

Accumulation is not a trivial act but an articulation of characteristic features of a human being dispraised in Qur'an (At-Takathur, 102/1–2) that might lead to individual punishment if the accumulated wealth is not used in the way of Allah (Tawbah, 9/34–35) and imbalances at the community level if it is circulated only among a small group of people (Al-Hashr, 59/7). If wealth is acquired lawfully and spent rightfully without greed, it is praised by the Prophet as narrated by Hakim bin Hizam: "I asked the Prophet (for some money) and he gave me, and then again I asked him and he gave me, and then again I asked him and he gave me and he then said, 'This wealth is (like) green and sweet (fruit), and whoever takes it without greed, Allah will bless it for him, but whoever takes it with greed, Allah will not bless it for him, and he will be like the one who eats but is never satisfied. And the upper (giving) hand is better than the lower (taking) hand'" (Sahih al-Bukhari, 6441). Hence, "being wealthy" is not a vice in itself. However, it can become a negative epithet depending on how and why wealth is acquired and spent. Based on the cited verses and hadith, it is clear that the accumulation of wealth through impermissible (haram) ways is forbidden.

Furthermore, the accumulation of wealth for the sake of accumulating more as an articulation of greediness is also a dispraised act since such an accumulation is contrary to sharing with others. It is important to note that the accumulated wealth is not a vice in itself but accumulation as a continuous act, particularly with greed, is a dispraised act. Hence, our discussion is not the permissibility or status of wealth one has, but the actions and intentions toward a never-ending accumulation process. This also includes a continuous accumulation of wealth (capital) with the purpose of production, as this becomes an end in itself rather than a means to achieve the objectives of Shariah.

Although the pre-modern mode of accumulation is mostly limited to the accumulation of wealth in terms of money, in the contemporary period, thanks to the advances in capitalism and moving from industrial capitalism to service-oriented capitalist modes of production, the act of accumulation is not limited to the wealth. The capitalist market system provides the individuals with opportunities to convert things beyond wealth into economic capital, such as human, cultural, and social capital (Bourdieu, 1986, p. 251).

For most of history, the accumulation of wealth had been an individual act motivated by the love of wealth itself. Following the commodification of money to sustain the unceasing production process after the industrial revolution (Polanyi, 2001), however, capital accumulation, through the financial system, particularly banking institutions, has become a necessity and social act, regardless of the amount of accumulation. In other words, financial institutions have played an intermediary role to channel the accumulated funds of the households or other market actors (lender-savers) to the parties in need of accumulated funds (borrower-spenders). Accumulation of funds and channeling them from savers to entrepreneurs efficiently lies at the heart of the modern capitalist market system as this ensures the growth of the economy, which is the primary goal of modern states. Hence, an individual vice of the pre-modern societies has become a virtue and a social act in the contemporary period. Although accumulation itself is problematic from the perspective of the morality of Islam, the way accumulated capital is utilized in financialized capitalism has become more problematic.

Financing is meant to provide the instruments and services as a means for production (Akgiray, 2019; Shiller, 2012a). In financialized capitalism, however, many corporates and financial organizations utilize their capitals to invest in various types of financial instruments instead of production (Lapavitsas, 2013), such as derivatives or similar instruments, invented through the commodification of risk, to increase their profit. The reason behind the shift from the utilization of capital in production to investment in financial instruments is that the latter provides more efficient and low transaction costs compared to the former (Deutschmann, 2011; Stockhammer, 2012). On the other hand, such financial instruments, which are beneficial for corporates in the pursuit of more profits at low cost, cause imbalances (e.g., due to the financial crisis) and inequalities (e.g., rich getting richer and poor getting poorer) in the society as the global financial crisis of 2008 evidence.

2.3 Interest

The prohibition of interest has become one of the central concepts of economic affairs in Islam, to the extent that people who keep interest-income are warned of war from Allah and His Messenger (Baqarah, 2/279). It is closely related to the previous two concepts since, in general, people are indebted in exchange for an interest payment in addition to the principal amount borrowed (whether it is borrowed for individual consumption or investment opportunity). Also, to provide a supply of credit in exchange for interest, particularly at relatively low-interest rates, the accumulation of money is required. Although the concept of interest has been practiced in pre-modern communities for centuries, after the commodification of money in the capitalist market system (Polanyi, 2001), it is located at the center of the economy. The ban on interest-bearing transactions in Islam has many pearls of wisdom, such as establishing profit-loss sharing between financier and entrepreneur (Chapra, 2006), "ensuring a just and equitable financial system" (Siddiqi, 2004, p. 34), avoiding exploitation, and decreasing the investment risk through equity financing (Iqbal, 2010). In this section, however, we only focus on the political economy aspect of the prohibition since this perspective helps us evaluating the outcome of the operations of the IFIs within the capitalist market system.

In financialized capitalism, the interest rate is the measure of everything; it is an indicator for the stability of an economy, the main parameter of the time value of money to calculate the present value of a money flow to compare alternative investment opportunities, and more importantly, the motivation to save money. Moreover, it is essential to point out the qualitative role of interest in a capitalist economy, which is, regardless of its rate, being the criteria for economic decision-making. Hence, although different levels of interest rate might lead to different decision outcomes, the interest is always at the center of each economic decision, even if the interest rate is zero (Mishkin & Eakins, 2018). In other words, although the quantitative value of interest rate is important for the functioning of a capitalist economy and may vary from one country to another, its qualitative role is similar in all capitalist economies. It is important to note that there are many interest-based instruments in a capitalist financial system. While one type of instrument might have a zero-interest rate (such as short-term treasury bills), there will always be other instruments with various risks and terms leading to non-zero interest rates. Even if one may claim that a zero-interest rate instrument is permissible since there is no interest payment, this is only a micro-level analysis of one type of contract. However, as we mentioned, it is important to dislocate the interest rate from its central position in the decision-making process. Therefore, an economy based on the morality of Islam cannot bestow the interest a central role in the decision-making process and establishing the relationships among individuals and institutions. In this regard, to establish an economic system based on the morality of Islam, it is important to promote profit-loss sharing (Chapra, 2006) rather than debt-based instruments, which lead to an increase of indebtedness of individuals and establishing "a just and equitable financial system" (Siddiqi, 2004, p. 34) that is not built upon the interest-based transactions.

The main characteristic of the IFIs is generally promoted as being interest-free. However, considering the above discussion, despite its Shariah compliance in terms of the form of the contracts, the market interest rate is still a determinant on "the price of every product and services" provided by the IFIs. From a political economy perspective, therefore, although the IFIs might provide Shariah-compliant products and services, due to conducting operations within a capitalist system, they do not remove the negative impacts of interest but only provides products and services that could be purchased by Muslim customers while obeying the formal aspect of the Islamic law.

3 Evaluating the Global Financial Crisis of 2008 through Indebtedness, Accumulation and Interest

During the last decade, plenty of research has been conducted to explore the reasons for the global financial crisis of 2008 and its characteristics with the hope that future crises might be prevented (e.g., A. Ahmed, 2010; Keen, 2017; Moshirian, 2011; Shiller, 2012b). Other researchers such as Mirowski (2013), however, argued that such crises are embedded within the capitalist market system, and it is impossible to prevent such crises unless a structural transformation takes place. We also advocate that financial crises are an inherent feature of capitalism. Furthermore, the regulations, though useful to alleviate the effects of a crisis, do not provide the ultimate solution for crises as the actors find a way out of the regulations (Aliber & Kindleberger, 2015). Moreover, the capitalists themselves are not affected in general due to the bailout mechanism of the states, but the everyday people suffer most from the consequences of the crises, which makes the capitalists more careless (Poole, 2009). Although it is impossible to narrow down the causes of a crisis, in this section, we discuss the global financial crisis of 2008 through three moral features of Islamic economics and how the absence of these features led to the crisis.

To make a profit, a seller must sell the products to customers who can afford them. However, if customers do not have the required money to afford a product, they can give up buying the product, delay buying the product until he/she has enough savings, or find financial support in the form of credit. The third option, taking loans from financial institutions, is the solution promoted in the financialized capitalism. Many investors earn interest income out of their accumulated capital through investing in debt instruments derived from distributed credits to the customers, such as "Collateralized Debt Obligation" (CDO), which had been popular during the crisis. To earn interest income through debt instruments, first, "the making of the indebted man" is required (Lazzarato, 2012). During the financial crisis of 2008, indebted man is made through the irrational assumption that house prices will increase forever (Aliber & Kindleberger, 2015).

In the first stage, "prime" customers with enough expected income to pay their debts in the long run are indebted. Although the morality of Islam discourages any kind of debt due to the vice it might lead, a capitalist social formation is built upon this vice to facilitate production, and hence, increase growth. The second stage of the process, however, had started due to the insufficiency of the eligible customers to exhausting the available sources for credit. In this stage, the credit was distributed to those who would probably not be able to pay the debt back; that is why the crisis is called "sub-prime mortgage crisis." Such generosity of credit expansion and the confidence of borrowers was due to the euphoria stage, as everyone irrationally expected that the house prices will always increase (Aliber & Kindleberger, 2015); hence, in the worst-case scenario, selling the house would compensate the expenses of the creditors and borrowers. However, in the end, the oversupply of the houses in the market led to the fall of the prices and then the crisis. While the first stage of the crisis should have mostly individual outcomes due to the commitment of long-term debt, the second stage, in which both creditors and borrowers undertake a higher risk, had consequences at the global scale due to the interconnectedness of the markets in financialized capitalism.

The existence of the second stage was mainly due to the high volume of accumulated wealth, which looks for and strives to create efficient ways to make a profit. Derivative instruments such as "CDOs" have been tools to make a profit through risky investments instead of using the accumulated capital for the productive investments that would benefit the society at large by creating employment in the market. Rather, debt contracts of individual customers are pooled together and sold to the investors hoping that cash flow will never be interrupted and profit income will continue. This is not a deviation from the aspirations of the market system but a consequence of the goal of profit maximization through efficient means by the corporates and investors.

During the industrial capitalism, the accumulated capital is used to make a profit through investing in the real economy for production. However, in the contemporary period, to achieve the same goal, accumulated capital is utilized in financial instruments to maximize profit. In the absence of accumulated capital at such volumes, the volume of the debt instruments would be less. However, since capital is accumulated at the hands of a small group of investors in capitalist societies, at the expense of the society, they strive to increase the wealth through interest. It is important to note the role of the state in capitalist societies as it is the state that bails out the big investors after a crisis. Hence, the debt becomes a burden on the shoulders of everyday people (Poole, 2009).

Last but not least, interest lies at the heart of the crisis and the capitalist market system. Thanks to interest, money becomes a commodity like any other commodity in the market instead of a medium of exchange. As a result, those who have accumulated capital have the options of both investing the capital for productive means and lending for interest income. Due to the efficiency and low-transaction cost, the financial instruments of the financialized capitalism provide better tools compared to the investment in productive projects. This has resulted in further financialization, leading to disembeddedness of finance from the real economy and society (Fimbel et al., 2015).

As mentioned earlier, the outcomes of financialized capitalism are not considered as perverseness since a political economy is based on interest. Efficiency and low-transaction cost at the core would lead to heavy usage of debt instruments to utilize the accumulated capital, particularly if the state bails out the investors and corporates in case of an unexpected negative outcome. The second stage of the crisis, in which the sub-prime customers are indebted, hence, was a necessity to utilize the funds otherwise invested with less return.

4 Islamic Finance: Some Moral Reflections in the Global Economy

From the 1970s onwards, Islamic finance performed a moderate transactional development, which is evident in most international reports on the IFIs.[1] This was interpreted as encouraging progress in terms of the material development of Muslim societies in the post-colonial period. The achievement also meant that Islamic finance has a great potential in securing its position in the global financial system. The quick implications of such an advancement recall the increase of social welfare and prosperity in the Muslim societies, and it did so, albeit partially. However, together with the appreciation of transactional development, Islamic finance today has also been expected to bring transformational development, which goes beyond material progress through reconsidering moral outcomes of financial transactions.

Recalling that Islamic finance has initially been envisaged as an ethically driven financial model that is shaped by the theoretical underpinnings of Islamic economics, which essentialize Islamic morality (Asutay, 2013), transformational development depends entirely on both financial performance and social performance.[2] The avoidance of *riba* (interest) and *gharar* (excessive uncertainty), the promotion of profit-and-loss sharing (PLS) and risk-sharing, for instance, are adopted as Islamic financial principles, not because of their efficient outcomes in various financial operations, but more importantly, due to their just and equitable consequences on economies, and in a broader sense, on societies. The recent historical experiences show such an orientation. Before the expansion of Islamic finance as commercial banks in the second half of the 1970s, local banking and finance initiatives in the post-colonial Muslim lands were formed under cooperative structures, which prioritized PLS and risk-sharing. Tabung Haji and Mit Ghamr, the two well-known successful experiences are today still remembered and cherished in the related academic studies (see, for instance, Alonso, 2015; Hegazy, 2007; Orhan, 2018) due to their transformational developmentalist potential despite they remained local in Malaysia and Egypt, respectively. The two examples showed how Muslim financial alternatives could bring welfare, justice and equity altogether without mimicking global financial capitalist practices. Notwithstanding such ideals, the local political agenda played an adverse role on the viability and sustainability of Mit Ghamr (Mayer, 1985), while Tabung Haji still operates successfully in Malaysia with ever increasing savings of pilgrim funds.

Global finance is not as it was in the 1970s. When Islamic commercial banks mushroomed in the 1970s all over the Muslim world, global finance was experiencing heavy financialization,[3] which brought domestic finance a significant share in the entire economy. The vital question in the minds of Muslim economists was about the way to widen Islamic finance without succumbing to the financialization trend that makes a clear distinction between the real economy and the financial economy. If a crossroad is sought in the recent history of Islamic finance, this distinction can provide a fitting example. While financialized economies introduced new forms of financial instruments in the last decades, which are highly debt-based, more gambling oriented, and having risk shifting character, Islamic finance was expected to embrace PLS and risk-sharing objectives to create an alternative sector. However, convergence has occurred on the side of Islamic banks toward mimicking conventional financial operations under instrumentally moralized forms of financial dealings (Asutay, 2012a).

Islamic banks, by definition, aim to sustain profit maximization and capital accumulation, but due to some Islamic restrictions, they had to give up traditional financial instruments based on partnership; instead, they developed alternative instruments to maximize their profit, which are highly debt-based such as *tawarruq* and *sukuk al-ijara*. Since these two objectives could not be achieved simultaneously in the last 50 years and seem not to be achieved in the future, Islamic banks opted for sustaining their presence and growing within the global financial system with a more form-oriented understanding. In other words, it could be possible to develop debt-based financial instruments and eschew participatory financial dealings that require PLS and risk-sharing operations through form-based understanding. Therefore, instead of partnership models, Islamic banks offered debt-based alternatives such as *murabaha, tawarruq*, and *ijara sukuk*. These alternatives dominated Islamic money and capital market instruments. The consequence was the instrumentalization of Islamic morality to form-based understanding.

The convergence of Islamic finance toward the global financial system has still been criticized by various scholars due to the failure of bringing transformational development (see, for instance, Asutay, 2007; Azarian, 2011; Hoggarth, 2016; Mohamad & Saravanamuttu, 2015; Rethel, 2011). The barriers against such development exist because of the replication of conventional financial logic. For instance, *murabaha*, as the most common instrument used by more than 95% of all Islamic financial instruments, has similar effects on the economy with those conventional bank credits. While these credits increase the indebtedness of households and firms and hence the financialization of the economy, income disparities worsen both locally and internationally.

Although *murabaha* contract has a direct effect on the real economy since its subject is the exchange of some assets, it is a debt-based financial instrument that increases indebtedness and contributes indirectly to the "peripheral financialization" (see, for the concept, Becker et al., 2010). On the other hand, when looked at the share of Islamic finance sectors, sukuk is the second most used instrument. However, global sukuk applications are made mostly under *ijara sukuk*, which is mostly a short-term contract with minimum risk that resembles bonds. That is why it is also called an Islamic bond. When these two most used instruments are left behind for a while, the remaining constituents of Islamic finance, such as takaful (Islamic insurance) and Islamic funds, which are not more than 2% globally, are not different from *murabaha* and sukuk in the sense of going beyond efficiency-oriented financial logic.

Putting aside the formalistic view that attaches minimal transformative role to Islamic banks due to their nature as "banks," and therefore, having limited elbowroom, the expectations from Islamic banks now narrowed down to fulfilling at least instrumental morality comprehensively. By instrumental morality, we mean no ethical authority over the functioning of the economy with the manifestation of self-regulated market understanding. Instrumental morality mainly rests on no ethical ground, and its conceptualization corresponds to what Bauman (1994) states "self-founding morality" or "ethically unfounded morality" in our times. Substantive morality, on the other hand, challenges any form of instrumenting morality and its dissociation from ethical grounds and claims an embedded nature of moral understanding, which covers an entire field, including modes of production, social formation of society, and institutional articulations of knowledge.

Islamic finance would have made use of substantive morality to resist being part of conventional financial structure in terms of subtracting moral character from the core of financial activities. However, the experience has so far demonstrated that morality has been instrumentalized through a form-based understanding of Islamic finance.

5 Islamic Finance: What Moral Objectives Have Been Achieved So Far?

The short history of modern Islamic banking and finance evidence that a niche market can only grow fast within the global financial economy so long as it gradually converges toward the mainstream. However, it would also be possible for the IFIs to preserve their position and keep their authenticity through showing disruptive business character, which suggests alternative financial models in the light of sharing economy values and principles. The reasons behind the convergence are multifold, including political backwardness of Muslim countries, suffering from neocolonialist policies of the WB and IMF, political and social instabilities, etc. Due to the impact of these factors, the general conduct of affairs in economies of Muslim societies has been on the side of instrumental morality vis-à-vis substantive morality (Yılmaz, 2018).

Putting aside the authenticity loss concomitant with adopting instrumental morality, the achievements that Islamic finance reached over the decades and social and economic costs of performing such an achievement can be explored. When social dimensions of IFIs are raised amongst the critics, the general justification by the practitioners of the field cannot go beyond bringing moral issues as an exogenous layer. In other words, social contributions of Islamic finance toward the global economy are mostly addressed on a philanthropy basis, such as (i) interest-free loan (*qard hasan*) that cannot go beyond 1% amongst the Islamic financial instruments, (ii) Islamic microcredits as part of the objective of financial inclusion that shifted the entire risk to the small- and medium-sized enterprises and also made them more indebted, (iii) environmental-friendly investments such as green sukuk that have a long way to sophisticate, model, and diffuse all over the world, (iv) supporting education through scholarships which are raised by Islamic banks' particular gains from interest-linked income, (v) restorations of old Islamic historical buildings.

These contributions cannot be neglected, and individually they all show more concern on the side of the IFIs about social developmental issues. However, the overall impact of such social initiatives on society and the economy remains minimal. The reason is that instrumentally moral applications can hardly bring disrupting effects on breaking conventional financial model. Instead, it introduces some moral layers to the existing financial relations at the very outside. Islamic finance, in this sense, suggests a softer and more humane way of doing financial dealings compared to the global financial system. The idea with Islamic finance is that it may not contribute to preventing the fragility of the global financial system. Still, at least Muslim economies wherein Islamic financial operations have a considerable share remain less prone to the effects of global financial crises. Therefore, post-crisis impacts of the global financial system on the human, economy, society, and environment can be diminished.

The moral concerns against the nature of the global financial system are being raised strongly, especially in the last two decades. In response to this, some new financial objectives are seen in the global financial industry, such as environmental, social and governance (ESG), sustainable development goals (SDGs), and corporate social responsibility (CSR) (see: H. Ahmed et al., 2015). These developments aim to regulate the highly corrupted global financial industry based on some normative goals so that the new financial route lessens global inequality and finance serves better in line with the societal development (Akgiray, 2019; Shiller, 2012a). Islamic finance, similarly, adopted these objectives to strengthen its moral character. This morality, again, is incorporated into the Islamic financial sphere as an exogenous social layer. There are many academic studies that explore how Islamic finance has great potential in fulfilling SDGs or ESG compared to conventional finance (see: Ahmed, 2017; Aström, 2011; Aydin, 2015; Gundogdu, 2018 among others). Instead of bringing a critical approach to the consistency of SDGs with Islamic moral values, the general attitude is less cautious with the implications of SDGs, and hence, perceives the goals as modern articulations of Islamic values (Asutay & Yılmaz, 2018, p. 378). In fact, instrumental morality reiterates its superiority over the authenticity of substantive morality.

6 A Way Forward: Where Is Islamic Finance Heading to?

Global finance is in search of a new moral narrative for its justification in the 21st century. The social and economic catastrophes due to the frequent financial crises shake the trust in capitalist modernity, and hence financialized capitalism must find new inroads. Despite the short experience, Islamic finance similarly aims to increase trust in its financial instruments due to the harsh criticisms mentioned above. Since it has not yet generated paradigmatic change globally, the Islamic finance experts of the governmental boards in different countries announce new financial approaches to bring morality to the center of Islamic finance, albeit instrumentally.

IFIs in Malaysia, for instance, had a long experience with the objective of meeting neoliberal policies. It has been very successful when transactional development of Islamic finance is considered; global statistics also approve of this success. However, when transformational development is rendered,

128 *Harun Şencal and İsa Yılmaz*

the Malaysian government acknowledges taking further action to establish Islamic moral values within Islamic finance in an authentic way rather than mimicking universally accepted development goals, including SDGs, ESG, and human development. In this sense, a new policy was introduced recently by the Malaysian central bank (Bank Negara Malaysia) announced with a strategy paper known as "value-based intermediation (VBI)." VBI mainly aims to develop some strategies which strengthen the role of Islamic banks in Malaysia. What makes VBI different from other financial initiatives in different parts of the Islamic world is that VBI recognizes the urgent need to focus on "value creation and value-based businesses that reflect the true essence of Islamic finance" (Value-Based Intermediation, 2018, p. 2), as uttered by the governor of the Bank Negara Malaysia. Therefore, while VBI leads to grow Islamic business and finance and provides profitable opportunities to the shareholders, it also aims to generate impactful contributions to society. This objective is demonstrated in the future landscape in the strategy paper shown in Table 8.1.

The search for new morally oriented financial initiatives is also valid for IsDB group. The group recently announced a full commitment to the 2030 Agenda of the United Nations. The group advocates that 17 SDGs and 169 specific targets are entirely in line with the objectives and principles of Islamic development (IsDB, n.d.); thereby, it suggests all its member countries reshape their Islamic banking and financial structures in line with the SDGs. The call from IsDB shows another piece of evidence that the existing operations within Islamic finance did not go beyond profit maximization, shareholder value orientation, and adaptation to the market rules of efficiency, all of which further exacerbated the global inequality so far. Thus, the 2030 Agenda seems a good alternative for realizing the untapped potentials of Islamic finance.

Table 8.1 Value-Based Intermediation Objectives

Perceived Current Financial Landscape	Envisioned Future Financial Landscape
Driven by the short term and narrow bottom line	Driven by long term and wider objectives (profit, people, and planet)
Performance measurement focuses on the financial aspect	Performance measurement considers both financial and non-financial aspects
Innovation mainly to create a competitive advantage for shareholders and players	Innovation to create values for all
Good conduct driven by regulation	An impact-based approach that fosters good conduct
Minimal roles of other stakeholders	Meaningful and active roles of key stakeholders (consumers, employees, and public)

Source: Bank Negara Malaysia (2018, p. 10).

Malaysia and IsDB Group reflect two different models of Islamic finance, one is practiced in Southeast Asia, and the other is practiced in the Gulf Cooperation Countries. Turkey, on the other hand, has a more hybrid road in its Islamic finance experience. While the increase of Islamic banks owes much to the trade liberalizations adopted in the 1980s in Turkey, and hence adopting neoliberal logic to strengthen its development, the last 40 years of experience brought moral considerations into the fore not much different than the experiences of other Muslim countries. Islamic banks in Turkey are known as "participation banks," which give special emphasis on the implications of participation to the profit and loss in banking activities. Yet, prevailing financial practices cannot escape from the typical criticisms raised against global Islamic finance. Thus, while the Malaysian model is adopted in practice, a morally authentic alternative is still searched for a long time. Recently, some new Islamic finance departments were established under Istanbul International Finance Center. These departments are all using the discourse of "Participation Finance," which is consciously chosen to give an image that Turkey's Islamic finance is not limited to banking sectors, but a broader sectoral development is aimed. Also, the use of the participation concept is aimed to evoke that the model appeals not only to Islamic economies but also to the broader economies in the world as a universal truth.

The examples given above show the current trends in global Islamic finance in locating Islamic morality at the center of financial dealings. While substantive morality has a long way to be achieved, instrumental moralities are seen in different Islamic financial centers all over the world. It is, of course, debatable whether the authenticity of Islamic finance is gained by adopting a hybrid financial model with a mix of traditional Islamic contracts and conventional financial contracts. Yet, it is more important whether the sector's development brings transactional and transformational development together. It seems that unless a paradigmatic shift takes place with substantive morality, instrumental morality can only provide Islamic finance with a softer and more humane way of doing financial dealings.

7 Conclusion

The nexus between morality and finance has a hard task to fully comprehend, especially in the age of finance. By looking from the angle of conventional understanding, there is no substantial role given to the morality in the global financial system since a harmonical interaction within the economic system is assumed to prevail thanks to Smithian notions of the invisible hand and interdependence through the division of labor. Market is believed an area that has no ethical considerations due to the value-free character of the capitalist system. However, an Islamic economic system, including the Islamic financial industry, puts morality at the center of its theory. In this manner, Islamic economics gains its authenticity from being a value-loaded system.

The global financial outlook does not seem promising in terms of creating an equitable environment for the future. Thus, moral objections against the global financial system are being raised more frequently in the last two decades. Islamic finance, amidst such developments, gains particular importance due to its moral promises within the financial system. Despite having a very small share within the global financial system, it has a significant transactional development in the last 40 years. Not just transactional, but also transformational development is now expected from IFIs to suggest an alternative to the ongoing inequalities, social and environmental problems. This chapter argues that the normative dimensions of Islamic finance provide authentic solutions to the most common moral problems of the conventional financial system, such as indebtedness, accumulation, and interest. As elaborated thoroughly in this study, the moral objectives of IFIs have been practiced very limitedly. It is necessary, hence, to develop some policies within the IFIs to reconstitute substantive morality.

This chapter suggests some short-run and long-run objectives that IFIs should fulfil as the developmental goals of the Islamic economics. Amongst the short-run objectives, developing equity-based structures such as private equity, venture capital, project and trade finance are essential for an equitable and just financial system. Therefore, Islamic banks should increase their participation investments where banks behave as capital partners with a share in projects within PLS arrangements. In addition, Islamic banks must increase direct investments where they employ funds independently in profitable projects.

Under its social performance objectives, Islamic banks should further finance "unbankable" individuals through microfinance and other financial instruments such as *zakat* funds and *qard al-hasan* (charitable giving). Moreover, to better perform socially, other forms of sophisticated and structured financing like SMEs financing, Islamic pawnbroking, Islamic crowdfunding and fintech, and green sukuk should be considered operational objectives.

The long-run objectives, on the other hand, should mainly challenge the logic of conventional banking and finance. While commercial and transactional performance is significant in expanding the capacity of Islamic finance, this achievement is only meaningful if it leads to the transformational development of societies where Islamic banks are operating. This consequentialist approach necessitates an objection toward the hegemony of debt-based understanding, which Islamic banks inherited from the conventional economic system, by which Muslim societies are getting more indebted and hence financialized. Despite such a financializing trend, PLS and risk-sharing alternatives can be modelled and turned into new financial instruments as the main thrust of Islamic finance (Asutay, 2014).

Additionally, regulatory and institutional renewing is another must for creating Islamic finance as resilient finance. Therefore, there is a need to develop new financial standardizations by Islamic international bodies in the light of authentic Islamic principles. Moreover, the logic of the corporate

Morality of Finance: An Islamic Economics Approach 131

governance model shaped Islamic banks should be reformed from shareholding value maximization to the stakeholder model. Lastly, the social responsibility roles of Islamic banking institutions should not be relegated to charitable giving. Instead, the social and development character must be expanded toward the operations of Islamic banks in the form of PLS and risk-sharing (Asutay, 2014).

The short-run and the long-run policy suggestions put forward above can be catalysts for Islamic finance to move toward the initial aspirations, which considers Islamic finance as embedded in the real economy and operating for stakeholder-centered development.

Notes

1 See some popular annual reports on global Islamic financial development published by, for instance, The Banker: Top 500 IFIs, Islamic Financial Services Board (IFSB) Industry Stability Reports, ICD Thomson Reuters Islamic Finance Development Report, amongst many others.
2 Evaluation of banks' operations' impacts on environment, society and other social institutions like family etc.
3 There is a rich literature on financialization in the heterodox economy. Some prominent studies are Epstein (2005), Krippner (2011), Lapavitsas (2013).

References

Ahmed, A. (2010). Global financial crisis: An Islamic finance perspective. *International Journal of Islamic and Middle Eastern Finance and Management, 3*(4), 306–320. https://doi.org/10.1108/17538391011093252

Ahmed, H. (2017, November 18). *Contribution of Islamic Finance to the 2030 agenda for sustainable development.* High-level Conference on Financing for Development and the Means of Implementation of the 2030 Agenda for Sustainable Development: From country initiatives to global advances – mobilizing financing for sustainable development, Doha, Qatar.

Ahmed, H., Mohieldin, M., Verbeek, J., & Aboulmagd, F. (2015). *On the sustainable development goals and the role of Islamic finance* (No. 7266). The World Bank.

Akgiray, V. (2019). *Good finance: Why we need a new concept of finance.* Bristol University Press.

Aliber, R. Z., & Kindleberger, C. P. (2015). *Manias, panics and crashes: A history of financial crises* (7th ed.). New York: Palgrave Macmillan.

Alonso, I. M. (2015). Mit Ghamr: Pioneer in Islamic Banking. *10th International Conference on Islamic Economics and Finance,* 30–31.

Aström, Z. H. O. (2011). Paradigm shift for sustainable development: The contribution of Islamic economics. *Journal of Economic and Social Studies, 1*(1), 73–82.

Asutay, M. (2007). A political economy approach to Islamic economics: Systemic understanding for an alternative economic system. *Kyoto Bulletin of Islamic Area Studies, 1*(2), 3–18.

Asutay, M. (2012a). Conceptualising and locating the social failure of Islamic finance: Aspirations of Islamic moral economy vs the realities of Islamic finance. *Asian and African Area Studies, 11*(2), 93–113.

132   *Harun Şencal and İsa Yılmaz*

Asutay, M. (2012b). Locating Islamic moral economy within emergence economics and evaluating the Islamic banking and finance in relation to the aspirations of Islamic moral economy. *Presented at the Kyoto University-Durham University Joint International Symposium 2012: Emergence and Feedback in Physical and Social Systems,* 27–29th November 2012.

Asutay, M. (2013). Islamic moral economy as the foundation of Islamic finance. In V. Cattelan (Ed.), *Islamic finance in Europe: Towards plural financial system.* Edward Elgar Publishing.

Asutay, M., & Yılmaz, I. (2018). Re-embedding Maqasid al-Shari'ah in the essential methodology of Islamic economics. In M. T. El-Mesawi (Ed.), *Maqasid al-Shari'ah: Explorations and implications.* Islamic Book Trust.

Aydin, N. (2015). Islamic social business for sustainable development and subjective wellbeing. *International Journal of Islamic and Middle Eastern Finance and Management,* 8(4), 491–507.

Azarian, R. (2011). Outline of an economic sociology of Islamic banking. *International Journal of Business and Social Science,* 2(17), 258–268.

Bauman, Z. (1994). Morality without ethics. *Theory, Culture & Society,* 11(4), 1–34.

Becker, J., Jäger, J., Leubolt, B., & Weissenbacher, R. (2010). Peripheral financialization and vulnerability to crisis: A regulationist perspective. *Competition & Change,* 14(3–4), 225–247.

Bourdieu, P. (1986). The forms of capital. In J. G. Richardson (Ed.), *Handbook of theory and research for the sociology of education* (pp. 241–258). Greenwood.

Chapra, M. U. (2006). Why has Islam prohibited interest? In A. Thomas (Ed.), *Interest in Islamic economics: Understanding Riba* (pp. 95–110). Routledge. http://site.ebrary.com/id/10163547

Deutschmann, C. (2011). Limits to financialization sociological analyses of the financial crisis. *European Journal of Sociology,* 52(3), 347–389.

Epstein, G. A. (2005). *Financialization and the world economy.* Edward Elgar Publishing.

Fimbel, E., Binninger, A.-S., & Karyotis, C. (2015). Demateriality: A key factor in the embedding of society within commodification and financialization. *Society and Business Review,* 10(1), 76–90. https://doi.org/10.1108/SBR-03-2014-0011

Gundogdu, A. S. (2018). An inquiry into Islamic finance from the perspective of sustainable development goals. *European Journal of Sustainable Development,* 7(4), 381–381.

Hallaq, W. (2012). *The impossible state: Islam, politics, and modernity's moral predicament.* Columbia University Press.

Hegazy, W. S. (2007). Contemporary Islamic finance: From socioeconomic idealism to pure legalism. *Chicago Journal of International Law,* 7(2), 581–603.

Hoggarth, D. (2016). The rise of Islamic finance: Post-colonial market-building in central Asia and Russia. *International Affairs,* 92(1), 115–136.

Iqbal, M. M. (2010). Prohibition of interest and economic rationality. *Arab Law Quarterly,* 24(3), 293–308. https://doi.org/10.1163/157302510X508346

IsDB. (n.d.). *Sustainable development goals.* Retrieved April 26, 2021, from https://www.isdb.org/what-we-do/sustainable-development-goals

Keen, S. (2017). *Can we avoid another financial crisis?* Wiley.

Krippner, G. R. (2011). *Capitalizing on crisis: The political origins of the rise of finance.* Harvard University Press.

Lapavitsas, C. (2013). *Profiting without producing: How finance exploits us all.* Verso Books.

Lazzarato, M. (2012). *The making of the indebted man: An essay on the neoliberal condition.* Semiotext(e).

Mayer, A. E. (1985). Islamic banking and credit policies in the Sadat era: The social origins of Islamic banking in Egypt. *Arab Law Quarterly, 1*(1), 32–50.

Mirowski, P. (2013). *Never let a serious crisis go to waste: How neoliberalism survived the financial meltdown.* Verso Books.

Mishkin, F. S., & Eakins, S. G. (2018). *Financial markets and institutions.* Pearson.

Mohamad, M., & Saravanamuttu, J. (2015). Islamic banking and finance: Sacred alignment, strategic alliances. *Pacific Affairs, 88*(2), 193–213.

Moshirian, F. (2011). The global financial crisis and the evolution of markets, institutions and regulation. *Journal of Banking & Finance, 35*(3), 502–511. https://doi.org/10.1016/j.jbankfin.2010.08.010

Orhan, Z. H. (2018). Mit Ghamr Savings Bank: A role model or an irreplicable Utopia? *The Journal of Humanity and Society, 8*(2), 85–102.

Polanyi, K. (2001). *The great transformation: The political and economic origins of our time* (2nd ed.). Beacon Press.

Poole, W. (2009). Moral hazard: The long-lasting legacy of bailouts. *Financial Analysts Journal, 65*(6), 17–23. https://doi.org/10.2469/faj.v65.n6.8

Rethel, L. (2011). Whose legitimacy? Islamic finance and the global financial order. *Review of International Political Economy, 18*(1), 75–98.

Shiller, R. J. (2012a). *Finance and the good society.* Princeton University Press.

Shiller, R. J. (2012b). *The subprime solution: How today's global financial crisis happened, and what to do about it.* Princeton University Press.

Siddiqi, M. N. (2004). *Riba, bank interest and the rationale of its prohibition.* Islamic Research and Training Institute.

Sipon, S., Othman, K., Ghani, Z. A., & Radzi, H. M. (2014). The impact of religiosity on financial debt and debt stress. *Procedia - Social and Behavioral Sciences, 140,* 300–306. https://doi.org/10.1016/j.sbspro.2014.04.424

Stockhammer, E. (2012). Financialization, income distribution and the crisis. *Investigación Económica, 71*(279), 39–70.

Thornton, P. H., & Ocasio, W. (2008). Institutional logics. *The Sage Handbook of Organizational Institutionalism, 840,* 99–128.

Value-based intermediation: Strengthening the roles and impact of Islamic finance (Strategy Paper BNM/RH/DP 034–2). (2018). Bank Negara Malaysia.

Yılmaz, I. (2018). *Essays in Islamic moral economy: Developmentalist promises, the delusion of financialisation and methodological dilemma* [PhD Thesis]. Durham University.

9 Issues and Practical Solutions of Shariah Governance in Islamic Financial Institutions

Burak Çıkıryel

1 Introduction

Corporate governance can be defined as a system of rules, relations, and processes by which companies are managed and directed. In a conventional sense, good corporate governance promotes capital formation, fosters involvement in value-maximizing behavior, reduces the cost of capital, and encourages disclosure and transparency. Conventional corporate governance takes its roots from socially derived *"secular humanist"* values rather than relying on religious and moral authority. The main driving forces of conventional corporate governance are the *"self-interest"* and its manifestation, *"agency theory"* (Lewis 2005).

On the contrary, the basis of Islamic corporate governance (ICG) differs from that of conventional corporate governance. ICG takes its roots from the Shariah. It literally refers to the *"way"* of life while it means, in a broad sense, Islam's legal system that encompasses all aspects of an individual's life. Shariah claims sovereignty over all ethical and social aspects of life, including both criminal and civil jurisdiction. As every act of an individual life must conform to Islamic principles, the same is expected for the corporation to follow Shariah and observe its ethical standards. These principles describe what is true, fair, and just, and they guide us to find a general framework of corporate governance, its business ethics, responsibilities, financial principles, and standards. Thus, ICG is a set of rules and practices (derived from the guidance of Shariah) that define the rights and responsibilities of corporate members and explain how to control and operate a company.

Since equity-based financial contracts are very important and constitute the backbone of the ICG mechanism, good corporate governance requires more attributes in ICG than its conventional peer. Given the moral hazard and agency problems closely related to the equity-based financial contracts, the good ICG needs respect for property rights and trustworthiness, truthfulness, faithfulness to the terms and conditions of contracts, sufficient disclosure and transparency, noninterference with the functioning of market and price mechanism. Abiding the market rules provides a sound economy where the information flows are uninterrupted, and market participants perform

DOI: 10.4324/9781003377283-9

their transactions confidently with minimal concern for the uncertainty associated with the other participants' actions and reactions (Askari et al. 2012).

Iqbal and Mirakhor (2004) revealed that two fundamental principles of the Islamic economic system, property rights and contracts, make up the basis of ICG. These two concepts also mandate the objective function of economic agents, including legal entities. Furthermore, Iqbal and Mirakhor (2004) presented that a corporation in an Islamic economic environment can be considered as "nexus-of-contracts." Whose main objective is to minimize transaction costs and maximize profits and returns to its investor contingent upon the restrictions that these objectives do not contravene property rights[1] of others whether it is associated with the corporation directly or indirectly.

Basically, the ultimate objectives of the Islamic economic system are to attain falah[2] and to establish social justice and fairness among the members of society. To achieve those objectives, corporations would play significant roles as economic agents in an Islamic economic system. There are four main institutional components of ICG: Shura (consultative council), Hisba, Shariah supervisory process, and audit (Lewis 2005). Shura refers to the collective decision taken by explicit members of a corporation. By expressing explicit members, it means those who get affected directly by a corporation's decision, such as shareholders and employees. Implicit members of the corporation, say environment or its representatives, do not necessarily participate in the decision-making process and do not directly get affected by a corporation's decision, but their rights are protected through sound institutional arrangements and market rules. Therefore, institutional arrangements should take these considerations into account and be carefully framed. They must ensure that market rules do not leave any loopholes that may lead to the violation of any individual's rights. In a nutshell, Hisba is a government institution and ensures that the corporations maintain ethical principles of Islam during their market transactions. If there is a breach detected over the course of market dealings, it would take necessary corrective measures and monitor the observance of those measures. As for Shariah supervisory process, it offers the maintenance of effective Shariah compliance, just and fair relations of a corporation with its constituents, enough disclosure and transparency, honest bookkeeping process, proper advertisement contents, calculation and distribution of zakat, protection of the rights of every interested party, and so on. Finally, auditors are responsible for overall Shariah compliance of operation, preparing reports, and submitting them to the board of directors. The auditing process can be carried out internally or externally, or both.

1.1 Shareholders versus Stakeholders

Another important theoretical discussion about corporate governance is which group's interest should be prioritized among different interested parties within the institutional framework. There are mainly two different views

136   *Burak Çıkıryel*

that emerged in the literature, Anglo-Saxon and European models (Cernat 2004; Ooghe and de Langhe 2002; Pillay 2013). On the one hand, the Anglo-Saxon model is commonly practiced in individualistic business societies such as the United States, Great Britain, and Commonwealth Countries. This model prioritizes the interest of shareholders over all interested parties in the corporation. In other words, shareholders are given vested rights to control the corporation, and they have managers serve their fiduciary duties for shareholders' best interest alone. In this model, the main objective of the corporation is to maximize the shareholder's wealth. On the other hand, the European model offers the right to all stakeholders to participate in the corporate decision-making process that has an impact on them. Managers discharge their fiduciary duties to serve the interest of all stakeholders such as employees, suppliers, and distributors. The objective of the firm is to serve the interests of all stakeholders.

The stance of most authors discussing the subject from the Islamic economics point of view takes the side with stakeholder approach or modified version of it (Askari et al. 2012; Bhatti and Ishaq 2008; Chapra and Ahmed 2002; Grassa 2013; Iqbal and Mirakhor 2004). Even this can be understood from the core of ICG's institutional arrangements, where a corporate decision is taken by a consultative council that includes everyone directly gets affected by a corporate decision. However, this section briefly highlights the important differences between the conventional and Islamic stakeholder approaches, shows how ICG conceives it, and recommends how to improve the ICG framework considering other approaches.

In ICG, having all the stakeholders join a decision-making process emanates from the divine authority itself (property rights of Islam), not because of the "secular humanist" approach. The main difference here is that the ultimate accountability of a board in ICG is not only to a company or stakeholders but also to the God (Allah SWT), the ultimate authority who leads to success and welfare (Ginena and Hamid 2015). ICG needs to be inclusive enough during a decision-making process so that cooperation among economic agents spills over the social life of Muslims, leading to the fulfilment of spiritual and worldly needs of the Islamic community. For instance, French law stipulates that large publicly listed companies allow employees to elect the directors (Ben Bouheni, Ammi, and Levy 2016). Such an example can also be applicable to ICG as well. This has two major impacts on corporate employees. First, employees feel that they are part of the company at which they are serving, and they have a right to exert influence on the company's future. Second, the company's management makes them express their problems and look for possible solutions at a higher level, which will make them feel considered. Such an inclusive approach of the corporate framework will lead to strengthen the social bond among the communities serving mostly to the spiritual atmosphere.

On the whole, any individual or group with whom a corporation has implicit or explicit contractual liabilities may qualify as a stakeholder. Because of certain constraints, everyone cannot take part in a decision-making process unless they are directly affected. It is worth recalling that those who do not directly get affected are called above as implicit members of the corporate governance framework. Their rights should be protected through a sound institutional framework and market rules. There is always deviation of the expected behavior of economic agents, but this can be handled through a well-established incentive mechanism in the economy. Lastly, apart from being inclusive, ICG protects the rights of small shareholders by institutionalizing their rights into the institutional framework without leaving it to the discretion of the individual corporation. Since the rights of small investors are embedded into the legal framework, it will prevent the abuses of the controlling shareholder position on them.

This chapter attempts to address the issues of Shariah governance (SG) in Islamic financial institutions (IFIs). It begins with the definition of Islamic and conventional corporate governance, and it is followed by making a comparison between the two frameworks. The fundamentals of ICG are explained in detail, emphasizing the components of its institutional framework. Then, the stance of ICG on the shareholder versus stakeholder model was identified. After highlighting that SG can be considered as part of the ICG framework, the issues related to SG are discussed, paying more attention to the Shariah supervisory board (SSB). Finally, the chapter ends by proposing a new SG framework to overcome the current issues and bring a unique perspective on the Shariah supervisory process in IFIs.

2 The Issues of SG in IFIs

The above-mentioned ICG comprehensive institutional framework has not been fully implemented yet. However, IFIs, throughout their development, have come up with some divisions within their institutional framework to carry out Shariah compliance procedures such as SSB, Shariah review, Shariah audit, and Shariah risk management units. These concepts as a whole are called SG in the literature. There should be no confusion between ICG and SG. ICG refers to a set of rules and practices (derived from the guidance of Shariah) that define the rights and responsibilities of corporate members and explain how to control and operate a company. In other words, ICG explains how an Islamic corporate system works in a broad sense considering Shariah principles. However, SG can be regarded as a part of the ICG framework, and it mainly concentrates on the Shariah compliance of IFIs in the course of their operation. In modern IFIs, the SG's scope of work usually revolves around product development, preparing contractual templates, overseeing transactional flows and advertisements, assessing Shariah non-compliance risks, detecting Shariah non-compliance income and its purifications, calculation of zakat and its distribution, reviewing, and auditing. As explained above, the ICG is beyond these activities and represents the corporate system itself. The important message that should be emphasized here is

138 Burak Çıkıryel

that since the IFIs ensure the Islamicity of their activities, their management and governance must also reflect the Islamic identity, which rationalizes the significance of forming sound and sustainable ICG (Sencal and Asutay 2021).

The objective of this chapter is to address the issues of the SG, paying more attention to the SSB that plays a significant role in the Shariah compliance procedures in IFIs. SSB is one of the components of the SG framework in modern IFIs. Its responsibilities include verifying permissible financial instruments and contractual templates, overseeing transactional flows and advertisements, assessing Shariah non-compliance risks and reporting, detecting Shariah non-compliance income and its purifications, calculation of zakat and its distribution. IFIs in some countries only have one SSB at the institutional level, and they are not held responsible for their decision to any higher authority at the government level (regulatory body). However, some countries have a two-layer SG framework where SSB is established at both institutional and governmental levels. In this framework, SSB at the institutional level usually seeks the approval of their decision from SSB at the governmental level. It is a two-sided process. In this section, the issues of SG are discussed by paying close attention to the SSB.

2.1 Financial Practices Causing Social Injustices

Sometimes, there are some flawed decisions implemented by the SSB that cause injustices in the industry. Some examples can be provided here to clarify what kind of decisions result in injustices. We can look at the example of banking. There is a reserve account called Investment Risk Reserve (IRR) used by Islamic banks widely. IRR implies the amount earmarked by an Islamic bank out of the profit of the investment account holders (IAHs), after the mudarib's (bank) share is allocated. In other words, in good times, Islamic bank transfers the profit of the IAHs to a reserve account (IRR) to cushion against future losses in bad times. In this case, there is a high possibility that deducted profit amount of customer A is used to cushion against future losses of customer B. Thus, it leads to the transfer of wealth from customer A to B, causing injustices against customer A who has contributed to the reserves but has not utilized them. Furthermore, the deduction for the reserve is only made out of the IAHs' profit, excluding the bank's profit causing injustices against IAHs since there is a partnership contract between the bank and IAHs.

The second example from the banking industry can be the accounting treatment of IAHs funds on the Islamic banks' balance sheet. Some banks treat IAHs funds on the balance sheet under liabilities, while others report them as part of equity. There is a third group reporting the funds of IAHs as off-balance sheet items. Even if IAHs funds are combined with the shareholders' funds in the same pool of assets (musharakah), IAHs funds are to make up potentially a larger share of the investment in the pool, but the choice of investment strategy still reflects management's view of shareholder preferences in terms of risk-return characteristics (Archer and Karim 2012). Under the mudaraba agreement, a financier provides the funds, and a bank acts as an entrepreneur by accepting them. Neither a certain rate of return nor the capital (invested funds) is guaranteed. Thus, IAHs effectively become shareholders. However, their status has a peculiar sort of shareholder in that they do not have voting rights and influence on the management. Normally, someone who owns a share can express their dissatisfaction with a firm, either selling off their stock or in some way showing their disappointment (Lewis 2005). Hirschman (1970) expresses these choices as that between exit and voice. Considering these explanations, non-voting IAHs have little exit and no voice. Thus, this gives rise to injustices against the IAHs.

Another example can be related to the structure of the legal entity, whether the way in which the modern corporate system is constructed with its distinct legal entity is acceptable under Shariah. For instance, in the event of (Islamic or conventional) bank failure, the losses of shareholders are limited to their share in the bank's capital. If the liabilities of a bank surpass its total assets, some of the debts belonging to the bank must be written off. Since the losses of shareholders are limited to their share in capital, they cannot be held responsible for compensating the funds of the lender. This casts serious doubts on the modern structure of corporate governance and causes severe injustices against the creditors. It is possible to proliferate these examples, but we stop here since this is not the main subject of the chapter.

The last example would be from the takaful sector. In case of a deficit in the takaful fund in T1, the takaful operator extends the qard al-hasan (interest-free loan) from the shareholder's fund. When there is a surplus in the following years, say T2 or T3, the takaful operator will take back the qard al-hasan given in T1. Suppose that the customers in T1 leave the takaful fund at the end of the contractual term and do not maintain the takaful contract next year. In this case, the qard al-hasan will be compensated from the surplus of customers in T2 or T3. This causes wealth transfer from the customers in T2 and T3 to customers in T1, leading to injustices among the customers.

2.2 Shariah-Compliant versus Shariah-Based Products

There is a widespread belief that IFIs bear a close resemblance to conventional financial institutions. This idea has emerged from the fact that the practices of IFIs are similar to those of their conventional counterparts. Usually, SSB members pay attention to the formal validity of contractual arrangements ignoring the economic consequences of the transaction. Focusing on contractual formalities for the formal validity is different from that of the economic consequences of the transactions. The latter requires economic expertise, which Shariah scholars are lacking. Thus, those products offered by IFIs fulfil the formal validity, but they do not satisfy equitable income distribution, full employment, economic stability and sustainability, balanced

140   *Burak Çıkıryel*

growth, and so on. Taking those commonly used conventional products and forming them in a way to meet the contractual framework of Shariah make the products Shariah-compliant. However, this process does not make those products Shariah-based unless they take those mentioned economic objectives into consideration. For instance, even though organized tawarruk,[3] a controversial Islamic financial product, is prohibited by many scholars worldwide, many banks consider it permissible by claiming its fulfilment of formal validity and use this instrument to restructure debts. It is a commonly known fact in Shariah that if the debtor becomes insolvent, he/she should be given some grace period to recover its financial hardship. However, some institutions employ this product to restructure the debt of their customers and raise the burden on them. This consequently leads to a disruptive effect on the aforementioned economic objectives.

2.3 Regulatory Issues

Depending on size, business model, and complexity, the SG framework and its components may vary from one institution to another. Moreover, the scope of the SG framework may differ from one country to another, subject to the nature of market conditions, economic realities and IFIs' current stage of development (Al-Jarhi et al. 2020). The absence of a unified SG framework shows the need for a unique regulatory framework for Islamic finance at the international level.

The absence of a genuine regulatory framework for Islamic finance at the international level is one of the formidable obstacles IFIs face over their development stage. For instance, if there is a dispute among the participants of Islamic finance in the UK, the UK law will be considered governing law of an agreement since Shariah is not recognized as a legal system that can supervise a contract. There have been no effective international standards[4] that are held binding for all participants so that it can fill the gap between different practices and rulings.

2.4 Inconsistency in Rulings and Standardization Issues

The issue of inconsistency in rulings arises because of different decisions of SSBs on the same matter. It cannot be acknowledged that some IFIs are more tolerant than others regarding Shariah compliance. Sometimes, even inconsistencies occur among the rulings of Shariah scholars in different countries. Some countries are recognized as lenient in their Shariah rulings than others causing severe damages to the reputation of IFIs. Besides, the more contradictions have emerged among the decisions of SSBs, the more people have become skeptical about Islamic finance, as they suspected that the differences between Islamic and conventional finance are merely in terminology (Al-Jarhi et al. 2020). This tragic situation underlines the need for immediate action for standardization.

2.5 Transparency and Disclosure Issues

There have been critics of IFIs on inadequate disclosure of information and being untransparent in their operation. The critics usually revolve around the inadequate disclosure of duties, transaction flows, contractual framework, integrity in accounting, the composition of SSB, decision-making process, and rulings. Full public disclosure and transparency help discipline the institutions and prevent asymmetric information and uncertainty in financial markets and, thus, market failure. However, the lack of providing the information mentioned above deprives the stakeholders of risk mitigation and undermines the customer's confidence.

2.6 Independence and Objectivity

The independence of SSB members in IFIs is another issue of SG. The issue arises here because the financial institution determines the appointment, dismissal, renewal, and paying the remuneration of SSB members at the institutional level. Reliance on the decision of financial institutions on these issues may jeopardize the independence and objectivity of SSB members in their decisions. Because, by instinct, nobody would like to lose his/her job, and they often choose the way of reconciliation with their institutions by doing their best to resolve the issues they face. The chapter does not claim that such a process takes place under all circumstances, but it underscores the high probability of such consequences occurring due to human nature.

Through semi-structured interviews, Abidin et al. (2021) conducted a research on the independence of SSB members during the discharge of their duties. One of the participants in the research stated as follows

> so that from the very beginning I am ready to be terminated anytime so that I have no conflict of interest. This is how I protect myself from dependency on the bank, and I do not use the money from the bank to support my daily needs.

This statement of SSB member provides compelling evidence that there are considerable risks of the above-mentioned issues to impair SSB members' independence and objectivity. The issue does not arise here because he finds ways to protect his independence, but the issue barely exists, and we can claim that everyone is not as successful as him to cope with the concerned problem.

In practice, SSBs base their decisions on the judgement of the bank's Shariah audit and review divisions. Usually, these divisions conduct an audit, prepare reports on Shariah compliance, and present their findings to SSB for their investigation. Such practice occurs mainly because of SSB's time constraints since most scholars serve many banks by sitting on various boards. Furthermore, this is considered a part-time job by many institutions. In fact,

142　*Burak Çıkıryel*

this practice poses great concern about the legitimacy of their decisions since their opinions about the institution lack independence and objectivity.

2.7 Confidentiality Issues

The lack of confidentiality may arise when SSB members sit more than one SSB of IFIs. Naturally, being members of more than one SSB of IFIs may lead to the duplication of product structuring, research, due diligence from one institution to another, disregarding business secrets, and intellectual property rights. On the one hand, some believe that allowing SSB members sitting on multiple boards provides IFIs much leeway in finding qualified Islamic finance experts in the industry. On the other hand, it is obvious that dealing with one institution requires a significant amount of time considering the responsibilities of SSB members. Because of time constraints, it is expected for SSB members to implement the same processes for all institutions, and this may severely affect their confidentiality.

2.8 Competency and Skill Issues of SSB

Lack of banking and financial knowledge of SSB members has been a cause for concern since the inception of IFIs. Because the IFIs would require the opinion of SSB about the banking and finance on which members are not specialized. While IFIs were evolving, they had two options to choose the specialization of SSB members, either having depth knowledge (expert) of banking and finance in addition to knowing Islamic commercial law (fiqh muamalat) or having depth knowledge of Islamic commercial law without knowing banking and finance. The industry has opted for the latter group, leading to the convergence between Islamic and conventional financial institutions. Besides, conventionally trained employees of the financial institutions have guided the latter group to concentrate more on contractual arrangements ignoring the consequences of their judgements on the macro-level. Even though the inherent deficiencies of the latter group was obvious, by this way, some invisible hands have deflected the attention of Islamic finance away from its core principles. Apart from the lack of knowledge on banking and finance, the latter group (Shariah scholars) causes controversy in the industry by focusing on the micro-juristic approach considering only the contractual framework. They ignore the macro-level implications of their works, decisions, and rulings, and there is also a little attempt by these Shariah scholars to conduct ex-post analyses on their own works (Farook and Farooq 2013). Abidin et al. (2021) have revealed how serious the situation is by the statement of Shariah scholar participated in semi-structured interviews in his research, "*but the longer I am at this bank the more independent I am. At first, it's kind of not independent, it's that we are kind of afraid, but again we soon get to know how the banking system operates.*" Even though the supervisory role of SSB is expected to avoid or at least mitigate realized convergence, they are rather regarded as facilitators of the divergence of IFIs from their core principles (Sencal 2017).

Moreover, the IFIs, at least some of them, would like to hire lenient and less costly Shariah scholars without considering their level of competencies and skills. This situation enables those IFIs not to encounter any issue while getting SSB approvals by fulfilling a ceremonial role rather than undertaking vigilant monitoring. As Al-Jarhi (2010) stated, "the market can be a bad judge as those who charge less for their services and are willing to provide more convenient opinions from the point of view of shareholders, will be chosen over the more knowledgeable." This is a very serious issue that needs to be tackled.

3 Practical Solutions to the SG Issues in IFIs

This section tries to address the aforementioned SG issues and recommend possible solutions. Before touching upon the solutions, this session would like to propose a new SG model that can operate more efficiently than existing models in the industry. The purpose of presenting the new model before the solutions is because some of the issues will disappear automatically with the new model. The solutions do not follow the same order as issues, but we assure all the issues highlighted above will be tackled.

The model is composed of a pool of SSB members at the central bank[5] level. The number of SSB members in the pool depends on the need of the Islamic financial sector. Any institution that offers Islamic financial products must obtain the services from SSB members in the pool. A group of SSB members will be assigned to the institutions by the central authority. The number of board members appointed to any institution may vary depending on the institution's size, sector, and business model. For instance, the number of SSB assigned to the takaful sector may differ from the banking sector. Among the pool participants, the five most senior economists would be chosen to preside over the meeting of groups. This group of economists is called central authority. One of the senior economists will be elected as a chairperson. If any dispute or contradiction arises among the SSB members appointed to the institutions or any advice is needed for any issue regarding the operation of institutions, these five most senior economists will provide the guidance and act as an arbitrator for the dispute resolution. In other words, there must be a dispute resolution mechanism to provide clarity about the disagreements over interpretation, application, or breach of rules.

Since there is an urgent need for product standardization, the member of pools, including the five senior economists, must prepare a booklet that contains the major products with its Shariah basis, product development methods and processes, contract samples, manuals for financial products, ethics and Islamic financial principles. However, this booklet should not be an obstacle to the development and innovation of new products. SSB members first evaluate any newly developed financial instrument within the institution, and this evaluation is reported to the product development department. If this assessment includes any modification in the product, the institution should make necessary changes to satisfy the Shariah requirements. The final product is submitted to the central authority for their approval, and if it is approved, the product is put on the market as a result of their comprehensive evaluation. If the central authority detects any issue about the financial instrument, they can return it to the financial institution for its revision. Thus, the booklet will grow in size with the addition of newly developed products. This process facilitates the accumulation of knowledge in the field of Islamic finance and a high level of standardization. Figure 9.1 illustrates the general framework of SG, the content of which has been described above.

Before assigning any SSB member to the institution, the central authority must conduct training programs for all SSB members in the pool. The purpose of launching programs is to train all members about approved Islamic products and their possible mixing and matching. It must also include the doubtful products with reasons for their prohibition. This will make SSB members more prudent and consistent. The composition of SSB must include a majority of economists and financial experts with adequate knowledge in Islamic commercial law and a minority of Shariah scholars with sufficient knowledge in banking and finance. Developing the necessary human resources in the field can be achieved with more comprehensive training programs if there are not enough human resources according to the aforementioned criteria. The training programs should be organized by the central authority and designed to fulfill the need for human resources in the field according to the aforementioned standards.

The reason why a majority of SSB members must consist of economists and financial experts is that the decision to be taken is related to banking

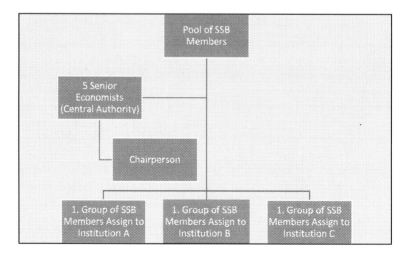

Figure 9.1 General Framework of Shariah Governance.

and finance. In fact, being an expert in banking and finance, in addition to knowing Islamic commercial law, enables SSB members to meet the formal validity of contractual arrangements and interpret the economic consequences of the transaction. Every group of SSB appointed to the institution must include and be limited to one Shariah scholar so that they may provide further clarification about the Shariah matters. For example, if the central authority decides to assign three members to a banking institution, only one (not more than that) must be a Shariah scholar.

There are two different layers of SSB in this model, the central authority and appointed SSB members to the institutions from the pool. Their roles and responsibilities differ as expected. The roles and responsibilities of the central authority will be explained first. Given the title of the advisor to central authority implies that the board has an advisory function rather than a supervisory function. Thus, this gives IFIs the right to accept or reject the advice. The current practices have demonstrated that considering the central authority as an advisory and delegating the full authority to the institutional SSB members have resulted in a convergence of IFIs to their conventional peers. This situation has damaged the credibility and reputation of IFIs in the eyes of the Muslim community. In this current model, the central authority is under the control of the central bank and has mainly four functions. The first function is to oversee the entire operation of IFIs as a supervisor. The absence of an effective monitoring mechanism on Shariah matters might have negative consequences for the stability of the Islamic financial sector. This stresses the major role that the central authority plays in the SG mechanism. Second, it is the supreme authority to endorse all Shariah-related matters. The third function is to be a bridge between the regulator and industry players, providing guidance to the regulator on how to ensure that IFIs adhere strictly to the Islamic paradigm. Lastly, they arrange training programs for appointed SSB members whenever it is necessary.

As for the roles and responsibilities of SSB members appointed to the institutions from the pool, they have both supervisory and advisory functions. On the one hand, in a supervisory capacity, SSB members are responsible for verifying permissible financial instruments and contractual templates, overseeing transactional flows and advertisements, assessing Shariah-non-compliance risks and reporting to the board, detecting Shariah non-compliance income and its purifications, calculation of zakat and its distribution. On the other hand, an advisory function of SSB members requires their guidance during the stage of product development and preparation of contractual templates and swift response to the inquiries from IFIs on their daily operations. Besides these responsibilities, they also need to arrange training programs for the IFIs staff. These training programs are based on the booklet that contains the major products with its Shariah basis, product development methods and processes, contract samples, manuals for financial products, ethics, and Islamic financial principles. In other words, all the IFIs staff will be trained about Islamic finance business ethics, principles, and standards. Participation

146   *Burak Çıkıryel*

in these programs must be mandatory for all staff, not just the management. The programs should be arranged in the form of video conferencing, considering the distances among branches. Thus, the entire IFIs staff will be aware of how the institution can be run according to Islamic principles, as there are harsh criticisms of their awareness about the business operation. SSB members are expected to resolve disputes between customers and institutions as arbitrators. Moreover, if there are newly developed products, they must take them to the central authority for endorsement.

There is a dire need for regulatory bodies both at the national and international levels. Central authority in this framework plays the role of the supervisory body. In fact, there must be auxiliary departments under the control of central authority reporting necessary contexts to the regulators to enact the laws and put them into effect. Those departments bridge the gap between supervisors and regulators and include law, banking, insurance, accounting, monetary and capital markets, nonbank financial institutions, information technologies, and financial innovation departments. The central authority must revise all the regulations governing Islamic finance and recommend that regulators should amend necessary parts to create a better environment for Islamic finance. Furthermore, the absence of a genuine and consistent regulatory framework for Islamic finance at the international level is one of the formidable obstacles IFIs face over their development stage. Setting a genuine regulatory framework at the international level has two major impacts on the Islamic financial sector. First, it will help enhance the consistency among IFIs across jurisdictions. Second, in the absence of an Islamic legal system or genuine Islamic finance laws, countries make direct reference to international Islamic financial laws to operate IFIs and resolve disputes.

The competencies and skills of SSB members would differ between Shariah scholars, and economists and financial experts. Shariah scholars must meet the conditions to be scholars, including a PhD from an accredited university, interest in banking and finance, graduate teaching experience for five years, and a banking and finance certificate.[6] Economists and financial experts must also fulfill the requirements to be scholars, including a PhD from an accredited university, graduate teaching experience of Islamic economics and finance for five years, conducting research in the field of Islamic economics and finance for ten years. Some claim that there is a lack of qualifying SSB members in the market, but this seems to contradict the widespread existence of universities and education programs almost all over the world for a long time. These programs have led to the development of a qualified labor force in the markets. If there is a shortage of SSB members fulfilling the conditions in a country, the length of the experience period can be revised, and the rules can be stretched. Furthermore, when central authority assigns SSB members to institutions, they must consider their area of specialization. For instance, if a person is specialized in the area of takaful, he or she must be employed in the takaful sector, not the banking sector.

Issues and Practical Solutions of Shariah Governance 147

Forming SSB with the majority of economists and financial experts will lead Islamic financial products to meet the requirements of Shariah, both the contractual formalities and the anticipated beneficial economic consequences of transactions. The latter implies the positive economic effects of the transactions, such as equitable income distribution, full employment, economic stability and sustainability, and balanced growth. The products cannot be considered Shariah-based unless these two objectives are achieved. Therefore, it is very important to have SSB members strong in both aspects to manage the financial system efficiently.

A group of SSB members must be appointed to only one institution by the central authority. In this framework, being a member of SSB cannot be considered a part-time job since dealing with one institution requires a significant amount of time, taking into account the responsibilities of SSB members. Thus, this framework does not permit SSB members to sit on the boards of more than one institution to avoid any conflict of interest and protect confidentiality in the industry. This will also help protection of business secrets and intellectual property rights. Moreover, the relationship between immediate family members of SSB and the institution should also be monitored carefully not to cause any information leakage. Therefore, the central authority must take measures to ensure that confidential information is not revealed to unauthorized parties.

The issue of independence arises because the appointment, dismissal, renewal, and paying the remuneration of SSB members are usually in the hands of financial institutions. In this model, IFIs would purchase the service of SSB from the central authority. So, the SSB members are the employees of the central authority. The central authority determines the appointment, dismissal, renewal, and remuneration of SSB members. As decisions regarding the position of the SSB members belong to the central authority, this situation will enable them to preserve their independence and impartiality.

It is important for IFIs to communicate diligently with their stakeholders because this will strengthen stakeholders' confidence and, thus, the credibility of the institution. The central authority must hold IFIs responsible for making accurate information available to their stakeholders at regular intervals to avoid inadequate disclosure of information. Duties, transaction flows, contractual framework, integrity in accounting, the composition of SSB, decision-making process, and rulings must be accessible to all stakeholders. Full public disclosure and transparency help discipline the institutions and prevent asymmetric information and uncertainty in financial markets and, thus, market failure.

One of the serious challenges of SG is the absence of consistency among the different rulings of Shariah scholars, boards, and institutions. The preparation of the booklet and the submission of new additional products to a central authority for their approval will help overcome this problem and facilitate a high level of standardization because the central authority will maintain the harmony and avoid the occurrence of contradictions among the different

148 *Burak Çıkıryel*

products that IFIs offer. Since the central authority trains all SSB members in the pool about the fundamentals of product development before starting their work, that would hinder the emergence of problematic products and establish compatibility and integrity in the market. This will contribute toward enhancing the credibility of Islamic finance and, thus, establishing an unshakeable reputation.

SSB members appointed to the institutions cannot base their decision on the judgement of the bank's Shariah audit and review divisions. As explained in detail, SSB members have very distinct responsibilities within the corporate structure compared to other employees. Their duties cannot be conducted by any department in the institution. Besides, SSB members are not allowed to hold many seats on different boards. Therefore, they will have enough time to fulfill their obligations.

As mentioned above, there are some flawed practices of IFIs that lead to social injustices in the industry. While the first example is related to the wrong decisions of SSB, the last two examples are associated with the flawed design of the conventional corporate structure. The first case usually emanates from the lack of SSB ability to identify the ultimate economic consequences of the transactions. This issue will be mostly resolved if SSB composition includes a majority of economists and financial experts with adequate knowledge of Islamic commercial law. In addition, if there are objections or opposing reactions to the rulings of SSB among the public, members must take these negative perceptions into account. And, they must either provide clarity about the problem or remove the controversial issue causing unrest throughout the industry. Last but not least, the Shariah scholars who have initiated all currently known and approved controversial Islamic finance products must be excluded from the boards, and they must not be employed in the industry. The second case is mainly derived from the flawed design of the conventional organizational structure. First, it is expected that there exists an objection among SSB members to the current corporate structure, and they propose feasible and viable alternative frameworks that can fit the Islamic finance paradigm. It is unfortunate to say that there is not enough data or arguments to prove such a claim. Second, this situation underlines the urgent need for a comprehensive and genuine ICG, which is beyond the scope of this research.

4 Conclusion

This chapter mainly discusses SG issues surrounding IFIs and provides a broader perspective by recommending a new SG approach to resolve those issues. First, we defined Islamic and conventional corporate governance and presented the distinctions between them. Then, the principles of ICG were covered in-depth, with an emphasis on the components of its institutional framework. The position of ICG on the shareholder versus stakeholder model was determined. It is important to note that SG can be regarded as a part of the ICG framework, and it mainly concentrates on Shariah compliance of IFIs during their operation. The main issues raised in this chapter were related to social injustices, Shariah-compliant versus Shariah-based products, regulation, inconsistency and standardization, transparency and disclosure, independence and objectivity, confidentiality, competencies, and skills.

This chapter proposed a unique approach that contains a two-layer SG framework under the control of the central bank. First of all, a pool of SSB members must be formed to meet the sector's needs. Out of this pool, the five most senior economists would be chosen as a central authority, who must be the supreme authority to endorse all Shariah-related matters. The rest of the SSB members in the pool would be assigned to the institutions by the central authority to maintain effective Shariah compliance throughout the operation of institutions. Sector players, such as Islamic banks and takaful companies, must purchase the services of SSB members in the pool, who are the central bank employees. This research offers unique solutions for each of the aforementioned problems, and this mechanism is conducive to establishing and maintaining a robust SG system.

Notes

1 Property rights of Islam has a broader meaning than that of conventional encompassing many elements. For instance, zakat is the right of impoverished people on the wealth of the rich. Thus, readers should be careful about the property rights in Islam since they are completely different from that of conventional structures.
2 Falah refers to the success and happiness that a person will achieve in this world as a result of fulfilling his/her religious and moral obligations, and the eternal salvation and happiness that he/she will reach in the hereafter (Bebek 1995).
3 Organized tawarruq refers to a sale contract in which the buyer purchases item on installment and then sells it at a loss to the original seller for cash.
4 This issue stems from particularly different contractual interpretations of the four schools of thought.
5 Islamic finance composes of mainly three sectors: banking, money and capital markets, and takaful. In this model, the assignment of SSB members to any institution is performed by a central bank. However, this can vary based on the organizational structure of the concerned country. In addition, semi-autonomous establishments can be founded, and the processes can be operated differently for each sector. Although the organizational structure remains the same in this case, only the relevant department working under the semi-autonomous establishments will carry out the execution of the process.
6 One of the officially recognized national institutions can offer certification programs by providing Islamic banking and finance courses to develop in-depth understanding and application abilities in the field.

References

Abidin, Nor Hafizah Zainal, Fatimah Mat Yasin, and Ahmad Zainal Abidin. 2021. "Independence from the Perspective of the Shari'ah Committee." *Asian Journal of Accounting Research* 6(2):196–209. doi:10.1108/ajar-07-2020-0053.

150   *Burak Çıkıryel*

Al-Jarhi, Mabid. 2010. "Reviving the Ethics of Islamic Finance." *Munich University Library* 66732.

Al-Jarhi, Mabid Ali, Abdurrahman Yazıcı, Şahban Yıldırımer, Tawfik Azrak, Adnan Oweida, Ahmad Al-Hersh, Ömer Faruk Tekdoğan, Hüsnü Tekin, Burak Çıkıryel, and Fatma Sayar. 2020. *Improving Shariah Governance Framework in Islamic Finance*. Ankara.

Archer, Simon, and Rifaat Ahmed Abdel Karim (Eds.), 2012. "Specific Corporate Governance Issues in Islamic Banks." Pp. 310–41 in *Islamic Finance: The Regulatory Challenge*.

Askari, Hossein, Zamir Iqbal, Noureddine Krichne, and Abbas Mirakhor. 2012. "The Role of Institutions and Governance in Risk Sharing." Pp. 201–24 in *Risk Sharing in Finance: The Islamic Finance Alternative*, edited by H. Askari, Z. Iqbal, N. Krichne, and A. Mirakhor. Hoboken, NJ: John Wiley & Sons, Inc.

Bebek, Adil. 1995. "No Title." *TDV İslâm Araştırmaları Merkezi*.

Bhatti, Maria, and Bhatti Ishaq. 2008. "Toward Understanding Islamic Corporate Governance Issues in Islamic Finance." *Asian Politics & Policy* 2(1):25–38. doi:10.5040/9780755608584.ch-003.

Ben Bouheni, Faten, Chantal Ammi, and Aldo Levy. 2016. "Mechanisms of Corporate Governance, Banking Governance and Islamic Banking Governance." Pp. 89–113 in *Banking Governance, Performance and Risk-Taking*. Hoboken, NJ: John Wiley & Sons, Inc.

Cernat, Lucian. 2004. "The Emerging European Corporate Governance Model: Anglo-Saxon, Continental, or Still the Century of Diversity?" *Journal of European Public Policy* 11(1):147–166. doi:10.1080/1350176042000164343.

Chapra, Umer, and Habib Ahmed. 2002. *Corporate Governance in Islamic Financial Institutions*. Islamic Development Bank.

Farook, Sayd, and Mohammad Omar Farooq. 2013. "Sharī'ah Governance, Expertise and Profession: Educational Challenges in Islamic Finance." *ISRA International Journal of Islamic Finance* 5(1):137–160. doi:10.12816/0002761.

Ginena, Karim, and Azhar Hamid. 2015. "Corporate and Shari'ah Governance of Islamic Banks." Pp. 57–102 in *Foundations of Shari'ah Governance of Islamic Banks*. Wiley.

Grassa, Rihab. 2013. "Shariah Supervisory System in Islamic Financial Institutions: New Issues and Challenges: A Comparative Analysis Between Southeast Asia Models and GCC Models." *Humanomics* 29(4):333–348. doi:10.1108/H-01-2013-0001.

Hirschman, Albert O. 1970. *Exit, Voice and Loyalty*. Cambridge: Harvard University Press.

Iqbal, Zamir, and Abbas Mirakhor. 2004. "Stakeholders Model of Governance in Islamic Economic System." *Islamic Economic Studies* 11(2):43–63.

Lewis, Mervyn. 2005. "Islamic Corporate Governance." *Review of Islamic Economics* 9(1):5–29.

Ooghe, Hubert, and Tine de Langhe. 2002. "The Anglo-American versus the Continental European Corporate Governance Model: Empirical Evidence of Board Composition in Belgium." *European Business Review* 14(6):437–449. doi:10.1108/09555340210448794.

Pillay, Renginee G. 2013. "Anglo-American Model Versus Continental European Model." Pp. 100–105 in *Encyclopedia of Corporate Social Responsibility*, edited by S. O. Idowu, N. Capaldi, L. Zu, and A. Das Gupta. Berlin, Heidelberg: Springer.

Sencal, Harun. 2017. "Essays on the Shari'ah Governance System in Islamic Banks: Disclosure Performance of Shari'ah Boards and Historical Evolution of the Roles of Shari'ah Scholars." Durham University.

Sencal, Harun, and Mehmet Asutay. 2021. "Ethical Disclosure in the Shari'ah Annual Reports of Islamic Banks: Discourse on Shari'ah Governance, Quantitative Empirics and Qualitative Analysis." *Corporate Governance (Bingley)* 21(1):175–211. doi:10.1108/CG-01-2020-0037.

Index

Note: **Bold** page numbers refer to tables, *italic* page numbers refer to figures and page numbers followed by "n" denote endnotes.

Accounting Auditing Organization for Islamic Financial Institutions (AAOI FI) 85, 86, 90, 92
accumulated capital 120, 122, 123
active ratio 15, 24–25n2
Adjustments to Policy Shocks 37–38
Alliance Islamic Bank Bhd. 55
alternative finance 105–106
Anglo-Saxon model 136
aqilah 81, 86, 95
asset quality 69, 71

Baitul Maal Wat Tamwil (BMTs) 5, 66, 67; competitive positioning 72; cost management 71–72; funding structure 73–74; human resources management 68; linkage programs 70–71; management information systems 74–75; microfinancing techniques 68–70; regulation and supervision 72–73
Bank Charter Act of 1844 21
bank deposit multiplication 10
Banking Act 17, 22
banking business models 45–49
banking crisis 22, 46, 48
Banking Regulation and Supervision Authority of Turkey (BRSA) 24–25n2
banking structures 58–60, *59*
banking system 8, 9–10
bank lending 8, 10, 19
banks, definition of 7; *see also individual terms*
banks stability 36, 38
Basel Committee on Banking Supervision (BCBS) 17, 102

blockchain technology 57–58, 61n9, 101, 106, 108, 109, 113
business model 44, 60; *see also* banking business models

capitalist market system 117–121, 123
central authority 143–149
central bank 10–13, 15, 17, 21–24, 33, 35, 38, 39, 41, 70, 105, 112, 143, 145, 149, 149n5
central deposit certificates (CDCs) 33, 34
Central Deposits (CDs) 33
Chicago plan 21–23
classical loan contract 4, 28, 31, 32, 35, 40–42
collateralized debt obligations (CDOs) 47, 48, 122–123
commercial-based insurance system 85
competency and skill issues, SSB 142–143
competitive positioning 72
confidentiality, SSB 142
conventional banks 7, 15, 17, 19, 21, 33, 36, 40, 44, 47, 48, 51, 52, 60n1, 111, 125, 130
conventional corporate governance 5, 134, 137, 148
conventional debt 40
conventional finance system 31–32, 38, 40–41
conventional insurance 82–84, 92, 95, 96
core moral principles, Islam: accumulation 119–120; indebtedness 118–119; interest 120–121
corporate governance 38, 134, 139
cost management 67, 71–72, 75

154   *Index*

credit creation theory 10, 12, 19
credit money 8, 9, 14, 15, 21, 24
criticisms: banking business models
  5, 45–49; Islamic banking business
  models 49–52, *50*
crowdfunding 53–56, *56,* 60, 104, 106,
  111, 130
cryptocurrencies 54, 103, 106, 111

debt 21, 37, 38, 69, 118; based-money 9,
  33; instruments 36, 37, 122–125, 130;
  sustainability 40; trade 42n4
decentralized finance (DeFi) 103, 106,
  111
decision-making process 38, 94, 121,
  135–137, 141
deposit multiplication 10–12
dichotomy 36–37
digital banking 105, 107, 113
direct spending 37
disintermediation 46, 106
efficiency 34–36

Electronic Fund Transfer (EFT) 12–15
equity 38–40
equity-based financial contracts 58, 134
equity-based money 33, 34, 39, 41
equity-based structure 24, 51–52, 130
Ernst and Young report 102
Ethereum blockchain 106
Ethis Crowd Indonesia 55
European model 136
e-wallets 48, 104, 107, 111

falah 135, 149n2
family takaful model 86, 89, 95, 96
fatawa 81, 97n1
financial accounting standards (FAS) 85
financial crises (2008) 51, 100
financial institutions 36, 39, 119–120
financial intermediaries 7, 9, 12, 21, 32,
  58, 66, 101
financial intermediation theory 10
financialization 45–48, 60, 123–125, 131n3
financialized capitalism 120–123, 127
financial market 3, 34, 35, 37, 47, 54, 102,
  141, 147
financial sustainability: of Baitul Maal Wat
  Tamwil 68–75; of Islamic microfinance
  institutions 5, 65–76
financial system 4, 5, 9, 10, 21, 22, 24, 28,
  35, 42, 100, 101, 105, 110, 117, 119,
  120, 121, 147

financial technology (fintech) 5, 48, 49,
  54–55, 57, 60, 100, 101–102, 109–110
financing 37, 120; for micro and small
  enterprises 72, 75; with murabaha 17,
  19, 21, 51, 53; peer-to-peer 106; tools
  23–24; *see also* microfinancing
fourth industrial revolution 100–101
fractional reserve theory 4, 7, 10, 11, 15,
  17, 21, 23, 24, 38–39
full (or 100%) reserve banking (FRB) 4,
  21–23, 24
full-reserve system 4, 7, 15, 23, 24, 33, 54
funding challenges 112
funding structure 73–74
fund mobilization 37–38

Gen-Z 96
German inflation (1923) 9
global finance 124, 126, 127
global financial crisis (2008) 5, 117,
  121–123
global financial system 5, 117, 124, 125,
  127, 129, 130
Global Findex Database 65
Global Islamic Fintech Report 103
Great Depression 8, 21, 31

Hisba 135
homo ordinarius 29
Hosios inefficiency 32, 35
human resources management 68
hybrid takaful model 85–86

ibaha 91
Ibn Abidin 81
ijara sukuk 32, 53, 125
income redistribution 39–40
indebtedness 118–119
independence, SSB 141–142
Indonesia: Baitul Maal Wat Tamwil in
  68–76; Islamic financial institutions
  in 66; microfinance institutions in 65,
  66, 67
industrial capitalism 119, 123
inequity 38–39
information asymmetry 35–36, 40
infrastructure availability 113
institutional changes 41–42
instrumental morality 5, 117,
  125–127, 129
insurance: conventional 82–84, 92, 95, 96;
  in Islam 81–82
interbank clearing 14, *15*

interest 120–121
interest-based finance system 32
interest-free banking 50
interest rate theories 28–31
International Financial Crisis of 2008 41
investment account holders (IAHs)
138, 139
Investment Account Platform (IAP) 56, *56*
investment banking 22, 47–49, 53, 59
Investment Risk Reserve (IRR) 138
Islamic banking 2, 44, 50; conventional
finance system 31–32, 38, 40–41; interest
rate theories 28–31; Islamic finance
environment 1, 33; qualitative research
methods 45; *see also individual terms*
Islamic (Shariah) Banking Act 17
Islamic banking business models
54, 60; criticisms 49–52, *50*; with
crowdfunding platforms 54–56, *56*;
with different banking structures
58–60, *59*; P2P (Peer-to-Peer)
platforms 56–58; smart PLS contracts
56, 56–58; suggestions for 52–54, **53**
Islamic banks 7, 23, 24, 33, 35, 36, 39–41,
51, 57, 58, 60, 104, 107, 125, 129, 130;
equity-based structure 51–52; money
creation by 15, 17–21, *18, 20*
Islamic commercial and rural banks
(BPRSs) 66, 70–72
Islamic commercial law 86, 89, 142, 144,
145, 148
Islamic corporate governance (ICG) 6,
134–137
Islamic development bank (IsDB) 113,
117, 128, 129
Islamic economic system 4, 19, 23, 28,
35, 124, 129, 130, 135, 136, 146;
configuration of 33–34; *see also*
morality, of finance
Islamic finance: debt sustainability 40;
description of 32; efficiency 34–36;
equity 38–40; financial market
under 34; fund mobilization 37–38;
moral reflections in global economy
123–126; objective morality 126–127;
objectives of 1–2; stability 36–37;
systemic integrity 38
Islamic finance development report
(2021) 2
Islamic finance environment 1, 33–34
Islamic financial framework 5, 100, 102;
Islamic fintech solutions support for
108–109

Islamic financial institutions (IFIs) 3, 5,
24, 66, 102, 103, 111, 112, 117, 118;
Shariah governance in 134–149;
Shariah governance issues in 134–143;
social dimensions of 126
Islamic Financial Services Board (IFSB)
17, 50, 85, 131n1
Islamic financial system 1, 82, 100,
102; fintech applications 109–113;
fintech solutions 105–109; framework
103–105, *104*, 108–109; *see also*
technology
Islamic financial technology/Islamic
fintech 100, 105, 109–110; definition
of 102; funding challenges 112;
infrastructure availability 113; Islamic
financial system framework 103–105,
104; lack of knowledge centers 111–
112; methodology and research design
102–103; policy recommendations
113–114; regulatory and legal issues
110; Shariah compliance 110–111;
talent shortage 111–112
Islamic fintech solutions 105; secondary
financial services 107–108; support for
Islamic financial framework 108–109;
traditional Islamic banking 105–107
Islamic Insurance Company 84
Islamic investment banks 58, 59, *59*, 60
Islamic moral economy (IME) 52
Islamic morality 124, 125, 127–129

Judeo-Christian approach 31

Keynes liquidity preference theory 31

lemon problem 35–36
liberalization 44, 46–48, 60, 129
linkage programs 70–71, 75
long-run objectives 130
long-term investment 58, 59, 96

macroeconomic stability 36
Malaysia: Islamic banks in 104, 128;
payment method in 107; takaful
regulation in 84; TakaTech in 109
management information systems (MIS)
67, 70, 74–75
Maqasid-based approach 1
marketing issues, takaful 96
market structure 35
maysir 1, 82–84
"*Mecmûatii'r-resâil*" 81

156 *Index*

Medici Bank 46, 49
micro-enterprises 69–70
microfinance 52, 53, 55
Microfinance Institutions (MFIs) 5, 65
microfinancing techniques 68–70
Ministry of Cooperatives and Micro
and Small Medium Enterprises
(MoCMSMEs) 66
Mit Ghamr Savings Bank 44, 50, 53, **53,
124**
monetary authority 33, 34
monetary expansion 34, 37
monetary policy 33, 34
money creation process 4, 8, 10, *11,*
11–15, *13, 15, 16*; by Islamic banks 15,
17–21, *18, 20*
money supply 7, 9, 12, 14, 15, 17, 20–24,
34, 36–37
morality, of finance 5, 117–118;
accumulation 119–120; in global
economy 123–126; global financial
crisis (2008) 117, 121–123;
indebtedness 118–119; instrumental
morality 5, 117, 125–127, 129; interest
120–121; long-run objectives 130;
objective morality 126–127; short-run
objectives 130; substantive morality
126, 127, 129, 130; transactional
development 123, 124, 127–128, 130;
transformational development 124,
125, 127, 129, 130
moral reflections, in global economy
123–126
muawalah 81
mudarabah 52, 86, 89, 90
murabaha 7, 17, 19, 21, 32, 52–55, 125
musharakah 32, 57

narrow banking 21, 54
National Acts of 1863 and 1864 21
neoclassical model 28–29, 31, 42n1
nihd 86, 97n4

objective morality, Islamic finance
126–127
off-balance-sheet 46, 61n2, 138
online digital finance 105–106
Otoritas Jasa Keuangan (OJK) 66, 70, 73

participation banks 17, 25n2, 129
"Participation Finance" 129
payment systems 22, 67, 105, 107–108
peer-to-peer financing 105, 106, 107

Permodalan Nasional Madani (PNM) 70,
71, 74
policy recommendations, Islamic fintech
113–114
political economy 120, 121, 123
P2P (Peer-to-Peer) platforms 56–58
profit-and-loss sharing (PLS) 44, 52, 58,
86, 94, 124, 125
property rights 134–136, 142, 147, 149n1
Prophet Muhammad 42n5, 84, 95,
118, 119
pure risk trading 42n4

qard al-hasan 53, 86, 90, 92, 94, 130, 139

rate of interest 4, 28–31, 33, 34, 41
ratio regulation 24–25n2
Real Bills Doctrine 20–21
"*Reddü'l Muhtar*" 81
RegTech *see* regulation technology
(RegTech)
regulation, BMT 72–73
regulation technology (RegTech) 105,
109
regulatory and legal issues, Islamic fintech
110
regulatory issues: in Shariah governance
140; takaful 88, 95–96
retail banking 47, 49, 53, 61n5
retakaful 86, 89, 90, 94, 95
risk management 48, 49, 60, 82, 84, 85,
95, 137
risk-sharing 1, 35, 38, 51, 84, 92, 95, 124,
125, 130

sale finance 32, 35, 39–40
Samuelson-Friedman's inefficiency 32, 35
sandboxes 104, 110
secondary financial services 107–108
shareholders' funds (SHFs) 86, 90
shareholders *versus* stakeholders 134–135
Shariah 117, 135; compliance 1, 3, 110–
111, 114, 121, 135, 149; conformity
1, 33; cryptocurrencies 106; issues in
takaful 91–95, *93*; rules 40
Shariah governance, issues in IFIs 5,
134–149, 137–138; competency and
skill issues 142–143; confidentiality
issues 142; inconsistency in rulings
140; independence 141–142;
objectivity 141–142; practical solutions
143–148, *144*; regulatory issues 140;
shareholders *vs.* stakeholders 134–135;

Index 157

Shariah-compliant *vs.* Shariah-based products 139–140; social injustices 138–139; standardization issues 140; transparency and disclosure issues 141

Shariah supervisory board (SSB) 137–149; *see also* Shariah governance

short-run objectives 130

short-term investment 96

Shura (consultative council) 135

smart PLS contracts *56,* 56–58, 57, 58, 106

social injustices 138–139

SocioBiz 55

socio-economic outcomes 44, 52, 53, 60

Sonnenschein Mantel Debreu (SMD) 31, 42n3

sovereign money 22, 24

spatial colonization 118

stability 36–37

substantive morality 126, 127, 129, 130

sukuk 3, 32, 34, 58, 89, 125, 126, 130

supervisory issues: Baitul Maal Wat Tamwil 72–73; takaful 88, 95–96

systemic integrity 38

Tabung Haji 124

takaful 5, 82, 103, 104, 139; awareness 88; contemporary issues in 88–91; definition of 83; development of 95–96; difficulties and issues 88–91, **92**; fund 85, 86, 89–92, 94, 95, 139; investment 89; marketing issues 96; public perception 88; regulatory and supervisory issues 88, 95–96; Shariah issues 91–95, *93*; Shariah supervision 88–89; theoretical framework of 83–88, *87*

Takaful technology (TakaTech) 104, 108–109

talent shortage, Islamic fintech 111–112

tawarruq 125, 149n3

technology: financial technology 5, 48, 49, 54–55, 57, 60, 100, 101–102, 109–110; fourth industrial revolution 100–101; *see also* Islamic financial technology/Islamic fintech

time preference 29, 30

traditional commercial banks 58

traditional Islamic banking 105–107

transactional development 123, 124, 127–128, 130

transformational development 124, 125, 127, 129, 130

Turkey/Türkiye: consumer Loans in 19, *20*; conventional banks in 17, *18*; Islamic banks in 52, 129; participation banks in 17

Turkish Financial System 9, **9**

universal banking 53, 54

unproductive credit creation 19

value-based intermediation (VBI) 128, **128**

wakalah-cooperative takaful model 82, 85, 89, 90, 92, *93,* 96–97

wakalah fee 86, 92, 94

Wakalah or agency finance 32, 52

waqf model 55–56, 90

wealth management 108

wealth redistribution 39–40

WealthTech 108

wholesale banking 47, 61n5

World Bank Group 65

World Economic Forum 101

Zakah 39, 61n8

zakat 135, 137, 138, 145, 149n1

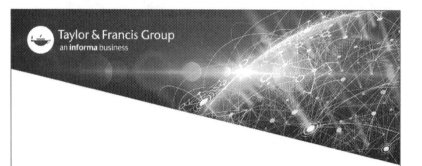